Does This Diet Make My Butt Look Fat?

Does This Diet Make My Butt Look Fat?

A New Perspective on Dieting and Weight Loss

BARBARA R. MCCOURTNEY, M.S.

Gotham Books
30 N Gould St.
Ste. 20820, Sheridan, WY 82801
https://gothambooksinc.com/
Phone: 1 (307) 464-7800

© 2022 Barbara McCourtney. All rights reserved.

No part of this book may be reproduced, stored in a retrieval system, or transmitted by any means without the written permission of the author.

Published by Gotham Books (February 2022)

iSBN: 978-1-956349-18-4(sc)
ISBN: 978-1-956349-19-1(e)

Library of Congress Control Number: 2022901922

Any people depicted in stock imagery provided by iStock are models, and such images are being used for illustrative purposes only.

certain stock imagery © iStock.

Because of the dynamic nature of the Internet, any web addresses or links contained in this book may have changed since publication and may no longer be valid. The views expressed in this work are solely those of the author and do not necessarily reflect the views of the publisher, and the publisher hereby disclaims any responsibility for them.

Table of Contents

PART I: A NEW PERSPECTIVE 9

A Letter to Yo-yo Dieters, Including Me 10
If Dieting Is So Easy, Why Am I Still Fat? 12
Former Fat Lady Finally Fesses Up 17
My Ten-Year Illness 20
The Psychology Behind My Fat Behind 25

**PART II: TEN THINGS I USED TO
BELIEVE WHEN I WAS STUPID** 33

How and Why These Things Kept Me Fat 34
Lie #1: I'm the Exception 37
Lie # 2: I'll Start My Diet Tomorrow 42
Lie #3: I Don't Eat That Much 49
Lie #4: I Don't Look That Bad 55
Lie #5: It's Hereditary 58
Lie #6: I'm Too Stressed 63
Lie #7: Diets Don't Work for Me 67
Lie #8: I Get Too Hungry! 74
Thing #9: I Don't Have Enough Money 83
Thing #10: Fill in the Blank 95

PART III: NOW FOR THE HARD PART 101

One: God Made Me Completely Unique,
Just Like Everyone Else. 102
Two: If You Want to Win,
You Absolutely Must Do This. No Choice.. 109
Three: This Means War 117
Four: Counting Calories. It's Underrated. 119
Five: Exercise: It's Overrated. 134
Six: Fats and Carbs. Carbs and Fats. I'm So Confused. 153
Seven: The Fatal Four, Plus a Few More 162
Eight: The Truth About Fruit. 188
Nine: Mama Was Right Eat Your Vegetables 194
Ten: It Doesn't Take a Rocket Scientist to Flush a Toilet 202
Eleven: Scrub the Toilet 209
Twelve: Vitamins, Minerals, Herbs, Food Supplements,
and Whatever the Heck Else You Want to Call Them 213
Thirteen: The Only Book Better Than Mine 226
Fourteen: When All Else Fails 232
Fifteen: The Joy of Fasting 237
Sixteen: Five Pounds by Friday 251
Seventeen: Accountability and Support. 254
Eighteen: The Whole Enchilada. 263

PART IV: LEFTOVERS 273

1: My Favorite Recipes 274
My Seven Favorite Tea Recipes. 275
My Seven Favorite Smoothies. 281
My Seven Favorite Oatmeal Recipes. 285
My Seven Favorite Soups 291
My Seven Favorite Salads 298
My Seven Favorite Main Dishes. 305

My Seven Favorite Snacks
(which sometimes doubles as a small meal)................311
My Seven Favorite Desserts (Actually Eight) 314
Definitions..320
Shopping List 321
Recommended Reading
(a.k.a. Books You Can't Live Without) 327

PART I

A New Perspective

A Letter to Yo-yo Dieters, Including Me

Dear Fellow Dieters,

You'll be glad to know that this is not an "I Have Arrived" book, because I'm still fighting that last four, no wait, five, or uh, maybe five-and-a-half pounds, depending on what day of the week it is. That's why, if you've tried every diet on the planet, or you can't seem to stay away from junk food, we are probably sailing along in the same boat. Sometimes the wind quits blowing, and we're just sitting there, waiting for something to happen. Other times we are taking on water (literally), but we are all floating in the same body of water, hoping to get to the other side without sinking.

I need to make it clear, I don't have all the answers, but over the years, (many, many years) I have learned so much about dieting and weight loss, that I feel compelled to share them with anyone who wants to lose weight. Each pound lost is a struggle, but I will never stop trying. Keeping it off is just as hard. In other words, I've come a long way, but I'm not there yet. I know I couldn't do it without God and my friends, who are also struggling with their weight.

Now I have two things I would like you to do. First, stop beating yourself up for all your diet mistakes and failures. Second, sit back in your favorite recliner and have fun with this book. Learn as much as you can but be ready to smile. And stop taking life so seriously, please.

Sincerely,
Barb McCourtney
Former Fat Lady (and still working on it)

If Dieting Is So Easy, Why Am I Still Fat?

You may look at me and think, *You aren't fat.* At least I hope that's what you're thinking, but I have a TV that implies that I am. That's because the lady advertising her newest weight-loss gimmick is six-foot, two; weighs 98 pounds, and is usually eating chocolate cake. But worse than that, there's one lady who says, "I used to be a size 10. I was so embarrassed, but now I'm a size two!" Really? Size ten is my goal! I'm 5' 9" with broad shoulders and big bones. If I was a size two, I would look like a giant spider. I will probably be a size two, five years after I'm dead (but only if I'm lucky).

This skinny lady assures me that all I have to do is just pop one of her pills (for only $19.95) and WHAM! I look like a *Victoria's Secret* model and IT'S EASY! She has the magic pill, that is "guaranteed" to make me thin. It works as well as a two-year-old, trying to help Daddy mow the lawn. The poor little guy doesn't know his *Fisher-Price* lawn mower is just a fake, but he keeps pushing it around, with a big smile on his face, believing it works. I do the same thing. I buy the fake *Fisher Price* diet pill. Then I go around with a big smile saying, "I'm going to get skinny." Then that TV-lady adds, "IT'S EASY." Since she's skinny, I should believe her, right?

Do you know what another skinny lady said? She said, "I got skinny in six weeks." Wow! Guess how she did it? She ate more and exercised less! That's right. She ATE MORE! Then, on top of that she EXERCISED LESS! And IT'S EASY! How cool is that? That's the diet I want, because I hate exercising and I love to eat, and I really, really want to be skinny just like her. And no matter how much I have to lose, it will only take me six weeks, at least that's what she implies. I'm so excited!

When I told my cousin (who is an attorney) she said, "It was a joke, right, like *Saturday Night Live*?" When I told her it was real, she didn't believe me. She laughed. "Nobody would believe that." Somebody obviously does or they wouldn't pay millions of dollars to keep airing that same commercial. I won't say that lady lies, but she does give you a distorted sense of reality.

Then there's the commercial that tells us "Diets don't work," but if you join their group, you can, "Stop dieting. Start living." I can? Oh boy! I'm so glad that they told me that I could stop dieting. Finally! More important, they told me that I could start living. I didn't know I was dead, but apparently, I am. Not to worry. They will resurrect me, and they aren't even religious. When I come back to life, they won't even put me on a diet. I just have to "start living." Who wouldn't want that? Because of them, I can have new life, and can eat what I want. All I need to do is to go to their meetings for forty-five minutes a week. That's it. Without dieting, I will have a life and perfect figure, just like the skinny lady. Oh, I forgot the important part, IT'S EASY!

Have you heard the one that says, "the pounds will melt off"? Of course they will, if you live in an incinerator. I got so desperate to lose weight, that this commercial hypnotized me and turned me into an idiot. I ran to the phone hoping to be "one of the first one-hundred callers," so that I could get free shipping and handling. What a deal! If I pay them $39.95, they would take care of the two-dollar postage. When my magic pills arrived, the instructions said, "This pill works best if you stick to our diet." Of course it would. Their diet was painfully difficult. When I stuck to it, I lost weight, but the pill was worthless although they made me believe it would help. One thing I know about popping a pill: IT'S EASY.

A NEW PERSPECTIVE ON DIETING AND WEIGHT LOSS

In 2006 there was a commercial saying that I could look like *America's Next Top Model* if I would be willing to exercise "two minutes a day!" Actually, that was my favorite commercial, because I could eat like a pig and only had to donate two-minutes-a-day to look like that skinny TV lady. Just as I decided to order their program, the commercial disappeared. What a disappointment! Just two-minutes-a-day and I could have had the perfect body. I wonder why that commercial isn't on any more. (If you happen to see it, let me know, because I have been working diligently toward a perfect figure for fifteen years and would love something a little easier.)

Remember phen-fen? This one really worked because dead people are thin. They are skin-and-bones (without the skin). By the way, Phen fen was approved by the FDA. I don't trust the feds.

I even heard a commercial on the radio that said we are all fat because we don't know how to breathe right. I'm serious! I can eat anything I want, as much as I want if I just learn how to breathe. And one thing I know about breathing. IT'S EASY!

One time when I was watching one of those get-skinny-quick commercials, I got down on my hands and knees, crawled over to the TV, and read the teeny, weeny print along the bottom. It said, "Results are not typical." Really? Results-are-not-typical my fat butt! "Results are not typical" translates as, "This only works on .001% of the people, but we can't tell you that or you won't buy our product and we won't make any money." The commercial forgets to mention the thousands of people who tried their product and failed. Where are all the people who are still fat? Why don't we hear their stories? I met one. I is one!

Think about people who you know personally. Have you **ever** met anyone ever who said, "I ordered this thingy from TV and that's how I lost 150- pounds?" I don't know anybody like that (and I'm old). I've tried most of them, and none of them work. I have a friend who keeps ordering these things. Sadly, she's still waddling around, looking for that magic pill or something "easy."

When you watch those commercials, do you really believe it? I used to. Here's the truth:

If any of those pills or programs were easy, we would all be skinny. I know I would be. Wouldn't you? We struggle with our weight because dieting and losing weight is tough, even painful. But when it comes to losing weight, the old expression, "No pain, no gain" (or loss) is true. In my own life, I have found that losing weight is, without a doubt, the most difficult endeavor I have ever taken on, in spite of what the skinny people on TV keep telling me.

On the other hand, I have two friends who have lost more than a hundred pounds each. Both told me the same thing. "IT'S NOT EASY!" Quite simply, it was year-after-year of changing their eating habits, making sacrifices, and often being hungry. Neither of them ever said, "It's easy." Instead, they continue to watch their weight and their diet so they don't gain it back. They will both tell you, "Losing weight and dieting is neither magic nor quick. It's hard work and takes time."

If you really want to get serious about losing weight, stop letting the TV commercials lie to you! Stop thinking that these people care about you! They want your money! Next time one of those commercials comes on, change the channel, burp the baby, wax your eyebrows, run out of the room screaming. Better yet, turn off the TV Then go find something constructive to do.

If you want to know the truth about dieting and weight loss, watch *N.B.C.'s The Biggest Loser*. It's the only reality show that gives you an accurate perspective on dieting and weight loss and how hard it is.

Here's how the show works. They have about six obese contestants who need to lose about 100 pounds or more, but all are determined to lose weight. As the weeks go on, these contestants slowly begin to comprehend the painful truth about losing weight, and I mean painful. As the weeks go on, some of them get so hungry or frustrated they pack their bags, and walk out cussing. They say, "I'm never coming back," but they usually change their mind and return. Others break down and cry because their muscles are sore from exercising, or they're craving junk food. They just can't stand it another day. Some just want to go home and pig out because they are so hungry. They are not actors! They are real people. (Sorry. I guess actors are real people too.) The people on this show are just ordinary people who are tired of being fat but slapped in the face by the bitter truth of what it means to diet.

Reality screams out, "Losing weight is hard work. Get used to it!" Watching these people wrenches your gut, because their tears and frustrations are so real. It's sad, but it's like spanking your child for running out in the street. Truth helps people change direction, make better choices, and save lives.

At the season finale, there's more crying from the ones who are still there, but now they are slender, healthy contestants with tears-of-joy. As they choke up, they say things like, "I had no hope. Nothing has ever worked before." (Boo hoo hoo.) "But I'm so glad I stayed with it because now" (nose blowing) "I know what to do." They finally understand that it's possible to lose weight, but it's work. They get it. They know there is no magic pill or easy plan.

When *Biggest Loser* is on, I sit in front of the TV with a box of tissues and cry along with them. It's so real. The people are genuine. I identify with them. I know exactly what they're talking about. Dieting is hard! It takes time and effort, but it feels so good when it finally works.

Here's the verifiable truth: there is only way to lose weight. Work at it and don't give up. There are no simple answers, but when we get desperate, we believe almost anything, especially when it sounds easy. We want to believe in a magic pill or a quick fix, but please stop listening to these lies! Don't let the skinny people on TV dupe you anymore. Dieting is hard work, but there is hope. However, it only works when we give up our fantasy of an easy answer or a quick fix. To lose weight, we must understand that dieting takes time and daily sacrifices, despite what the commercials tell us. IT'S NOT EASY!

Former Fat Lady Finally Fesses Up

Many years ago, I met a lady who told me she was an alcoholic. Then she proudly announced, "I've been clean and sober for twenty-five years." What? I almost laughed, thinking, *You mean you **used to be** an alcoholic.* After all, if she hadn't had anything to drink for twenty-five years, she obviously wasn't an alcoholic anymore. What is wrong with that woman?

Now after fifteen years of dieting, I understand exactly what she meant. I understand that her temptation to drink is always there, just like my temptation to overeat or to eat the wrong food is always there. Although it gets a little easier with time, she could never say, "I **used to be** an alcoholic." She knew it and because of her, it's my turn to confess.

Hello. My name's Barbara (Barb for short), and I'm a food-a-holic, also known as a compulsive eater, a foodie or a food addict, or a piggy in disguise. If you saw me today, you would look at me and probably say, "You don't look like someone with a food addiction." The problem is that I'm a medium-sized lady, with a big, fat, lady trying desperately to burst out. She and I constantly battle. She's like a fat devil warring against my belly (or soul) saying, "It's only one little brownie." Sometimes she tempts me by saying, "Wouldn't your family love to come home to the smell of chocolate-chip cookies baking in the oven?" Of course, when I hear that little voice, what do you think

I do? I stand up straight and say, "What a great idea. It's all for the children." Then I head for the kitchen, but not always. I'm learning how to reject this demanding devil, but it's a process.

No matter what, this little she-devil refuses to leave me alone, but here's what I learned. The less I feed her, the quieter she gets. She thrives on junk food, generous proportions of mashed potatoes with real butter. She loves compulsive eating. But she grows faint when I eat healthy, smaller portions. She almost disappears when fix a salad with low-fat dressing. She hates it when I pray, but she never totally goes away. Never. Brat!

When I first started my diet, I knew there were food addicts, but I never considered myself one. That's because I thought I knew what one looked like. You know, the lady on *Dr. Oz*, who eats six double-beef cheeseburgers, a half-gallon of soda, and a box of cookies every day **for breakfast**, then continues to eat the rest of the day! Anyone could look at her and see that she cooperated 100% with her she-devil. But I was nothing like her! After all, I was only forty-five pounds overweight. At least I wasn't **morbidly** obese, like her.

I used to think, "I, Barbara McCourtney could not possibly be a food-a-holic because I am **only** forty-five pounds overweight. It's no big deal." It shocks me now that I could have ever believed that. What if I had said the opposite? What if I said, "I'm only forty-five pounds underweight? It's no big deal." You would say, "Crazy lady!"

Yes, forty-five pounds either way is too much. Forty-five pounds is the size of the average kindergartener. Did I think it was no big deal to carry around a five-year-old kid all day? Let's see. Would I strap the little tike on my back, or would I just have them hang on to my ankles as I went about my day? Maybe I could carry the little thing in my arms. And then, when I went to bed, I could have the little stinker sit on me. Yet I kept telling myself, "forty-five pounds is no big deal."

Forty-five pounds is three bowling balls! I spent the day lugging around three bowling balls and wondered why I was so tired at the end of the day.

I also had a hard time with this "food-a-holic" concept because I was almost always on some sort of diet. The huge lady I saw on *Dr. Oz* never deprived herself of anything. She had no self-control and no desire to control herself. I wasn't like her at all. I ate very little junk food, rarely took seconds, and made a point to eat fresh fruits and vegetables every day, so how could anyone call me a food-a-holic?

I look back now and see how deceptive my way of thinking was. I was like the alcoholic who only gets drunk twice a month, holds down a job and goes to church. They think, *Well, of course I'm not an alcoholic. Alcoholics get drunk every weekend and they can't hold down a job, and I know they don't go to church.* Like the alcoholic, I wasn't just deceived. I was stupid.

The one thing that helped opened my eyes more than anything else was counting calories. (More about that later.) When I weighed and measured everything I ate and wrote it down, I realized that I was eating more than I thought, **way more**! Slapped in the face with a calorie counter, helped me realize that I had a problem, a serious problem. I finally understood that I was and always will be a food-a-holic. That's how my journey began.

My Ten-Year Illness

Don't you hate it when people sit around whining about their health? Me too, but I need to mention this because it's a big part of my life, my weight gain, and interference with my weight loss. I also mention it off-and-on throughout my book. I will however, make this as brief and un-boring as possible. (I hate putting my readers to sleep.) Here's the rest of the story.

On my fiftieth birthday, I took my 100-pound chocolate lab for a run, came home, put dinner in the crock pot for me, my husband and all my foster kids, made phone calls, attended appointments, did laundry, mopped the floor, and cleaned the house. About 5:00 p.m., I put on my make-up and went to my big 50th-birthday bash. In other words, I was busy, strong and healthy. That was my lifestyle, nonstop about15-hours a day.

Six months later, I woke up seriously ill, and thought I was dying. I was so weak I couldn't roll over. I couldn't lift my hand to scratch my nose. I didn't have the strength to press the buttons on the remote. I didn't even have enough energy to talk (which is bizarre for me). I laid in a pool of sweat most of the day. My throat felt like I had swallowed a bag of razor blades, and I had a fever, 99.8. (Anything more than 97.6 is unusual for me.) When I went to the bathroom, I had to crawl, and stop to rest along the way. I felt like there was a 200-pound weight on each arm. When I wanted to roll over, it felt like a big fat man was sitting on top of me. I ached everywhere. I thought it was a severe case of strep, but when my husband called the advice nurse, she said, "It's probably the flu. If you are not better in a few days, come back."

After three days of this horrible sickness, I finally went to the doctor. Walking to the car felt like climbing Mount Everest, but I finally got there. I had to use a wheelchair to get from the car to the doctor's office. The doctor ran numerous tests. Everything was negative. Again, I was told, "It's the flu."

It didn't go away. Week-after-week, month-after-month, I could not get well. I had to find a home for my dog and all my foster kids. I didn't even have the strength to heat up soup.

Every two or three months I would "climb a mountain" to see a different doctor. That's when I started meeting the world's dumbest doctors. (That should be my next book.) One doctor proudly announced, "You're just going through the change." Weird because I had already done that two years earlier. Does it come back? Sounds like a scary movie. *The Revenge of the Change.* Besides, what does a sore throat and a fever have to do with the change? A few months later, that same doctor shouted in my face, "There's nothing wrong with you!" Two different docs told me, "You're healthy." I wonder how many healthy people are so weak they can't scratch their nose.

One doctor told me that this was a classic case of depression, even though he couldn't explain the fever and sore throat. I tried several antidepressants. I got all the side effects and none of the benefits. Another doctor said "fibromyalgia." That didn't explain the sore throat. Yet another doctor said, "You can't be that sick. You keep gaining weight." That's what they told him in medical school so he thought he should pass it on to me.

After two years, I found a doctor who said, "chronic fatigue." That was a good guess and it fit my symptoms, but she couldn't tell me the root cause or what to do about it. My illness finally had a name, but no hope and no cure; just a name.

I tried vitamins and minerals to no avail. Nothing worked. Over the years, I continued my search for a cure. It was so hard, but I wanted to get well. I prayed too. Four-and-a-half years of laying around, begging God to either heal me or kill me, I found my first answer, Paul Rosen. He had been trained in something called "Nutrition Response Testing," although it's MUCH MORE THAN NUTRITION. Providers who do this testing call themselves "Herbalists." I call them a-light-in-the-darkness. They are similar to a naturopath, but not able to prescribe drugs, and much, much cheaper than a naturopath. Legally, an herbalist is not allowed to diagnose, but that's pretty much what they do. They just can't call it that.

After my Herbalist, Paul Rosen ran his strange, nontraditional tests, he gave me answers. He said I had parasites and food sensitivities (like allergies but less severe). He also said that my adrenal glands were failing. After that, he put me on a specific diet that he created just for me. He told me which foods to stay away from and which foods to eat more of. He also gave me herbs and food supplements.

It was the first time in four years that I started to feel better! I couldn't believe it! **My health turned at a snail's pace, but clearly a turning point.** I could walk across a room without passing out. I could scratch my nose. I could heat soup and sweep the floor without feeling like a walking zombie. I could work for ten minutes and then had to rest for an hour, but it was a huge improvement. My sore throat and fever gradually dissipated. The fatigue was still there; better, but not gone, but I had hope.

<u>Something supernatural:</u> I was incredibly grateful that I felt better, but after several years of being on herbs, I hit a plateau. Although I was able to do simple things, I was still weak. I wanted to get completely well and couldn't seem to figure out how.

There were a lot of little things that helped, but one of the biggest turning points was in the eighth year of my illness, I went to a healing service at my friend's church. Filled with anticipation, I hoped for a supernatural touch from God, so my healing would be complete. Instead, God spoke to my heart. He said, "Stop acting like a sick person." I was so disappointed! It wasn't what I wanted to hear. In fact, I felt annoyed. Couldn't God just touch me and heal me? But His words were exactly what I needed. I had been laying around for so many years that I didn't know how to act like anything except a sick person. I would do a few chores, then sit for an hour. Then I would get up and do a few more things and sit for two hours. After God spoke to me, I started forcing myself to work harder. My muscles were weak. Therefore, everything I tried to do was grueling, but I gradually improved. A few years later, I joined the YMCA and started taking the "low-impact" exercises classes. I remember my first class. I made it through six whole minutes watching the clock the entire time, thinking, *One more minute. One more minute.* When I quit, I thought I was going to faint, but I didn't. I started out small and slowly worked up. I improved, little-by-little.

I'm still working on my health. I study nutrition, read, and pray, always looking for new answers, refusing to give up. I tell people it took me ten years to get healthy, but I'm still not where I should be. At the end of ten years, I still had a few symptoms and still do. I'm about 75% better, but I'm shooting for 100%. The problem now is that I'm in my 60's. That usually means less health, not more. I don't care. I won't accept poor health even though I'm aging. If Benjamin Button can do it, so can I.

Here's why I shared all this with you. Because **my book repeatedly refers to this strange illness in different places.** I also shared this with you because I wish more than weight-loss for you. I wish you health. I've learned about both, and I did it the hard way, not from a book. I learned from personal experience.

You probably know thin people who are not necessarily healthy. I was one. Before my illness hit, I was at my ideal weight, running a mile-a-day, aerobics three-times-a-week, and thought I was healthy. Looking back, I can see that I made a lot of "eating errors," but I'm hoping that you can learn from me. The old saying, "what doesn't kill you, makes you stronger" seems to be true.

I used to ask God why He allowed me to be so sick for so long. There's a verse in II Corinthians 1:3-5 that explains it. It says that God allows us to go through tough times, so that we can help others when they go through the same thing. God allowed me to be sick and fat so that I could help others. That's what I'm hoping to do; help you lose weight and get healthy.

The Psychology Behind My Fat Behind

My friends expect something intelligent from me because I have a Bachelor's Degree in Psychology and a Master's of Science Degree in Counseling. In addition to that, I'm always on some sort of diet. Consequently, people want to know, from a psychological viewpoint, how I got so fat. I have an answer, but it's probably not what you think, because most psychology tries to convince us that our problems (such as overeating) have something to do with our past. This leads people to believe that they are fat because their mother yelled at them. If that were true, we would all be fat. Unfortunately, psychology is often used as an excuse for bad behavior. In other words, most psychology is crap. Just my opinion.

Each and every psychotherapist has their own ideas about what causes obesity, but personally, I believe that overeating has very little to do with our past. (If you had a painful past, I'm not making light of it and I'm sorry that happened to you, however, not everything you do is about your past.) Millions of people with a horrible past have healthy eating habits. So much for that theory.

The good news is that there is one branch of psychology that has been studied and scientifically proven called **Behavioral Psychology.** This type of psychology has nothing to do with your past and not based on guess work. It's tested, common sense, and extremely effective. It started in the 1800's with tests done on dogs (Pavlov's dogs) and other animals. Later these studies were generalized (transferred) to humans, and it clearly explains why we eat too much.

Now, get ready because I'm going to tell you what this intelligent form of psychology has to do with poor eating habits. First, I will tell you what it is not. According to *Behavioral Psychology*, you are **not** fat because your grandma spanked you or because you didn't have a dad. Plain and simply, *Behavioral Psychology* does not deal with your past, no matter how painful. Instead, it's based on consequences.

Here it is. There are two types of consequences, rewards and punishment. The first one, "rewards" feel good, so it naturally increases certain behaviors (similar to a bribe). The second type of consequence is "punishment." If it's painful enough, it decreases or stops certain behaviors. Both must be applied correctly in order to work. (Remember, I said it was simple.) Here's what a Behavioral Therapist says about people who eat too much and why. Ready?

1. They get hungry.
2. Hunger is uncomfortable and they want to get rid of it or stop it.
3. They eat.
4. Food satisfies their craving and their hunger goes away.
5. It feels good.
6. They have just rewarded them self with food.
7. It feels good, so they continue eat whenever they are hungry.

That's it. People eat because they're hungry, and food is a reward. Now aren't you glad I told you that. Otherwise, you would have been clueless. Now you can become a Behavioral Psychologist.

Seriously, food is the perfect reward for being hungry, and we naturally respond to rewards. Everyone! We love rewards. They motivate us. When your child cleans his room, you give him a hug, or a star on his chart, or something that makes him feel good. You reward your child so he will be more likely to repeat that behavior.

That's the goal. People go to work because they want their reward at the end of the week, a paycheck. Rewards not only motivate people. They make us continue the same behavior so we will continue being rewarded and keep feeling good. HOWEVER, THIS IS A BIG PROBLEM WHEN IT COMES TO EATING. Food is a wonderful reward when you are hungry. The problem is that it seems like it's your **ONLY** reward. How else do you get rid of your hunger besides eating?

But wait! There's more bad news! Another thing you must know about rewards is this: **If a reward is not immediate, it's not effective.** That's why diets don't work and why they are so difficult. When you get hungry and eat, you feel rewarded **immediately.** On the other hand, if you get hungry, deny yourself because you are on a diet, and a week later you lose a half-a-pound, that doesn't feel like a reward because it's not immediate. There is too much time between the "pain" (hunger) and the reward (weight loss). The brain doesn't associate those two as something that goes together. Dieting (being hungry) feels more like a punishment. I'm hungry and deny myself my favorite foods seven days in a row, and then only lose a half-a-pound? The natural response is, "I give up." I've been punished for being good. Why bother?

However, I have good news, finally. Behavioral Psychology was done on dogs and animals. It's based on instincts and responses to those instincts. The difference is that we are intelligent human beings with the ability to think logically. So, repeat after me. "I am smarter than a dog." Yes, you are and don't forget it!

If a dog sees a steak, he runs over and eats it. He wants it; therefore, he eats it. He's an animal. He doesn't have the ability nor the desire to reason. He cannot tell himself, "I better not eat that steak. I might get fat." But you are not a dog. You can talk yourself out of eating something, especially if you know you shouldn't. You know how to exercise self-control. If you don't know, you can learn.

Isn't that what we constantly teach our children, self-control? When they are little, we teach them to share. They don't like it and don't understand it, but we keep teaching them kindness, and thinking of others until they grasp the idea. When they are teenagers, we tell them to stay away from drugs and to control their sexual urges. Throughout life, we are all taught to control our animal urges. Unfortunately, we often forget to teach our children (and ourselves) to ignore our eating urges. It's natural to eat, **but we have control over it.**

This is how I deal with it. I use logic. When I get hungry, I talk to myself. I say, "If I ignore that brownie, I will lose weight, look good, and feel better." Then, I look at a picture of Jennifer Aniston and say, "If I stop eating brownies, I will look like her . . . someday." I look at the Brownie, then at Jennifer. The thought of looking like Jennifer Aniston is a reward for being hungry. In other words, I use my common sense, rather than my instincts. So can you. If not, you put yourself on the same level as a dog.

I would like to have a bracelet that says, "WWJAE," which stands for "What Would Jennifer Aniston Eat?" I would wear it and look at it often. As an intelligent human being, I can figure out ways to reward myself. Now that you understand part one of psychology, let's go on to part two.

Stopping Bad Behavior:

According to Behavioral Psychology, the best was to stop bad behavior is to administer a painful consequence (or punishment) after the bad behavior. If your child reaches out to touch the hot stove, what do you do? You grab his hand and shout, "No!" Maybe a swat on the hand. The goal is to make sure the child stops this behavior. Therefore, the consequences must be so painful that the child will never do it again. Some countries allow the child to touch the stove or fire. The child remembers. (Don't do that in our country. You will get arrested.)

What's important is this: the painful consequences must be administered immediately after the deed in order to be effective. **If it's not immediate, it's not effective.** If a child reaches for the hot stove and two hours later, you yell, "No," your kid will think, *What is wrong with Mommy?* The parent must give the painful consequence **immediately** in order for the child's brain to associate the consequence with the action. So do we.

However, this is a major problem when it comes to eating or overeating. How am I going to apply an immediate painful consequence if I pop a big brownie in my mouth? What am I supposed to do? Bend over and spank myself? (Might be a problem if I've been invited over for dinner or am eating in a classy restaurant.) Eating delicious, unhealthy foods, or eating too much is not painful at all. It's pleasurable and makes me want to keep eating. A brownie is a reward.

Wouldn't it be great if I ate a batch of brownies and **immediately** got a horrible stomachache and started barfing my guts out? Guess what would happen? I would stop. I wouldn't do it anymore. No one would. Who wants to be doubled over in pain, kneeling by the toilet? Unfortunately, the stomachache comes an hour or two later. Consequently, our brain doesn't connect the two. That explains why hangovers don't stop people from drinking. The person gets drunk and has a great time, laughing and hanging out with friends. The hangover comes the next day. The brain does not associate the two as going together. You would think the drunk would get a clue, but food addicts don't, so why should anyone else?

I have two choices. I can either be logical, or I can respond to my animal instincts. That's it! I must constantly remind myself that I am an intelligent human being, smarter than a dog.

But how can I punish myself if I cheat? This is what I do. After I bite into a brownie, I look at a picture of a fat lady (me, a few years ago) and say to myself, "Just keep eating this and you will look like her again. Do you want to look like her?" (This is the opposite of the Jennifer Aniston picture.) Something else that works for me is to look up the calories and carbohydrates and write it down. **Now that's painful!** A large brownie has enough calories to be a meal and enough carbohydrates for two days. Checking the calories and carbs hurts, and stops me from having more. Another painful consequence is to picture myself getting on the scale and seeing that I've gained back what I worked so hard on losing. Am I going to ruin my diet in one day by eating a plate of brownies? That's what's going to happen. How painful is that? Worse yet, brownies have no nutritional value. If I eat a plate of brownies, I either have to skip a few meals, or gain weight. This leads to poor health too.

So, what are you going to do? How can you administer a painful consequence after eating badly? A friend of mine puts a rubber band on her wrist. Every time she bites into something unhealthy or takes seconds, she pulls back the rubber band and snaps it, hard. It works for her. No thanks. I'm not a masochist. There are other things you could do, but you have to figure it out for yourself. Ask yourself, "How can I make something delicious, painful?" It's up to you. Be creative, but don't spank yourself. You might get caught.

Now, there are four things you learned about Behavioral Psychology.

1. Your painful past has nothing to do with overeating.
2. You overeat because it feels good.
3. You are smarter than a dog.
4. Brownies taste good.

Now that you understand the psychology behind your behind. Let's move on to a clearer understanding of how "stinking thinking" affected my eating habits and how it kept me fat.

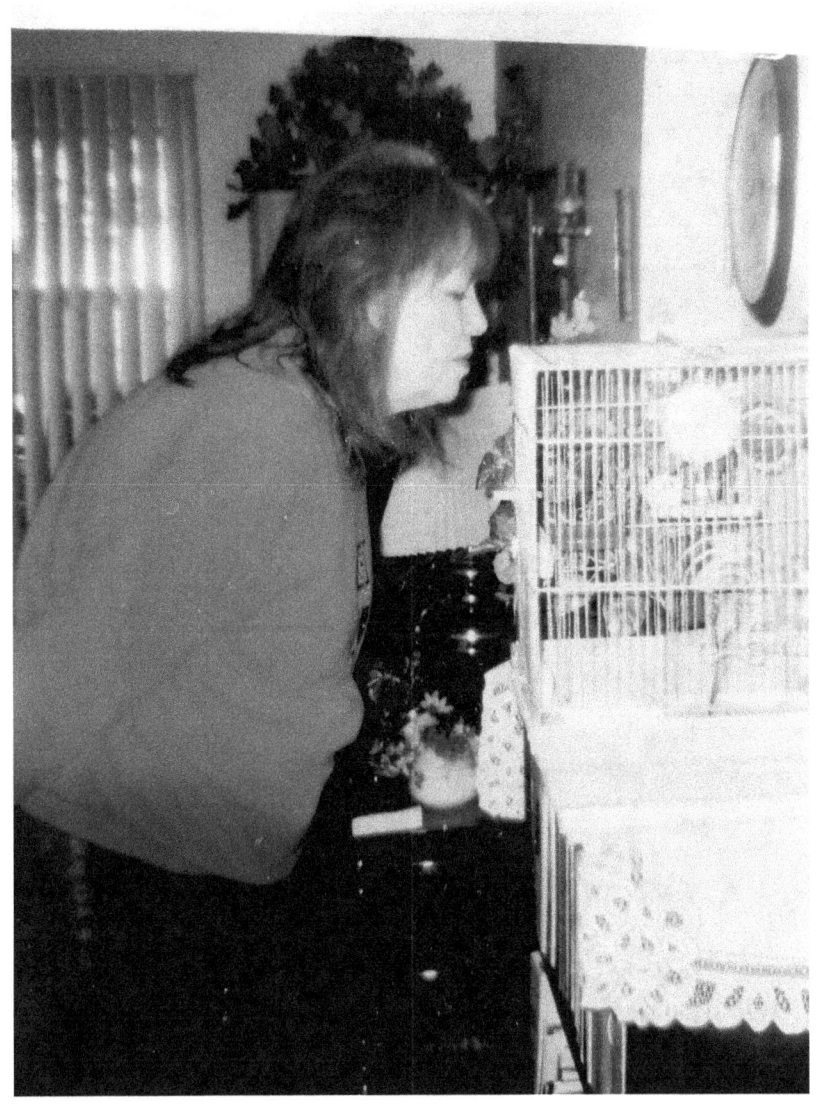

This is me at 200 pounds. Embarrassing!

This is me seven years later.

PART II

Ten Things I Used to Believe When I Was Stupid

(But Now I Smart)

How and Why These Things Kept Me Fat

These "things" I used to believe have a name, called "logical reasons," logical and good. Don't we all have logical reasons why we can't lose weight? They really aren't logical and they aren't good either. The correct name for these "things" is "denial," such a civilized word. If you talk to a therapist or psychologist, they politely say, "My client is having difficulty reconciling reality with their psyche." Isn't that nice? In other words, they just can't help it. The poor little creatures. They're so human.

But a more accurate term for "denial," is "excuse." I know, because I was the Queen of Excuses. (Aren't you glad I didn't say Queen of Denial?) Sometimes my excuses for eating too much were good excuses, like, "I'm so hungry," or "I don't really eat that much." But whatever the excuse, it kept me from getting serious about losing weight. Worse yet, it kept me gaining. Excuses allowed me to behave badly and then excuse myself, like the kid at the dinner table who passes gas as loudly as he can. Then, in a sweet little voice says, "Excuse me."

The definition of "excuse" is "to seek or serve to justify a fault or offense." How saint-like. We do whatever we want, then justify it. That's what a sociopath does. He kills someone, then excuses it by saying, "It's not my fault. I couldn't help it." I wasn't much different. I didn't kill anyone, but I was a food addict and food addicts excuse their behavior. I said, "It's not my fault. I just can't help it." Whatever I told myself was a poor justification for my weaknesses, namely over eating. I think most people are like me. They lie to themselves when it comes to food. (This is good information, coming from The Queen.)

It's important that we stop calling it 'a logical reason,' or 'excuse,' or even 'denial.' **It should be called "bull plop."** When I make an excuse for bad behavior, I call it what it is, lying. Maybe I'm only lying to myself, but I'm still lying. A lie is a lie. Yes, when I try to convince myself that I really want to change, and then don't, I lie, but I don't have to. I can fix myself. I start by recognizing that I'm lying and making excuses. **When I get honest with myself, that's when change begins.**

Where do I get my ideas about excuses? Actually, there is a little plagiarism going on here. This idea (lying to yourself) is all over the Bible, especially in the book of Proverbs. This chapter of the Bible was written by King Solomon, the wisest man who ever lived. He wrote the book of Proverbs so that his people would know how to live and how to act in every circumstance. Here are two of my favorites verses that explains denial.

> *"There is a way that seems right to a man,*
> *but its end is the way of death."*
> (Proverbs 14:12, NKJV)

Even back then people lied to themselves. (Thank God, it's not just me.) The Bible says it again a little differently in this verse.

> *"We can always 'prove' that we are right,*
> *but is the Lord convinced?"*
> (Proverbs 16:2, The New Living Bible).

I can pretend that I don't know, and make all kinds of excuses, but I can't hide from God. He knows. Without Him, I would still be in denial, and still be fat.

Do you know what else the Bible says about people who make excuses? It says they're lazy. Look at this verse.

> *"The lazy man is full of excuses. 'I can't go to work!' he says. 'If I go outside, I might meet a lion in the street and be killed.'"*
> (Proverbs 22:13, The Living Bible).

I would comment on this, but it's so clear that lazy people make excuses, and **dieting is hard work!** (I think I mentioned that.) To lose weight, I had to stop making excuses, stop being lazy, put my nose to the grindstone, and work. It's worth it.

I used to make up a lot of excuses. Sometimes I still do, but here's My Top Ten List:

LIE #1

I'm the Exception

That's me. I had no doubt that I was the exception. I had always watched my weight, but started gaining two-or-three-pounds-a-year when I was in my forties. I continually gained no matter what I did. I had always been on some-sort-of-a-diet, but it felt like I was eating almost nothing and still not doing well.

When I was in my late forties, I joined a weight-loss group at my church. It was only six weeks, but it put me on the right track. I finally did it. I hit my goal, but it was such a serious and constant battle that I felt like something was terribly wrong with me. Was dieting and losing weight really supposed to be this hard?

Then, tragedy struck. Two years after striving and fighting to maintain my ideal weight, my ten-year illness hit. I started gaining again, about a pound-and-a-half-per-month. I was trying to be careful, but I couldn't exercise anymore. I couldn't even walk to the kitchen without resting. In addition, I was so sick that I couldn't shop or cook or even fix myself a bowl of soup. Well-meaning friends and family would come over with a plate of homemade cookies or a big batch of spaghetti. After lying in bed all day, I was so hungry when the food came, I ate too much, and most of it was unhealthy, fattening or both. Because I couldn't exercise or even walk, it all went to fat.

That's when I realized, I was that person who was destined to be fat no matter what I did.

In many ways, I really did have an excuse. When I talked to my doctor, she said my thyroid was low. That definitely makes a person fat, but there was a problem. My thyroid was at the absolute lowest end of normal, right on the edge. I had all the symptoms of a low thyroid, but the doctor couldn't prescribe anything to boost my thyroid. She said, "You are still in the normal range even though it's on the lowest end and you have all the symptoms." A low thyroid slows your metabolism and causes weight gain. So, I had a good excuse. Then on top of that, I couldn't possibly exercise. The most exercise I got was to scratch my nose. However, after three years of gaining weight, week-after-week, month-after-month, I got tired of it and turned it around, despite my illness, lack of energy, and thyroid issues. How I did it is in the chapter, "When All Else Fails." I was still seriously ill and felt like I was dying, but **I didn't want to be a fat lady lying in my coffin**. For now, we need to focus on the excuse called "I'm the exception," and why it doesn't hold water. (No pun intended.)

There are some of you reading this who really believe that your fat is not your fault. **Most** people who say that are full of it (literally). However, there truly are some exceptions, but they are rare, extremely rare.

One of my closest friends eats about half what I do, exercises more and is more-than a hundred pounds overweight. I have known her for thirty years, so I know she's not a compulsive eater and she doesn't deserve her excess poundage. Even her children don't understand it. Her doctors are baffled.

The most bizarre thing about her weight is that when she's pregnant, she begins losing a pound-or-two-a-week. She doesn't change her eating habits and doesn't have any morning sickness. She just starts losing huge amounts of weight. Pregnant women are supposed to gain about fifty pounds. Instead, she is usually about fifty pounds lighter by the time her baby is born. She's had five kids.

Each pregnancy her doctors throw a fit, telling her she needs to eat more or she will hurt her baby. She tells them, "I eat all the time and I eat healthily!" They never believe her. However, nine months later, she spits out an eight-or-nine-pound baby in perfect health. Unfortunately, as soon as her baby is born, her eating habits stay the same, but her pounds returned. Did you get that? When she's NOT pregnant, she gains. When she IS pregnant, she loses, without changing any of her eating habits. Clearly, something's physically wrong, probably a hormonal imbalance, but the doctors can't seem to figure it out. There's no logical reason for her excess weight, but until someone figures out what's wrong, she just has to keep eating well and doing her best. At this time, she is still overweight, but here is what's important. **She never gives up.** She eats healthy, small portions, but still gains. She doesn't care if she's the exception. She refuses to quit dieting.

Here's another story, one that inspires me. My daughter's friend has fatty liver disease and Cushing's Syndrome, a disease where her body makes too much cortisol. Cortisol makes you fat. When she told me her diagnosis, I said, "That explains why you are having so much trouble losing weight."

She responded, "No. That only explains part of it. The other part is that I eat too much." I was so proud of her. Her honesty about her weight was so refreshing and so unique. She had a great excuse for her obesity and didn't use it. She understood that part of her problem was her disease and part of it was poor eating habits. She's now dieting, barely losing anything, but she finally stopped gaining. She feels good about it.

Another friend, Colleen who's in my T.O.P.S. group (Take Off Pounds Sensibly) is about sixty pounds overweight. She diligently sticks to her diet, keeps a food journal, and exercises, but can't lose any weight. I couldn't understand. One time when I talked to her, this is what she told me. "I had a kidney transplant ten years ago. I take medication that causes weight gain. I don't have a choice. I have to take it. Either that or die." When she told me which medications she took, she was right. Two of them cause serious weight gain. I asked her if there was anything she could do about it. She stood up straight and said, "Of course. Stick to my diet and keep exercising. I may not lose anything, but I'm determined to stop gaining, no matter what. Otherwise, I'm going to be really fat." How inspiring is that? She had an excuse and was determined to work around it.

Another guy I know had been underweight all of his life. One time he had an abscess tooth. While at the dentist, he had a severe reaction to novocaine and nearly died. He was in a coma for a month. When he finally came out of the coma, he started gaining four or five pounds a week! The doctors couldn't figure out why, and never did. Now he lives on fifteen-hundred calories a day, exercises, and is still gaining. Did you catch that? He diets anyway, determined to do his best in spite of his situation. How many of us would be that diligent?

These four people clearly have legitimate excuses for being overweight, but none of them gave up. They had an obstacle but didn't use it for an excuse. Let their stories inspire you! Whether you are the exception or not, ask yourself this. Why give up? You only have one body. Take the best care of it possibly. Stop putting sugar and junk food in it. Stop stuffing it so full that it shoots up your blood pressure and overworks your heart. Take a few extra minutes a day. Keep a food journal. Use the tips and tricks in this book to make yourself the best and healthiest person you can possibly be no matter what's wrong with you.

I entitled this section of the book, *Ten Things I Used to Believe Back When I Was Stupid* **because I really believed these things.** I believed that losing weight was totally and completely hopeless because of my health. Impossible! I believed I was the exception. No matter what I did, I couldn't lose any weight. But when I started a food journal and counted calories, I found out that **most** of what I believed was untrue. Whining and making excuses was so much easier. When I let go of these excuses, I discovered it wasn't hopeless, just painful. I didn't like painful. Most of us don't. I also discovered that I tend to lose weight very slowly, about a half-a-pound a month, and only when I'm conscientious and consistent. (The two C's.) It doesn't seem fair, but I was and still am determined to stay on my diet and off the crap that causes weight gain and health problems. My thyroid is low. Exercising is nearly impossible. I have an excuse, but I refuse to quit. I'll continually stand my ground. I feel good about it.

After I got serious about dieting, something strange happened. I noticed that other people used the same excuses I had. I felt sad for them. Worse yet, I understood that I looked just like them when I used those excuses. I wrote this part of the book to wake up anyone who **really** wants to lose weight, but feels like it's impossible. I want people to be honest, so they can get healthy, lose weight, and feel good. No more excuses, even if you have an excuse.

LIE # 2

I'll Start My Diet Tomorrow

<u>Ode to a Diet</u>
I'll start my diet tomorrow.
I said as I stepped on the scale.
After it creaked and squeaked.
I felt like a whale.

I'll start my diet tomorrow.
I said as I made a plan.
Writing down every calorie,
Sugar and junk-food I banned.

I'll start my diet tomorrow.
I felt it to the depth of my soul.
This time I would do it.
Even if it took a toll.

I'll start my diet tomorrow.
Is that really what I said?
I sucked in my stomach
And realized, I don't look that bad.

Whenever I say I'll start my diet tomorrow, I mean it! It usually starts when I step on the scale and I'm up a few pounds or when I can't button my pants. I panic. I'm starting to gain back everything I just lost. Do I really want to do that? No! I refuse! I definitely will start my diet tomorrow, and this time I really will. I think. I plan. I write it out. I **will** overcome!

I wake up the next morning and reread the plan I made the night before. I go to the kitchen and eat a small bowl of oatmeal with molasses and flax seeds, almond milk, a few walnuts and a cup of hot tea. Protein, complex carbohydrates, fiber, healthy fats. Perfect! I plan to have a crisp juicy apple for my midmorning break. But an hour after breakfast, my foster daughter gets up and bakes homemade biscuits, the smell wafting through the house. I try to go about my business, but there she is slathering on the butter and honey, adding to the aroma. I think, *One little bite won't hurt.* So, I give in, just one. It tastes so good, so very good. As I approach the last bite of this hot, buttery biscuit, dripping with honey, I start thinking about my next one. Proudly, I stop after two, but then I wonder, do I skip the apple? Yes, of course. Two buttery biscuits loaded with condiments instead of an apple. Makes sense to me.

For the rest of the day I know that my plans are down the toilet, but now I have a new plan. Stop getting on the scale. Throw away my tight pants. Then I won't have to make that promise ever again. However, a week or two later, I bend down to put on my shoes, but can't see my feet. Finally, I go through the same routine. Tomorrow. I'll start tomorrow. Does any of this sound familiar?

Think of all the people who have said they were going to start doing something, or quit doing something tomorrow. . . eventually . . . someday . . . How many people have told you they were going to quit smoking? Some actually quit. Most don't. Have you ever heard anyone say they are going back to school? My favorite one is, "I've thought about writing a book." Most never start. But the one I hear most often is that they are going on a diet. (Me too.) The implication is "later" or "tomorrow." I believe they want to. So do I, but when?

Do you know why I told myself that I would start my diet tomorrow? First, I knew I needed to lose weight. I was sick of grabbing handfuls of love handles. I had no doubt that it was time to cut the junk food and start my diet, but I said "tomorrow" because I really didn't want to make the hard choices. My brain reminded me of the required sacrifices, painful sacrifices, and hunger pangs. I also remembered dieting takes time, planning, effort, work. I had so many mixed emotions, so I told myself that I will definitely go on a diet. "I promise, but not right now."

Usually when I say, "I'll start my diet tomorrow," (instead of now) it's because I'm driving by a *Dairy Queen* and I hear an Oreo Blizzard calling my name. When I used to say, "I'll start my diet tomorrow," it should have been followed with, "... but right now I'm going to eat like a pig." Consequently, I had two thoughts in my head, battling for first place. I want to lose weight, but I don't want to make the sacrifice. The food is available. Weight loss is years away.

Here's how I overcame this excuse. First, I decided to STOP SAYING IT, ever again. When I finally decided to get serious about losing weight, I started saying this instead: "**I'll *cheat on* my diet tomorrow.**" Then I followed it with "... **but today**, I'm going to stick to my diet." I only changed a few words, but what a difference!

I came up with this idea on my own, but alcoholics have a similar idea called one-day-at-a-time. (I thought of it first.) Alcoholics are often overwhelmed with the urge to drink, so they tell themselves that they will be sober for today only. They don't worry about tomorrow. It works! It has kept millions of alcoholics sober for over half-a-century. That's why Jesus said, *"Don't worry about tomorrow. Let tomorrow take care of itself. Just worry about today."* (Matthew 6:33, loosely translated.)

Something else that helps me when I start to lie to myself is this. If my foster daughter makes homemade biscuits, I set a timer. (A timer is one of my best friends when I'm trying to diet.) I tell myself that I can have half-of-a-biscuit in thirty minutes. It gives me time to think about it instead of eating mindlessly or responding to my animal instincts. Instead, I stay busy doing something constructive like cleaning the kitchen or folding clothes. But here's the amazing part. When the timer goes off, I have usually lost the urge to eat. I controlled myself for thirty minutes and it changes my thinking. My pride wells up and I feel inspired. In spite of it, I set the timer for another thirty minutes to see if I can do it again. In other words, **I continually postpone eating**. Some people call this "delayed gratification." (Sounds so intellectual.) Postponing junk food teaches me that I don't have to eat just because I feel like it. I take control over my impulsivity. This starts a new habit. Usually after one or two resets, I lose the urge. Then I put all the leftover biscuits in the fridge and forget about them. Try it. You'll like it. Not the biscuit. The idea.

An Excuse Disguised-as-Tomorrow:

How many times have you said, "I'll start my diet **after** the holidays." It's the same idea as "I'll start tomorrow," except the holidays are longer. I knew I needed to lose weight, but not now. Year-after-year, I told myself, **I will diet after the holidays.** The holidays started on Thanksgiving (or maybe Halloween) and ended on January first. Do you realize that excuse gave me permission to "pig out" for two full months? At the time, I didn't look at it that way. It sounded logical.

So, there I was, January 1st, five-pounds fatter, feeling physically ill and bloated, promising to start my diet. When that day finally came, I faithfully started up the newest weight-loss plan. I even looked forward to it, feeling confident that I could do it this time. Sometimes it lasted three or four days, sometimes a week, or even the whole month of January, but my good intentions, were undermined by two months of bad eating habits. I had just spent all that time without any boundaries on what I ate, and now because I flipped over the calendar, I was suddenly going to have this great self-control?

Where was that going to come from? I had to make some changes, but how?

Planned cheating:

Here's what I do now. I make a specific plan to cheat on my diet. Yes, you can read that sentence again. **I plan to cheat.** However, instead of cheating for two solid months, I pick four days during the holidays to cheat. This gives me power and control over my eating and cheating. I also have something to look forward to while I deprive myself. A few days before Thanksgiving, when I start thinking about cheating, I remind myself, *only two more days and then I can cheat; then one more day.* The self-control feels so much better than all the crap I was about to eat. And it's definitely better than waddling around, loosening my pants, and farting.

The Secret to Cheating:

How to cheat is my little secret, but I will share it with you. (Don't tell anyone.) On Thanksgiving Day (the biggest meal of the year), I have a small portion of everything with an emphasis on veggies. This is usually a good-sized plateful. No dessert yet! Afterwards, I put my plate in the kitchen, have a cup of hot tea or coffee, visit with my friends and relatives, and play with my grandchildren. Then I pick up the dishes, and refill everyone's coffee. In other words, I stay busy instead of focusing on food.

Now it's time for dessert, usually four or five delectable dishes. I choose a small portion of two of my favorites, Mom's cherry cheesecake and my sister-in-law's peanut brittle. (Mm mmm. I can still taste it.) I sit down and slowly enjoy each bite sipping coffee or tea between the bites. Yum! When I'm done, I jump up and start cleaning the kitchen. This keeps me occupied and my hostess adores me. After drying the last dish, I go back and get a small portion of one or two foods that tasted particularly good. I usually have seconds on Mom's Caesar salad and another sliver of that cherry cheesecake, of course. As I carry out this ritual, I know that I'm taking a day off from my diet, and that I will get back on it the next morning. It doesn't feel like cheating because I am in control. It's planned. If something looks really good, I take home that one food and eat it the next morning. (I love mashed potatoes and gravy for breakfast.) Then I look at my calendar and know that the next time I can cheat is my mom's Christmas party, two weeks after Thanksgiving. It gives me something to look forward to. My four favorite days to cheat during the holidays are Thanksgiving, Christmas, and New Year's Eve, and Mom's Christmas party. **It's planned.** But all those days in between, I stick to my diet, looking forward to those special days.

Another way to plan cheating is to eat less the day before and the day after the big day. If you are counting calories, you can cut 500 calories the day before and the day after. That allows you to eat an extra 1,000 calories!

Here's another idea. Center your big meal around vegetables. When there is a big meal or potluck, there are usually a lot of vegetable dishes. Load your plate with those first. If there's fish or poultry, do that next. Go easy on the potatoes and run from the dinner rolls. (You don't need all those carbohydrates.) Vegetables are a good way to stick to your diet and for that one day, you won't need to count calories.

If you really want to, you can pig-out on Thanksgiving, and then fast the next day. When you fast, you don't necessarily have to stop eating. Maybe have a low-cal smoothie for breakfast, and a light soup or *Horrible Soup* for lunch. (Recipe in the back.) But, decide how you want to fast ahead of time. (For more information, see the chapter "The Joy of Fasting.") Whatever you do, **plan out exactly how and when you are going to cheat,** but please, don't eat like a fat cow for two months. Your body will get very mad at you. So will your pants.

About Once a Month

There are many holidays, birthdays, pot lucks or family get-togethers that seem to come up every three or four weeks. Those are days I plan to cheat, but it's planned! That way, I'm not giving in to every eating-urge as it hits. I'm taking control. For me, the simplest way is to eat a lot of vegetables, cut back on the carbohydrates, and stay busy. The next day, I jump back on the wagon. You can make any plan you want, but do something.

Dr. Laura Schlessinger, a well-known talk-show host who is very slim and trim saves her dessert (cheating) for Saturday morning. She has something sweet with a cup of tea. Like me, she plans to cheat, then goes back right back to her healthy eating.

Some of the popular diet groups recommend taking one-day-a-week off. Too much for me. If I tried that, it would open a can of worms (or *Almond Roca*). I know myself well enough that once-a-week would give me too much leeway. However, I have a friend who takes every Saturday off. She's lost ninety-two pounds! She looks forward to her day off. It helps her stay on track. She told me, "If I couldn't have a day off every week, I could never stick to my diet."

Here's the key: figure out what works for you. Plan ahead, but whatever you do, stop giving in to all your urges. Then take a vow that you will never again say, "I'll start my diet tomorrow." Take control. Say, **"That food looks really good, but I will eat it tomorrow. TODAY I will stick to my diet!"**

LIE #3

I Don't Eat That Much

When I was fat, I thought I was doing a good job. I would skip dessert and think I was wonderful. Whenever I purchased anything that said "lite" or "sugar free" I burst buttons. And my head was the size of a watermelon when I bought 1% milk instead of 2%. One time I wanted to give myself a trophy when I decided not to have seconds. I was convinced beyond a doubt that I wasn't eating that much. But when I stepped on the scale, up another half-pound for the tenth week-in-a-row, I thought, *How is this possible? All I'm eating are salads and light yogurt. Maybe something's wrong with my scale.* That was another lie. If it was the scale, then why were my clothes getting smaller?

When I said, "I don't eat that much," the translation was, "I'm making all kinds of sacrifices, but I'm not losing weight." Or, "I don't eat nearly as much as my friends." I continued to modify my eating, but was still gaining. Not a lot, but about a pound a month. It doesn't sound like much, but gradually, over the years, I had packed on an extra forty-five extra pounds, or three bowling balls. When I said, "I don't eat that much," I was like the drunk driver who tells the officer, "I only had a couple of beers," but their blood-alcohol level doesn't support what they are saying. My pot belly and my scale refused to support me either. Darn tattle-tales!

I finally got in touch with reality when I started doing two things. First, I started writing down everything I put in my mouth. Just that one act alone stopped me from believing this lie. I honestly thought I didn't eat that much, but when I wrote it down, I realized how ignorant I was. **To be honest, I lied.** I was like those criminals on true-crime shows who lie so much that they believe their lies. Embarrassing! Writing it down (a.k.a. keeping a food journal) helped me see I was nibbling my way to obesity. Writing down **everything** I put in my mouth, especially my "nibbles," forced me into a new perspective.

When I began my first food journal, I cringed when I started to have a second brownie. I didn't mind writing down "1 small brownie," but did I really want to write down "3 brownies" or "4" or "5"? Before I started a food journal, I had convinced myself that I rarely ate junk food or **very** small amounts. (My grandkids were probably wondering why my pants weren't on fire.) I'm guessing that everybody and their brother knew how much I was eating, except me. A pencil and a piece of paper were the most powerful tools I have ever used to get me in touch with reality and help me understand that I was eating far more than I thought I was.

When I used to say, "I don't eat that much," it was ridiculous. How could I say "I don't eat that much" when I never wrote down anything? I just popped food in my mouth, but why bother with a food journal? I knew exactly how much I was eating because I kept track in my head. I was like a young adult with their first check book, thinking, *I know there's money in my account. I've been keeping track in my head.* But when they get their statement, the account is overdrawn. A young person spends and spends, then can't figure out where their money went, because they're keeping track in their head. (I know adults who do that too.) Like me, they needed to get out a pencil and paper and write it all down, whether it's food or money. Keeping track on paper is better than keeping track in your head.

Writing things down, helped me to stop nibbling and stop taking seconds, but that one act alone was not enough. The second thing I did to help me stop saying, "I don't eat that much," was to count calories. What a shock! Remember the kid with the overdrawn account? He may write down "I spent money on gas, groceries, and video games," but if he wants to know **exactly** how much he's spending, he needs to do the math. He has to write it down AND has to figure out how much he spent. Then he has to subtract the amount spent from what he has. That's when he knows precisely how much money he has (or doesn't have). It's the same concept with counting calories. It's precise. **For a complete lesson in calorie counting, see Section III Chapter 3**, but for now, here is a mini lesson in calories.

First, you might want to know what a "calorie" is. It's a different way of measuring food. Most of us would measure things by putting it on a scale, but that doesn't work with food. Think about this. Would you gain more if you ate a small apple or a tall bag of *Doritos*? They both weigh about seven ounces, but common sense tells us that the chips would cause weight gain and the apple wouldn't, but why? Because the chips have more calories (word-of-the-day). A seven-ounce apple has about seventy-five calories. A bag of *Doritos* has more than ten times the number of calories, 900 calories to be exact. However, if you want to compare these two foods in calories, it would look more like this:

One medium-sized apple: 80 calories
Twelve *Doritos*: 80 calories

DARN!

So, what is a calorie? Technically, a calorie is "... a unit of energy, specifying the energy value of food." In other words, calories give you energy, but if you don't burn them off, they give you fat. Or **if you eat more calories than you burn, you will gain weight. If you eat fewer**

calories than you burn, you lose. As the Scarecrow said, "I should have thought of it with my brain."

When I started counting calories, I discovered that I was eating FAR MORE than I ever imagined. Calories may not seem that important, but here is a simple fact. **An extra 100 calories a-day makes you gain ten pounds a year.** A hundred-calories is one cookie, or a tablespoon of butter, or a thin slice of cheese. Consuming a few extra calories without being aware of it is easy. However, if you write it down and count every calorie, your brain comes alive and you will become acutely aware of how much you are consuming.

Now for the good news: if you want to lose-ten-pounds-a-year, all you have to do is give up a hundred calories a day. It's simple, but you have to do the math. Here's my rule. If I don't count calories I can't say, "I don't eat that much?" How would I know if I should have that slice of cheese on my burger? (100 calories.) Can I afford to put cream in my coffee or not? (100 calories). Can I have a little cookie after dinner? (100 calories.) Is that one extra piece of food going to cause me to gain weight? Maybe. Is giving up that one piece of food, going to help me lose? Probably.

When I finally started counting calories, I was struck with horror when I found out how much I really ate. My first shock was when I read the labels and discovered how many calories a peanut butter and honey sandwich had, **especially the way I made it!** You see, I like butter on my sandwich, real butter, in addition to the peanut butter. Oh, yummy! And I use the super chunky peanut butter, which doesn't spread well, so I use twice as much. When I finally measured the peanut butter **and** butter **and** honey, on two slices of bread and then added up all the calories, I nearly fainted! It was more than six-hundred calories! That's worse than a Big Mac, dripping with animal fat and mayo! It was half my calories for the day! I thought it was a snack.

After I understood the calorie concept, I learned how to make a peanut butter sandwich. I used healthy margarine (Brummel and

Brown) instead of real butter, one slice of bread instead of two, measured the peanut butter, and easy on the honey. It took a little extra time, but it really wasn't that hard. Only 250 calories. Pretty cool, and a snack instead of a meal.

My next shock was my coffee, which of course has zero calories, but not the way I made it, with real cream, **and** French vanilla creamer, sugar free of course. (After all, I was on a diet.) My problem was this. I wasn't measuring my cream or creamer. I thought it was a few teaspoons of each. How wrong was I? Very wrong. I used three tablespoons of cream and a-fourth-of-a cup of creamer! My coffee tasted great but added up to two hundred-and-seventy calories! That's a lot of calories, when you are trying to keep it down to twelve-hundred a day. Two cups of coffee was nearly a half of my daily food allowance. Counting calories jolted me into reality and stopped me from saying, "I don't eat that much." To cut the calories, I switched to half-and-half and measured everything. Simple.

One time, when I was at a potluck, a very large man said, "I don't eat that much," as he went back for thirds on lasagna. Thirds! He really didn't know. Like me, he truly believed what he was saying. I felt so sorry for him, but on the positive side, he was the one who motivated me to write this chapter. It's a constant reminder for me and I hope it helps people who have been saying it.

A few years ago, I was watching the show "Fat," an interesting TV program about people who are hundreds of pounds overweight and want to lose. The doctor who worked with these morbidly obese people said that 100% of his obese patients said, "I don't eat that much." **One-hundred percent!** I was just like them.

Whether we eat an extra 100-calories-a-day or an extra 1,000, we have to figure out how much we eat, no matter how difficult.

I once met a lady who had lost ninety pounds, twelve years earlier, and kept it off. When I asked her what was her secret, she said, "I count every calorie and write it down." I asked her, "You mean you used to?" She emphatically told me, "No! As soon as I quit counting calories, I start gaining weight. I will count calories for life, otherwise, I'll get fat again." What a shock! And also, darn! I was hoping that I could quit someday, but she was a great role model for me and all people who love to eat.

Next time you are tempted to say, "I don't eat that much," please don't be like me or those morbidly obese people. Save yourself the embarrassment. Bite your tongue. (No pun intended.) If you aren't keeping track, then you don't have a clue how much is "not that much." If you want to know the truth, write it down. Educate yourself. Start a food journal. Study the chapter on calories. You may be shocked to find out how much you are eating. I certainly was. Most people are.

LIE #4

I Don't Look That Bad

I can't believe I used to think *I don't look that bad,* because when I look back at my "fat pictures" I looked bad. I had three chins, a pot belly, and jowls. Jowls are face-fat hanging next to your chin. Yuk! (Skinny people don't have jowls.)

The first time I was slapped in the face with the reality of my looks was when I saw a video of me dancing. Every time my rear end faced the camera, it looked like someone had stuffed a pillow in my pants. As I watched it, my eyebrows grew closer and closer until I had a unibrow. I kept wondering how that camera could make me look so fat. Even more puzzling was that my friends didn't look fat. I didn't understand! How was that possible? You would think that watching that video would have done it, but all it did was confuse me. "I can't possibly look that bad." So, I ignored it. (One more form of denial.)

My next reality check was when I was teaching Sunday school and one of my five-year-olds asked me, "Teacher, are you going to have a baby?" What was wrong with that little boy? His parents needed to get his eyes checked. Brat! Did that help me see the truth? Nope! I was not fat. That kid needs glasses. That's all.

Then there was the time I asked the lady at *Ross,* "Where are the lady's swimming suits?" She directed me to the *fat-lady* department. I was only a size sixteen, still two sizes away from having to shop for fat clothes. (However, the sixteens were too tight, so I probably was more like an eighteen or twenty.) Instead of reality, I was mad at that stupid sales lady, but at least I wasn't fat. Just mad, and clueless.

My turning point was when I got on the scale and I had finally hit two-hundred pounds! My first thought was, "Something's wrong with my scale, but I had watched it gradually creep up over the years and somehow knew that wasn't it. Two-hundred pounds terrified me. The bathroom scale screamed "FAT!" It yelled, "You don't look that good!" That time, I listened.

I'm convinced that most obese people are like me. I used to focus on the one part of my body I liked, like my legs. I'm one of those people who always has good legs, no matter how fat I get. I thought, *If my legs aren't fat, I must not look that bad.* Wrong! My belly stuck out like I was about to give birth, but at least I had nice legs. I was so deceived. I ignored my beer belly, my wings, my flubber, my whatever, but it didn't matter because I still had good legs, therefore, I don't look that bad.

There are **some** obese people who don't look that bad, but they are few and far between, like Kirstie Alley and Delta Burke. Those two women are natural beauties, but how many of us are that drop-dead gorgeous? By the way, both of those women are prettier when they're thin.

Here's how I know if I look bad. I stand in front of a mirror. At first, I think, *Not bad.* Then I take off my clothes. My reflection starts to plummet, but still not too bad. But then I stop sucking in my stomach. When I let it out and turn sideways, nothing looks good, not even my legs will save me now. Don't laugh. You try it.

And then there are my pictures. I thought I looked quite good until I saw those darn things. (I put on clothes on for pictures.) If you truly want a reality check, take your picture of yourself standing next to someone thin. Get a hard copy and hang it on your refrigerator.

Look at it often. I cringe when I look at myself standing next to my skinny cousin.

Another way to know what you look like is to step on the scale. The scale will tell you the absolute truth. Two-hundred pounds is too much (unless you are a linebacker for the Seahawks, or seven-feet tall). Most obese people refuse to weigh themselves. They don't want to know what they weigh. They make a choice to believe, "I don't look that bad."

You can also measure your waist line. The rule-of-thumb is at least ten inches less than your chest, but I would say if your waistline is more than forty inches, you probably need to lose some weight. Ask your doctor.

Instead of saying, "I don't look that bad," I say "I may not look bad, but I would look a lot better, if I lost some weight." Reality stinks, but it helps me to face the truth.

LIE #5

It's Hereditary

The "Heredity Leaves Me Hopeless Theory" usually means three things. The first, translates as, "I'm big boned." Sorry, but that excuse doesn't work. Have you ever seen a fat skeleton? Naturally, some of us have bigger bones than others. I'm one of them. My Swedish Grandmother who was born in the late 1800's was 5'9" with broad shoulders and big bones. I am built just like her. When I have a cousin's reunion, I walk into a room full of Amazon women tall, broad shoulders, and big bones just like Grandma Broughton. Some cousins are thinner than others, but about half of my cousins have Grandma's bone structure.

I also have some German on the other side of the family. The phrase "petite German girl" is an oxymoron. Consequently, even when I'm ten-pounds underweight, I still wear a size 10. I'm anything but petite and never will be. Even if I was anorexic, I wouldn't be tiny. However, **I won't quit dieting because of my bone structure.** How dumb would that be? Big-boned people like me can lose weight and be slender, but not tiny, just slim and trim.

Because I'm German and Swedish, I can't expect to look like a petite little Asian lady. I have learned to thank God for who I am, and how He made me. No matter how envious I might be, I still have to be nice to skinny people who inherited tiny bones.

Some say that heredity means, "I inherited slow metabolism." If that's true, there are two words to solve that problem. "So what?" If you really have a slow metabolism, then it's even more important to limit your food intake. Besides, the older you get, the slower your metabolism. You might be wondering, "Why are so many old people are thin?" It's because they just eat less. My mom is one of them. Slim and trim in her 90's.

My metabolism is about as slow as it gets. The first three years, I diligently stuck to my diet, and only lost twenty-four pounds. That's less than a pound-a-month year-after-year. That's slow! This was followed by two years of just maintaining my weight loss, but I didn't gain back what I lost. Another victory. After that it's been two or three pounds a year, but I refuse to give up. (The experts will tell you that you can speed up your metabolism by exercising, but it doesn't seem to work for me. More about that in the exercise chapter.)

Finally, heredity means, "My parents, siblings, and cousins are all fat. Consequently, it's hopeless. Fat is my fate." (Get the hankies.) If you look at family photos, then sigh and cry because you believe obesity is your lot in life, stop it! If that's what heredity means, it translates as, "It's 100% not my fault, so there's nothing I can do. Guess I'll go eat worms (or fudge.)" If you believe it's hopeless, then you are destined to be fat, whether it's hereditary or not.

Look at it this way. What if you **acted** as though it **wasn't** true. What if you said, "Everyone in my family is fat, but I refuse to be. I'm going to be the one who breaks this cycle." How much thinner and healthier would you be right now if you had lived your entire life that way? What if you had lived and acted like that for the past ten years? Just think how great you would look now.

What about this? Suppose heredity is only 50% of your problem, but you decided to ignore it and eat right. That would mean, instead of being a hundred pounds overweight, you would only be fifty pounds overweight, but **only** if you decided to diet in spite of your heredity. Wouldn't fifty pounds thinner be better than a hundred pounds overweight? You might not look like a super model, but you would feel better about yourself, be healthier, and have more energy.

How True Is It?

As someone who observes life and people, I have a hard time buying this "heredity concept." Here's why. Throughout history, people who live in poor countries are thin (underweight), and people who live in rich countries are fat. More money means more food.

Here's another reason. Sixty years ago, when minimum wage was a dollar-an-hour, only 5% of the people in our country were obese. People didn't have a lot of money for extra food or junk food. Now, nearly half of the people in our country are overweight. Could we be overweight because our minimum wage went up more than 700%? Having a lot of extra money usually means having a lot of extra food. It has nothing to do with heredity.

During the depression, the only fat people were the bootleggers and the Mafia. They had money and they ate well, while the rest of the country nearly starved. Consequently, the poor people were thin, and rich people were fat. Their pot belly didn't have anything to do with how much their parents weighed. Go figure.

I wanted to check out my theory, so I picked up a new hobby. Whenever I go to the grocery store, I watch what skinny people buy; then watch what others buy. What I noticed is that the thin people have their shopping carts filled with fresh fruits, veggies, low-fat yogurt, skim milk, "lite" products, and occasionally a cake mix, but healthy and low-cal overall. On the other hand, the obese people have carts-full of pop, chips, cookies, beer, *Top Ramen*, a lot of processed foods, whole milk, high-fat yogurt, and usually a few bananas or a head of lettuce. I've been watching people for years. It's not 100%, but it's at least 98% true. If you don't believe me, try it yourself.

One time I was in line behind a thin, healthy-looking lady who had a shopping cart filled with frozen pizzas, chips, candy, and pop. I was puzzled and hoped that she wasn't going to mess up my theory. I kept looking at her cart, then figured it out. I finally said, "Looks like you're having company." She smiled and said, "Yes, my daughter's soccer team is coming over for a slumber party tonight." I smugged a grin.

Now let's be honest. **Of course heredity plays a part!** It's a fact! I'm part of that group. My thyroid is low, metabolism slow, exercise is difficult, and I'm big boned. What does that mean? It means I have a choice. I can either cry all over my cookies, or ignore these excuses, and stick to my diet. **Should I eat like a cow just because I can never look like a Barbie doll?** The simple truth is that if I eat less than I burn off, I will lose weight, no matter what my heredity is.

I have a good friend, Sonya who is neither fat nor **thin**, but medium-sized. When I saw a picture of her family, I was shocked to see that they were ALL obese. I made a comment like, "Wow. You're lucky you didn't inherit your family's genes."

She said, "Luck has nothing to do with it! When I was a teenager, I made a decision that I wasn't going to get fat like the rest of my family. I work at it all the time," she said with gusto. "I'm very careful, always on a diet, and always will be. Besides, they eat too much." WOW! She could have used heredity as an excuse, but refused to fall into that trap.

I have made it my mission in life to disprove the "Heredity Leaves Me Hopeless Theory." If I can prove that this is a myth, then I can go on *Dr. Oz*, and be rich and famous and in addition, thin. (I love rich and thin; such a nice combination.)

I had to stop using "heredity" as an excuse to overeat. I didn't have a choice. I had to stop living as though it was all hopeless. Here's my advice. Grab a notepad and a calorie counter. Then in a year or two, after you've lost weight, call *Dr. Oz* and tell him you've disproved this theory. If you get on the show, don't forget to invite me. I want to be famous too.

LIE #6

I'm Too Stressed

Let's face it. Dieting is stressful. It's hard work, and (as I said before) NOT EASY! But when I thought it about it, how much sense did it make? "I'm so stressed, so I will just open my mouth and stuff it full of anything I want, any time I want. Let's see, cookies? No, wait. I want potato chips with lots of dip and, then wash it down with a *Coke*." Do you think I will be less stressed after I gorge myself with a bunch of garbage and no nutrients? How stressed will I be the next day when I'm nauseated or bloated? Worse yet, what happens when I step on the scale? That's major stress for me. (Stresses my scale too.)

When I use "I'm too stressed" as an excuse to avoid dieting, it wasn't logical. Here's why. First, eating junk food (a.k.a. garbage) puts huge amounts of physical stress on my body. Most junk food has so many chemicals that a person's body doesn't even recognize it as food. The stomach sees it coming and says, "Are you kidding me? Again?" It doesn't know what to do with it, so it says, "That's not really food. No thanks! Then it passes off to the liver. While all this is happening, the reproductive organs are watching, cracking up laughing because they know they don't have to deal with it. The other organs tremble with fear, hoping that they don't have to take it, because they can't figure out how to handle it either. Finally, the partially digest "food" arrives at the blood. The problem is that the blood desperately needs assertiveness training, because it sees all this garbage and thinks, *Oh dear. Here comes those chemicals and sugar again*. But then, ever-so sweetly it says, "Okay, come on in Mr. Sugar and Mrs. Junk Food. Make yourself at home." The blood sucks it up and is forced to hop onto a roller coaster, playing a game called "Diabetes, Hypoglycemia and Mood Swings." Finally, your skin is a big tattletale and a gossip too! When you eat unhealthily, your skin tells the whole world "Look at this person. Do you see how badly they eat?" Mine tells everyone, "See those zits? The two on the right cheek was soda. The three on the left was a king-sized *Mars Bar*. Isn't she a pudden-head?" The only way I can get my skin to shut up is to eat better. My herbalist, Paul Rosen calls your skin, "the third kidney." Whatever you call it, it will rat you out.

My nephew, struggled with severe skin problems during middle school and high school. He had those golf-ball sized, ugly, red zits. (That's stressful.) My brother and his wife took him to three different dermatologists and finally to Oregon Health Sciences University (OHSU), all of whom treated him with, creams, pills, and medication (also known as legalized drugs). **Nothing worked!** Finally, when he tried to get into the Army, they rejected him because his skin was so egregious. They wanted him because of his grades in high school, and he scored high on their written test, so they sent him to an old military doc who gruffly told him, "Stop drinking soda and coffee. Your skin will clear up." My nephew asked him if it was the caffeine or the sugar that caused the problem. The doctor said, "Neither! Soda and coffee are poison!" My nephew quit both. His skin cleared immediately. No drugs. No topical creams. No lotion. What I've learned from my nephew is that the healthier I eat, the prettier my skin. Less stress for me. Him too.

I understand that dieting is stressful, but so is overeating. I remember how stressed I felt after Thanksgiving dinner. My relatives and I would be flopped out all over the house, holding our stomachs, moaning and groaning. Obviously, I didn't eat like that every day, but any time I ate more than my body could use, I added unnecessary stress to my body.

Do you want to know what overeating does to you? Buy or borrow a blood-pressure kit. (Most drug stores have one you can use.) Take your blood pressure before you eat. Then eat a good-sized meal. Be sure you feel full. Then, take your blood pressure again. Your blood pressure goes from normal-to-dangerous. The more you stuff yourself, the higher your blood pressure. Stress, plain and simple.

On top of everything else, the more fat you carry around, the harder your heart has to work. (Your poor little heart.) The average **healthy** heart creates enough pressure to squirt blood thirty feet. That's like from one end of your house to the other. (Paints a creepy picture.) When you get fat, your heart has to pump even harder (all the way to your neighbor's yard). It's a miracle our hearts don't explode.

But it's not just your heart. All that extra poundage puts pressure on your knees, your ankles, and your back. It's only a matter of time before you need a walker or a wheelchair. (If I ever get so fat I have to use a walker, I'm really going to be stressed.)

Finally, being overweight is emotionally stressful. I don't know about you, but stepping on the scale and being up another five or ten pounds is stressful. How about trying to squeeze into a pair of jeans that fit perfectly six months ago? Worse yet, seeing an old friend, and being forty-pounds overweight makes me stressed . . . and depressed . . . and just plain embarrassed. Looking in the mirror at three chins and a pot belly doesn't help either, and I can hardly stand to look at my pictures.

This little white lie, "I'm too stressed to diet" not only kept me fat. It kept me unhealthy and far more stressed than dieting. Life is filled with all kinds of stressors. Putting boundaries on your eating is also stressful, but it's mildly stressful. Losing your health and looking unattractive is extremely stressful. We live in a free country. We get to choose our stress. You decide.

LIE #7

Diets Don't Work for Me

This one is not a bad excuse. Not good either, but it was one of my favorites when I was fat. It felt real to me because no matter which diet I tried, nothing worked. They all seemed to work a little at first, but then the pounds returned. Every time a new diet came out, I tried it. All the old ones too. I would try one, then another, then another. Then, I got tired of dieting, so I gave up. After all, I would struggle with sacrifice, and starvation with little or no success. Why would I bother dieting if it doesn't work? Can anyone relate?

Let me start by sharing some of the diets I tried. There are reasons why they worked (or started to work) and why they quit working.

Many years ago, I did the *Atkins Diet*, the one where you eat lots of protein, meat, fat, and vegetables, but no grains or sugars, and a decrease in carbohydrates. The principle is that your food digests faster when you eat protein by itself or without carbohydrates. At first, it worked. I lost four-and-a-half pounds the first week, but I started feeling very weak and sick. My body screamed for carbs. Someone told me to increase my carbs and I would feel better. I did. Then I gained back everything I had just lost, plus a few more.

A NEW PERSPECTIVE ON DIETING AND WEIGHT LOSS

One of the reasons why *The Atkins Diet* works is that you have to stop eating junk food, because they are loaded with carbohydrates, something you can't have on this diet. (You can have a little, but not very much.) Whenever you stop eating junkie food (especially processed food), weight loss naturally follows. People also feel better when they stop filling up on garbage. Those foods makes you feel sick and run down. But here's the problem. When I realized I had to give up **all junk food forever** in order to make this diet work, I couldn't stand it. The Atkins Diet tells you that you can add some of your favorite foods later. In the meantime, I was dying for it.

In addition to giving up almost all junk food, *The Atkins Diet* has three problems. First, most people who do *Atkins*, crave carbohydrates so badly that they can't stick with it. (That was me.) An occasional craving is okay, but when I did *Atkins*, I craved carbs so badly and so continuously that I gave up. Second, if you cut your carbs too low, you will mess up your keytones. Even if you don't know what that is, you don't want to mess them up or you could get sick or even die. Third, you can gain weight on the *Atkins* diet if you eat too much. They say that in the first chapter on the first page. Although your food digests better and more effectively, you can still consume more than you burn. I needed a diet with stronger boundaries. Most of us overeaters do. *Atkins* doesn't have enough for me. In other words, I don't know when to stop. Also, Atkins allows you to have unlimited cream (pure fat). I'm not sure why, but if I have cream, I gain weight even if I don't have any carbohydrates. Pork seems to make me gain weight too. Bad piggy.

When I did the *South Beach Diet*, which allows you to eat a lot of some foods, but sacrifice others, I ate too much. (No junk food on this one either.) They say that you can eat as-much-as-you-want of the foods they recommend, but they don't understand people like me and my "foodie friends." WE LOVE FOOD. We eat too much. Even if it's healthy, it has calories. However, I have a good friend who loves this diet and lost a lot of weight on it. Unfortunately, I saw her three years later and she had gained it all back. She missed the sugar.

I tried the blood-type diet from the book *Eat Right for Your Blood Type*. Here's a quick summary of how it works. The author, who is a doctor, discovered that certain foods cause **weight gain** for one blood type and **weight loss** for another. He has scientific facts to back up his studies. (Positive and negative blood types are not factored in.)

Let's look at people with Type O, since that is the most common blood type. Type O can eat a lot of meat, because their blood is high in acid. They actually lose weight by eating red meat! However, Type O blood doesn't digest carbohydrates very well. Carbs cause weight gain for them.

On the other hand, people with Type A blood (the second-most common blood type) do well as vegans. Type A doesn't digest meat or milk, but does digest most fruits, vegetables, and grains. I was so excited when I found out I was Type A blood. I figured that I could give up the foods that caused weight gain (red meat and milk). Then I could pork out on grains and potatoes. I was wrong. Porking out on any food, even the right food for my blood type, led to me be an oinker. I was eating more than I was burning, even though I ate exactly what the book told me to eat.

Another problem with the *Blood Type Diet* is that it encourages people to eat certain foods. For example, type-A people are supposed to eat a lot of soy and tofu. Since I'm Type A, it sounded like I could lose a lot of weight if I followed their advice. After two years of choking down tofu, I found out I was highly allergic to it. Instead of losing weight, I got sick. I was so happy when I found out I was allergic because I HATE TOFU. *The Blood Type Diet* has some good points but it still allows you to eat more than you burn off. Another one with poor boundaries. However, I still use a few of his ideas when I'm dieting.

I lost a lot of weight on the *HCG Diet*. This one alters your hormones. HCG is a hormone that is produced in a woman's body during pregnancy. Without going into a lot of details, here's how it works. You have probably heard that if you cut your calories too low, you will burn muscle instead of fat. However, **if a pregnant woman cuts her calories too low, she burns fat instead of muscle.** The pounds melt off like a snowman in the sun because the HCG hormone imitates pregnancy. So, when you take the HCG hormone, you cut your calories to 500-a-day and burn a lot of fat. Also, HCG curbs your appetite. It works! When I took HCG, cut calories, and followed their diet, I lost a lot of weight. **The problem is that you can't stay on it permanently.** Thirty days max. Any longer can be dangerous. Can you guess what happened when I stopped taking it? Go ahead and guess. That's right. I gained back all my weight. This diet doesn't teach you how to change your habits. They give you a diet to follow when you are done, but it's not an easy diet. (None of them are.) So here it is in a nutshell. HCG changes your hormones for thirty days. You follow their plan and lose weight. Then, when you quit taking the HCG hormones, you have to figure out how to keep off the weight. (The other problem is that when a man tries it, he gets a little cranky every 28 or 30 days.)

I didn't do any better on the ninety-five other diets I tried. Sometimes, I would follow part of their advice, but not all of it. Most of the times, there weren't enough boundaries for me. I overate. Some diets didn't allow me to eat my favorite foods. I felt cheated and gave up. (I hate being cheated.)

If all of these diets claim to have **a proven success rate,** then why do I fail when I try them?

Two Reasons My Diets Didn't Work:

First of all, not enough boundaries. (I think I may have mentioned that.) Healthy foods like bananas, or milk, or whole grains can still cause weight gain if you eat too much. Too many calories (healthy or not) causes fat retention. But here's the real reason. Ready? My diets don't work because I don't stick to it long enough.

Here's what I did. I would finally make a decision to diet because I hated being fat. Hated it! I want the fat to go away, as quickly as possible, so I tried a new diet for a week or two, get on the scale and would be down three pounds. (Most people lose a lot of water the first week.) The following week, I get back on the scale, but now I've only lost one pound. The next week half-of-a-pound. **Then, instead of being tired of my fat, I'm tired of my diet** and tired of getting on the scale and seeing the disappointing news. I want to lose more and faster. That's when I gave up and gained back the few pounds that I worked so hard to lose. **I give up too soon, then proclaim to the world, "Diets don't work for me."** Yes, they do! Like all the other lies, this was just another one I believed.

When I was much younger, I diligently counted calories. I was thin. As an employee of the school district, I had to get a physical every year, including my weight. One time, when my doctor announced my weight, I groaned in frustration. He said, "What's wrong? You've weighed exactly the same for the past seven years." I told him I wanted to lose a few pounds.

"No," he said. **"Weighing the same year-after-year is an accomplishment.** Most of your fellow employees gain about two pounds a year, every year, consistently." It doesn't sound like much, but over a twenty-year period, that's forty pounds! That was the first time I realized that all my dieting and sacrifices had actually worked. Even though I hadn't **lost** any weight, my sacrifices and dieting kept me from gaining. Unfortunately, I got tired of counting calories and quit. That's when I started gaining. Silly me.

When it comes to dieting, remember this. **Something is better than nothing.** Duh. Please, just do something. Stop taking seconds. Give up one or two unhealthy foods. Eat more vegetables.

Diets do work, but do it right and don't quit. Find a diet you like and believe in. Be patient. **Then in addition to your favorite** diet, count calories, especially if the diet you pick has unlimited boundaries.

Here's what I do. I eat a lot of veggies, and use some ideas from other books, but it's not enough, because most diets don't have enough boundaries. I have no choice. **To keep my diet in check, I have to count calories.** In addition, I avoid foods that guarantee weight gain for my blood type. At the same time, I don't gorge myself on everything else. What is more important, I don't quit.

So here I am, sacrificing my favorite foods, counting calories, feeling hungry and deprived. Guess how I'm doing? I lost less than a-pound-a-month for three solid years! Then, I had fifteen months where I didn't lose anything. I didn't gain back what I lost, but I didn't gain. I worked so hard, and made hundreds of sacrifices just to maintain my weight loss. Do you think I'm angry? Nope. (Well, maybe annoyed.) But I'm proud, too. I didn't gain back those pounds I lost. That's a victory for the fat lady! **Remember, most people can lose weight, but few can keep it off.** I didn't lose a lot, but I lost some and didn't gain it back! That's called success.

When it comes to dieting, there's two things to remember. First, find a diet that works **for you.** If there has been a diet in the past that works, was healthy, and you felt like you could stick to it **for life**, do that one. If not, try counting calories. It's proven. If you eat fewer calories than you burn, you will lose. Simple.

Second, don't quit! If you diet for five days, quit for three, then start and stop again, you will tell yourself and everyone else, "Diets don't work for me." Instead, make a plan. Then, don't give up.

Learn a lesson from skinny people who say annoying things like, "It's not a diet. It's a lifestyle," (but don't slap them). **Most thin people watch what they eat daily and regularly.** They don't quit. For them, it's just routine. Before they put anything in their mouth, they think about it. That's how they stay thin. They keep on keeping on. It becomes a way of life.

The bottom line is this: if you want to be thin, don't give up. Diets do work. Just think how cool it will be, ten years from now. You will be able to tell people who struggle with their weight the same thing I'm telling you. "Diets do work. You just have to find the right one; then stick to it." They will want to slap you, but it's okay. You will feel so good you won't care.

Here's how you know that your diet is working. First, find a diet that works for you or just count calories, or both. Next, make a plan and write it out. Then, weigh yourself. Stick to the diet 100% for a week. Then weigh yourself again. If you've lost anything, the diet works! Diets work if you stick to them **AND** they have the clear boundaries.

LIE #8

I Get Too Hungry!

You do? That is so sad! So do I. Let's get the hankies and violins and have a good cry. After many years of dieting, this is what I learned. Being hungry is like being horny. I had to ignore it. If not, I could get into a lot of trouble.

What if everyone treated their sex drive the same way they treated their appetite? Worse yet, what if we trained our children to treat their sex drive the way we treat our appetite. What would we tell our kids? "Okay, Sweetie. Whenever the urge hits, just grab a condom and go for it." Teen pregnancy and social diseases would be even worse than it is now. Instead, we teach our kids to control themselves, but are we good role models for them when it comes to our eating habits? What are we eating and how much?

I work hard to eat right, but often, I give my eating habits my power. If I get hungry, I eat. After all, what or who is going to stop me? No one will chop off my tongue if I eat thirty-five brownies.

The television doesn't help either. Most of the commercials are centered around food, one after another, after another. Everyone is eating and no one is fat! That's because those skinny actors don't eat those foods. They aren't stupid, but they're probably hungry.

Have you ever seen a commercial for a weight-loss group that says, "If you join our group, you are bound to be hungry?" Me either. Many come right out and say, "I joined this group and I'm not hungry." Really? So far, I haven't found any diets where I didn't get hungry. I'm still looking. I've never met anyone who said that. Stop and think about it. **If there was really a diet where you lost weight and didn't get hungry, we would all be on it and we'd all be skinny!**

I was in T.O.P.S. (Take Off Pounds Sensibly) for six years. It's a support group for people who want to lose weight. We got weighed (privately) before our meeting. When our meeting started, we acknowledged all the people who lost weight with applause. Then, the one who lost the most, put on a crown and we stood up and sang, "We Have a Winner in our Crowd." We used to ask our Loser-of-the-Week, "What did you do this week to help you lose weight?" At least half of them say, "I was hungry." The people in my TOPS group learned that being hungry is one of the "tricks" to losing weight. When was the last time you saw that on a weight-loss commercial?

Sometimes we think we are hungry even after we've had a decent meal. That's because it that it takes about thirty minutes for our tummy to tell our brain, (or our brain to tell our tummy), "You've had enough." For me, that's a problem. I wish I had a built-in alarm that beeped immediately after I had enough saying, "Beeeeeep! Stop eating. Your tummy is full!" It would be so helpful. Since that will never happen, I have another option. I can take what I've learned and use it for my benefit. I'm aware that it takes thirty minutes to know that I'm full, so I can use that information to my advantage. This is what I do. If I'm still hungry after I consume my calories, I set the timer for thirty minutes. Then I get busy doing dishes or laundry. Usually, when the timer goes off, I realize I'm not hungry anymore. Amazing! If I still feel a little hungry, I set the timer for another fifteen minutes and get busy again. Most of the time, when the buzzer dings, I can't even remember why I set it. I walk over, turn it off, and stare at it. Then, it's like, "Oh, that's right." I shrug and walk away because I'm not hungry anymore. If I'm busy scrubbing the toilet, or mopping the floor, I'm in a completely different mindset. (Besides that, my house looks like the maid just ran out the back door.)

However, if I'm really hungry, I'll have a light snack, like a cup of yogurt or an apple with a little almond butter. Yum! Sounds like cheating, but it's better than the taking seconds and thirds on mashed potatoes and gravy, then thirty minutes later feeling like I'm about to explode. One of my favorite things to do when the timer dings is to reset it for another twenty minutes. While I'm waiting, I plan my next meal. It works, because I'm thinking about what I get to eat in a few hours. I have something to look forward to.

Do you know what I used to think about hunger back when I was fat? I looked at hunger as an evil demon, something I had to fight and get rid of, fast! I was the "Hunger Exorcist," and I knew how to destroy this thing. All I had to do was to pull out the *Ben and Jerry's Double Chocolate Chip* to exorcize the dreadful "Demon of Hunger". I would do what I had to do no matter what the consequences, because hunger was the enemy. Food was my sword. I was so deceived.

Instead, I should have embraced hunger like it was a long, lost lover, running to it with open arms. I should have listened to hunger as it quietly whispered, *This is not a bad thing. You're resting your digestive organs and losing weight at the same time. Appreciate what I'm doing for you. Squeeze me to your bosom.* Okay. That's a sappier than a Hallmark movie, but you get the idea. When *The Hunger Demon* spoke, I should have stuck my fingers in my ears and said, "La la la la ... "

Now when I get hungry, I think, *I'm hungry. Praise God.* Actually, I don't, but it sounds nice. You think I like being hungry? No, but I like losing weight. When I get hungry, I tell myself, *You know you're hungry, but that's not necessarily bad. You've had enough calories and you can eat in three hours or tomorrow. Besides, if you're hungry, that means you are losing weight or keeping off those extra pounds. That's good. Now go find something to do.*

Another great way to get rid of hunger is prayer. (Actually, this should be first, since it's so simple.) Alcoholics use prayer to keep themselves sober. Drug addicts understand that they need help from their "Higher Power." But people who love to eat rarely consider praying when they feel tempted. More about prayer in a later chapter, but for now, I will tell you when I stop and pray, asking God's help, thoughts will pop into my head. I believe that's God's way of telling me what I'm supposed to do. Here are some of the things that pop in my mind when I get hungry and then pray.

<u>Eat something</u>. Does that sound strange, since I'm trying to lose weight? Of course, but there are healthy foods you can eat that won't make you fat, like vegetables. Better yet, they make you feel full and have very few calories. I know you're craving chips and cookies, but carrots, cucumbers, and celery won't cause weight gain. Hey! It's better than sitting around listening to your stomach growl. Sometimes I open a can of green beans, strain off the liquid, and put a little *Brummel and Brown* on it. It's quite filling. Green vegetables count as zero calories because they are mostly fiber and water, except for peas. A cup of *Progresso Lite Soup* is good too. It only has 100 calories per cup. Soup calms my hunger pangs and is low cal. In the old days, I would have eaten a whole pie instead. Pray and ask God for wisdom. Sometimes, after I pray, I'm not hungry anymore. Who says miracles don't exist?

<u>Drink water or flavored water</u> (More about flavored water in the chapter *It Doesn't Take a Rocket Scientist to Flush a Toilet*). Sometimes my brain lies to me. It tells me "You are hungry" when I'm actually thirsty.

Before I pig out or take seconds, I drink a few glasses of flavored water and maybe some green beans too, then set the timer for twenty minutes and find something to do.

Green tea is a great way to control your appetite and boost your metabolism. It also has calcium, iron, potassium, B1, B2, B3, B5 and C. I have recipes at the end to make it taste good (really, really good). I drink two-or-three cups a day with a little Stevia to sweeten it. Green tea not only **decreases** your appetite. It **increases** your metabolism, and I can tell you how to make it tastes good, honest. (I know I already said that, but no one believes me.) They also have green tea in a capsule and green tea gum, a quick substitute.

Chia Seeds: That's right. Those seeds that grow fake hair on ceramic animals and beards on *Duck Dynasty* figurines can decrease your appetite! Here's how. Chia seeds are like tiny sponges. When they get in your tummy, they soak up water and puff up. As a result, you feel full. Put a teaspoon of chia seeds in a cup of water or tea or "flavored water." Drink up. By dinner time, you will feel somewhat full. You can also sprinkle them on your oatmeal, yogurt, or salad, but there's one small problem. It takes a little time for these seeds to help you feel full. I like to eat these before a big party or potluck to curb my appetite, and they are healthy too! They have more Omega 3's than fish. It also has calcium, magnesium and zinc. Besides, it lowers your cholesterol. Wow. Decreases your appetite and healthy too! Better yet, it won't grow hair on your chest. By the way, you are supposed to do this BEFORE you get hungry, but if you are hungry after dinner, chia seeds take about thirty minutes to start working.

<u>Do Something</u>: I asked a very good friend of mine, Dolly how she managed to stay so thin. She said, "I stay busy." She has a lot to show for it besides her award-winning figure. She runs several businesses and owns six houses. She does most of the maintenance herself. Follow her example. Stay busy. Maybe you could clean your closet or drawers. Do your make-up (unless you are a man). Go for a walk. Write a symphony. Paint your house. Remember. You are smarter than a dog. You can think of something. When I stick to my diet, my house is cleaner, laundry done, and the garbage cans waxed. I can always find something to do.

<u>Brush your teeth</u>: When your mouth is clean and fresh, you are less likely to want to mess it up. I brush, floss, and use mouthwash. After all that, I don't want to contaminate my mouth. Sometimes, after brushing, I grab a piece of sugarless gum. Keeps my mouth busy and reminds me not to stick something in there.

<u>Take a nap:</u> If I'm tired, I'm hungry even if I've already eaten. That's because my body craves energy. Calories equal energy because they are "heat" (according to the dictionary). When I'm tired and hungry, the best thing I can do is take a nap or put my feet up. If that's not possible, I just need to be aware that my tired body is trying to force me to eat. If a nap is out, I do one of the other things on this list.

The Other Reason You Might Feel Hungry:

What I'm going to tell you might surprise you. You could be hungry because you are nutritionally starved. What does that mean? It means that you ARE getting enough calories, but AREN'T getting enough nutrition. Junk food and sugar have calories, but they contain something called "empty calories." That means you are eating calories that have little or no nutrition. If you've cut back to 1,500 calories a day, and half of those calories have no food value, your body is going to be unhappy and your tummy will complain. They will tell you that you are hungry, almost starving because you're not getting what you need.

Your body needs all of the following regularly: vitamins, minerals, good fats, good carbohydrates, fiber, fluids, and amino acids. When you count calories, they add up fast. There isn't a lot of room for empty calories, especially if you want to be healthy and don't want to be hungry. Food supplements or vitamins help, but don't depend on those. You have to eat right too. If you feel like can't live without junk food, keep it **less than** 10% of your total calories.

Here's the easiest way to figure 10% of your daily allowance of junk food. Write down how many calories you plan to eat. Drop the last number (usually a zero). So, if you plan to eat 1,800 calories, drop the last zero. That means you can have 180 calories in junk food, **absolute maximum.** Your body doesn't need any junk food. Neither does mine, but sometimes just a tiny bit keeps me from giving up on my diet, but not enough to starve nutritionally.

In addition to my diet, I take vitamins, minerals, and food supplements. (More about that in the chapter called "Vitamins, Minerals, and Food Supplements.") These tablets help fill the gaps, so I get the nutrition I need.

Eating right and eating healthy **helps** stave off hunger. So will vitamins, but remember this. **Anytime you cut back on calories, you will be hungry. That means you are doing it right. You are losing**

weight. That's good. Hunger is normal when you are losing weight! At least, that's my opinion. Some doctors disagree. Skinny people too.

If you've been looking for a sign that your diet is working, this could be it! Hunger isn't something to immediately get rid of. When dieting, hunger is to be cherished. When I stick to my diet, I get hungry, but I've learned to live with it, instead of using it for an excuse to binge. I don't allow my hunger to push me into the kitchen or talk me into eating a bag of chips. Instead, I ignore my hunger as much as possible.

If you still think being hungry is not normal, I would like to share a scene in a movie with you. In *Notting Hill*, Julia Roberts plays the part of a beautiful actress, trying to hide from the Paparazzi. She starts dating a shy English gentleman (Hugh Grant) who invites her to dinner at his friend's house. After dinner, there's eight people vying for the last brownie. They decide whoever has the best sob-story gets the brownie. They go around the table sharing their sad stories and bypass Julia Roberts, thinking she doesn't have to complain about since she's rich and famous. Finally, she says, "Wait! Don't I get a chance?" Do you know what her sob story was? She said, "I've been an actress since I was a teenager, so I've been hungry for more-than-a-decade." What? That can't be right? She wasn't anorexic, just conscientious. She knew the cameras were on her and she didn't want donuts hanging off her hips. Consequently, she was hungry. How long? **A decade!** She didn't have a choice. She had to stay thin and her secret was hunger.

Hunger isn't the goal, but losing weight is. It's hard to have one without the other. I just deal with it while I lose weight and look great. It's worth it.

More Bad News:

Now you've learned that feeling hungry means you are losing weight, but here is the other side. **If you feel full, you are gaining**

weight. Sorry. When you feel full, that means you ate too much and your body doesn't have the ability to burn it off. If you eat more calories than you burn, you gain weight.

Here's another problem with feeling full. When you eat too much, you are stretching out your stomach. If your stomach is larger, it takes more food to make you feel full. But you can only burn off a certain number of calories. It means you will be even hungrier next time you eat. Besides, I don't want my stomach stretched out.

Besides all this, I gain weight whenever I feel full. How do I know? Because I weigh myself daily. The next day, after I eat too much or feel full, I'm ALWAYS up, always. 100% and I've been doing this for years!

My body talks to me every time I eat. So does yours. **If you're hungry, you are losing weight. If you are full, you are gaining.** Are you listening to your body? Mine smacks me in the butt and says, "Wake up!" I hate when that happens.

One Last Thing:

If you are diabetic or hypoglycemic, you need to be careful about being hungry. You don't need to be fainting or dying. Talk to your doctor.

THING #9

I Don't Have Enough Money

When I was fat, this was one of my all-time favorite excuses. It didn't feel like an excuse because I thought it was the truth. (Most people think their excuses sound like truth.) I would watch those TV ads for weight-loss programs and diet pills with a box of tissues. I felt cheated because they were too expensive and I couldn't afford it. I would think, *If I was rich, I would be so skinny.*

Once, I sent for some pills that took my last $39.95. They sent the pills, along with their strict diet plan. I took the pills, but didn't want to do the diet. It didn't work. However, when the pills ran out, I tried the diet. It worked! It was a great weight-loss plan, but like it. I didn't stick to it and gained back what I lost. At the time, it didn't seem like I got anything for my money. Wrong! I got their ads and junk mail for the next five years, and it was free! But I was still fat. What those commercials don't tell you is that you have to do everything they say, exactly how they say, 100%, "Take our pill, but be sure to follow our diet plan as well." If you have as many excuses as I did, they can't help you. No one can. I've seen most of their plans and none of them are that much different from anything I'm telling you in this book.

Here is the truth: **there is no magic bullet.** No one has any special pill or plan that is much different from any of the others. If any of these diet plans or exercise machines had some magical potion, then everyone who was rich would be thin. All they would have to do is fork over the money and buy this amazing pill. In other words, **if all you needed was money, all rich people would be thin,** and I would still be fat because I'm poor.

There are other reasons why people think they need money to be thin. When I was fat, I was convinced that I couldn't afford expensive diet food, like fresh fruits and vegetables, rather than potato chips and cookies. Here's the part I didn't consider. How much does it cost to cut a sandwich in half? **If I'm eating 3,000 calories a day, then cut back to 2,000 a day, I'm actually saving money.** Duh! Also, I could stop buying the junk food and save even more. How easy is that?

It's important for my readers to understand that I was on a tight budget when I got serious about dieting. (Still don't.) My husband was barely making minimum wage and I had severe chronic fatigue so I wasn't able to work or earn any money. We were ineligible for food stamps. We made three-dollars a month too much. I had a small reimbursement for my two teenage foster daughters, but I used that money to pay them to do chores and housework. In other words, **we barely had enough money to survive, let alone extra money for special diet foods. The ONLY thing I could do was cut calories.** It worked, slowly and painstakingly, but it was better than gaining. So, if you are counting every penny like I was, there's hope.

If you just count calories, then everything you need to get started costs less than twenty bucks. You've already bought this book, so you have that out of the way. You need a calorie-counter booklet that costs about $5.95, unless you want to use an "app" on your phone. (That's free.) It actually does everything for you. Weird! Doesn't work for me. You need a food scale, about $10.00. If you don't have measuring cups and measuring spoons, you will need those too, both at *Dollar Tree*. While you are there, pick up a cheap calculator. (I think they're about a dollar.) And now for the expensive part. Are you ready? A pencil and paper, or if you are seriously neurotic, you can buy my food journal. It's quite helpful. That's it! And now for the free part. Prayer, where willpower comes in. (More about that later.)

So, if you're poor, you can still lose weight. Don't let those skinny TV people make you think that their product is the only way to look like them. Next time one of those commercials comes on, stand up straight and tell that skinny lady, "No thank you, Honey! I don't need your help, and you can't have my money. I'm going to get thin without your expensive crap!" Then stick out your tongue at her.

On the other hand, I have to admit that an apple costs slightly more than a candy bar, so I'm going to show you how to buy healthy diet foods on a budget. (I love saving money.) As I said before, you're going to be saving money because you will eat less and stop buying junk food. Start by cutting *Top Raman* and boxed mac and cheese out of your diet. There's no nutritional value, lots of calories and too many carbohydrates. Stop buying it, or buy half as much as you used to, and why are you buying potato chips, cookies, or other snack foods when you are trying to lose weight? Besides, you are throwing your money away. Stop it. Now, with all the money you saved, you've got a little bit extra to work with.

When buying food, you want food that is healthy, inexpensive, and won't make you fat. Sometimes it's hard to find all three of these in one food. The simplest way to start is to get the newspaper and shop the specials. If you have a Facebook account, ask your Facebook friends. I love telling my friends, "Hey, *Chuck's* has pears this week for forty-nine-cents-a-pound."

<u>Fruits and Veggies:</u> After checking out the sales on fresh fruits and veggies, compare them to what's in the frozen-food department. Sometimes frozen fruit is even cheaper. In the ads, I saw frozen strawberries for a dollar-a-pound. (My mouth is watering.)

Most of the larger towns have a produce store with great discounts. I can usually get apples for fifty-cents-a-pound. Apples last several months in the refrigerator. I usually pick up a few bananas, one of the cheaper fruits. Occasionally I splurge on a small package of frozen raspberries. They are so healthy and I'm saving money by not buying cookies or chips, so it's justified.

Vegetables are bought the same way as fruit. See what's on sale first. Ask your friends. Compare fresh veggies with the frozen. Be sure to see if there's a local produce store nearby.

People often ask me if fresh is healthier than frozen. It depends on which article you read. From everything I've read, the jury is still out. Fresh and frozen have about the same nutrients, because the frozen usually gets refrigerated immediately after it's picked.

Finally, if you are counting every penny, watch for sales on canned vegetables. There are four servings of vegetables in each can. (Avoid canned fruit. Too much sugar.) I'm aware that they aren't as healthy as fresh or frozen, but when they're three-cans-for-a-dollar, it's cheaper than a donut, healthier, fat-free, and very few calories. Other than that, it's terrible.

Finally, onions have dozens of vitamins and minerals, and so affordable. You can fry them up with celery and mushrooms or add them to almost any main dish or soup, or put a little soy sauce on fried onions and veggies. Makes a great side dish.

Protein: I've given you ideas on how to buy fruits and vegetables. Here is a list of foods that are loaded with protein and very reasonable. The six cheapest sources of protein are this (1) beans (2) peanut butter and peanuts (3) sunflower seeds (4) eggs (5) tuna and sardines (6) milk and milk products. **All very affordable!** Here is a little about each one.

1. Beans: This is one of the cheapest foods in the world! In addition, they are high in protein, and a great source of fiber with little or no fat. **However, they are high in carbohydrates.** We need carbs, but we don't need too many. They also have some calories, so you have to weigh and measure them, but **beans are cheap!** And if you put beans and rice together, they make a complete protein. That

means you don't have to have meat. Black beans and pinto beans are best and if you really want to save money, buy dry beans in a bag. Bring them home. Rinse. Soak. Cook. Cheap and healthy.

In the book "Eat Right for Your Type," they don't recommend kidney beans, lentils, or lima beans. They are hard to digest and cause weight gain for most blood types. Type O's shouldn't eat navy beans either because it "impairs caloric utilization."

At this point I always talk to someone who worries that beans will give them gas. Wait! Let me reword that. At this point I talk to *ladies* who worry about gas. (Doesn't seem to concern the men). Here's a tip. Beans give you gas because they have a lot of fiber and therefor have a cleansing effect. However, if you eat them regularly, two or three times a week, they will completely clean you out and no more gas, which means no more excuses. My best friend says it still gives her gas. Others say they don't. Beans are cheap and healthy, two things we all need when we diet, but you still have to count calories.

2 & 3: Peanuts, peanut butter, and sunflower seeds contain protein, vitamins and minerals and are inexpensive. Add nuts and seeds to any breakfast to get the healthy fats you need to give you energy and help you feel full. Better yet, peanuts and sunflower seeds are cheaper than those breakfast bars and healthier too. Many breakfast bars have sugar, corn syrup and a whole-bunch-of-words I can't pronounce. The better those breakfast bars taste, the more sugar or carbohydrates they have. Instead, eat nuts and seeds. Almost always cheaper and healthier than a granola bar.

I measure out three tablespoons of peanuts, a tablespoon of sunflower seeds and a tablespoon of raisins and put them in a zip lock bag. This gives me healthy carbs and fats, vitamins and minerals, and only 200 calories. If they are bagged up ahead of time, and I'm in a hurry, I grab my little baggie and go. It gives me the nutrients I need and helps keep me healthy. It's a great snack for the kids and grands. (When I have a little extra money, I use almonds or mixed nuts instead of peanuts. The calorie count is on the container.)

However, there is one problem with nuts and seeds. They are high in calories, but don't worry. That's easy to overcome. Just weigh and measure before you eat them. A tablespoon of nuts or seeds is about a hundred calories, packed with nutrition, filling and healthy. I like them with my morning coffee or tea and a bowl of berries. I love the taste of oatmeal sprinkled with nuts and seeds. One of my favorite quick snacks is to smear peanut butter on apple slices. YUM! Quite satisfying and economical!

4. <u>Eggs</u> are an almost perfect food and about ten to fifteen cents each. That's cheap! My herbalist says, "Eggs are the most nutrient-dense food in the world." Think about it. All life begins with an egg. One little egg becomes a whole entire chicken if it develops. Eggs: cheap and healthy.

Worried about cholesterol? There's some controversy but my doctor (my western doctor) told me that high cholesterol happens because of sugar and junk food, not eggs. (He's really smart.) Recent research confirms what he says. I eat a lot of eggs (probably six or more a week) and my cholesterol is good. Eggs are loaded with vitamins and almost every mineral necessary to nourish your body. (Although eggs are cheap, I spend a few extra pennies on eggs labeled "free range." I don't support people who abuse their chickens.) When I build a meal around eggs, I am confident that my family and I are getting essential nutrients and I'm saving money. **A veggie omelet, is a perfect meal.** I fry onions, mushrooms, and green peppers, then stir in the eggs. It's more like scrambled eggs with veggies than an omelet, but it's delicious, cheap, and filling. I keep hard-boiled eggs in the refrigerator. If I get hungry, I can just snatch it, crack it, and peel. Only 80 calories and no carbs.

5. <u>Tuna and sardines (in mustard, not soy)</u> are cheap, loaded with protein, very low in calories, and fat free! Did you know that the cheap tuna is healthier than the expensive white albacore tuna, because it has less mercury? Yup.

If you want a special treat, watch for canned salmon on sale, like four cans for five dollars. There's a great recipe in here for salmon dip; cheap, tasty, and low in calories and filling. Best of all, salmon has vitamin D and those amazing Omega 3's that Dr. Oz says we need to be healthy. Tuna has fewer calories than chicken, pork, or beef, and no fat. Most salmon does too, but read the label. Some salmon has more calories than others. The bones in sardines are high in calcium. All affordable.

6. <u>Milk and milk products</u> are filling, have vitamins, minerals, and almost all of the necessary amino acids and affordable. I usually buy 1% milk or low-fat milk products but not fat free. (Fat-free tastes boring.) When you're hungry, plain yogurt with fresh berries and Stevia can be so satisfying, and so much cheaper and healthier than other snacks. If I'm really hungry, I sprinkle a tablespoon of granola on the top.

However, there is one problem with milk. It's hard to digest, so here's what I do. I buy "lactaid," a little pill to help with milk digestion. This little pill allows me to have milk products, but I limit them, one or two serving a day.

Finally, I don't "drink" milk. I eat low-fat cheese, cottage cheese, and yogurt. If I want milk on my oatmeal, I use almond milk or coconut milk. I sometimes cook with milk, but I rarely ever drink it. (Except, I love a cup of hot chocolate when it snows.)

<u>Other protein:</u> If you want poultry, simply watch for the sales. My favorite is chicken breasts or thighs. If I get the ones that are boneless and skinless, I'm paying for pure meat, 99% fat-free, sometimes as low as a dollar-a-pound. Around Christmas and Easter, turkey goes down to twenty-three-cents a pound (as long as you buy $50.00 worth of groceries). A turkey will last my family three or four days and still some for the freezer. Also, when buying poultry, I use ground turkey, in place of hamburger, but read the label. Some ground turkey is 35% fat. Too many calories. Besides, some people believe animal-fat isn't healthy.

Finally, anything that walks on four legs (a.k.a. red meat) should be kept to once or twice a week. Red meat is usually more expensive and harder to digest. Dr. Oz only eats red meat once a week. When buying hamburger, get the 4% to 7% fat. The lower the fat, the more it costs, but use half as much because it has less fat and doesn't shrink. If you want cheaper red meat, there's usually an area of the grocery store that has day-old meat, often half price. It's still good, but keep red meat needs to a minimum in order to lose weight and be healthy. The only exception is if you have Type O blood. You can eat and digest red meat better than the rest of us, but be sure you count calories too.) Also, I don't eat any meat that comes from pigs. According to "Eat Right for Your Type," it's unhealthy for everyone. The Bible agrees.

Grains are cheap but most cause weight-gain:

To start with, you can live without grains. Repeat after me. "I CAN LIVE WITHOUT GRAINS." Yes, you can. Most grains have been hybrid, cross bred, or genetically modified (also called GMO). Consequently, our bodies don't recognize it as food and doesn't know what to do with it. What are grains? Here's a list of most of them:

Wheat	Rye	Quinoa
Corn	Soy	Millet
Rice	Oats	Buckwheat

Most bread, pasta, crackers, and cereal are grains, and you can live without them.

The two cheapest grains are wheat and corn. Those are also the two most likely to cause weight gain. Start cutting back on those two. (More about that in the chapter "The Fatal Five.")

My herbalist, who helped me get my health back, said this to me. **"If you want to eat corn or wheat I can't help you."** He takes ALL of his patients (clients) off wheat and corn, with no exception.

That's because the ALL of them show some sort of "sensitivity" to those two grains. Second, he takes most of his clients off of ALL grains. His diabetic clients are not allowed to have any grains. NO EXCEPTIONS! Interestingly, their health begins to return. Most of them stop shots and medication, and lose weight. His patients with autoimmune disorders can't have grains either.

The problem is that people in our country tend to center their meals around grains. Grains are often 50% of our diet or more. Consequently, it's hard to stop all grains. I've spent years cutting back, but I haven't quite mastered it yet.

Our bodies don't need a lot of grains, especially as we get older, but most of us overdose on grains and carbohydrates which is part of why we keep gaining weight. (In case you don't know, grains are mostly carbohydrates). Now I want to share a few of my favorite grains with you. Oh! That reminds me of a song (to the tune of *These Are a Few of My Favorite Things.*)

<u>My Favorite Grains</u>
Black rice
And brown rice
And oatmeal with coffee
Oat bran and rice bran
Tastes so good to me.
Oatmeal that doesn't
Cause me to gain
These are a few of my favorite grains.

When the urge hits
When I crave carbs
When I'm feeling sad
I simply start eating my favorite grains
And then I don't feel so bad.

That was a poor excuse for a song, but you probably noticed **my two favorite grains, rice and oats.** My herbalist often allows his clients to have these two grains and these two ONLY. This is especially good since I don't have a lot of money. They are cheap and satisfying.

Let's start with oats, one of the cheapest and healthiest grains in the world (oat bran too). I add oats and oat bran together when I make breakfast. Oatmeal with oat bran has five different types of fiber! All five types are needed to make healthy poop. (That's what Dr. Oz calls it. He is a big fan of a healthy poop.) Besides that, oatmeal decreases your cholesterol, and tastes delicious! In my recipe chapter I have seven different ways to fix oatmeal. Wait until you try my recipe for *Mocha Oats*. Yum! Now you can feed your family gourmet oatmeal on a budget.

One last thing about oatmeal. When I make cookies, cakes, or muffins, I substitute oats for half of the flour. If it calls for two cups of flour, I use one cup of flour and one cup of oats. (I use the "old-fashioned oats.") It adds a nice texture, gives it a uniqueness that makes my friends and family say, "Mmm. What is that?" By the way. I buy oat bran in bulk for 67 cents-a-pound.

The other wonderful grain on a budget is rice, healthy, gluten-free and cheap. But rice isn't just that stuff you use as a side dish. Now they have rice cakes and rice crackers, much healthier than other breads and crackers, both sold at most grocery stores. Also, if you like crackers they have one called "Nut Thins" grain free and wonderful with salsa or bean dip! (Recipes and snack ideas later.)

If you love dry cereal in the morning, the cereal companies have done us all a favor, making dry cereal out of rice instead of wheat. Look for the boxes that say "gluten-free," but read the label and make sure that it isn't made with corn. Corn is gluten-free but makes you fat and sick. Stick with cereals made out of rice or oats.

There is one more grain, a wonderful new grain called "quinoa." It's not exactly a grain. It's more like a cross between spinach and tumble weed, but it's healthy and a fun alternative to wheat, corn, and other unhealthy grains. I'm still learning about it, and it's a little more expensive than other grains, but very healthy and high protein. I plan to experiment with it and see if I can come up with some new recipes for my next book.

That's it. Rice and oats are cheap. Quinoa is healthy, but these three are the ONLY grains I recommend for people who want to lose weight and be healthy. No matter which ones you choose, you still have to count calories. Darn!

Cheap Fats:

Unlike grains, **we need fats to be healthy**. You might think that fat makes you fat. Wrong. Well, not entirely. The **bad** fats make you fat and too much of anything causes weight gain, but here's some good news. Fat gives you energy and feeds your brain.

Do you ever feel run down? Foggy? You may need some healthy fat in your diet. What are my favorite fats? (No song for this one.) I will discuss fats in detail in the chapter "Fats and Carbs." But for now, here are some of the healthier fats: **nuts and seeds, peanut butters, almond butter and other nut butters, flax, chia seeds, avocados, cold-pressed olive oil, palm oil, and coconut oil.** The healthiest bottled oils are "cold pressed." They are also more expensive.

I have more good-and-bad news about fats. The good news is that the unhealthy fats are cheap. The healthy ones cost more, but here's the good news. You will be spending less on everything else, so you can afford to spend a little more on fats. The most affordable fats are peanuts, peanut butter, and sunflower seeds. Those three are high in protein and healthy. I can afford these, but I have to budget in olive oil and palm oil. I watch for sales on everything else.

At the end of the book, I have a chapter entitled "Shopping List," This chapter will help you make a shopping list and save money.

A NEW PERSPECTIVE ON DIETING AND WEIGHT LOSS

In my recipe section, most of the meals are cheap, easy to make, low cal and low carb.

The bottom line is this: **It doesn't cost anything to eat half-as-much. If you cut calories, you will eat less, buy less, save money, and lose weight.** Sorry. You can't use "I don't have enough money" as an excuse anymore.

THING #10

Fill in the Blank

The reason I can't lose weight is because _____. You won't even believe some of the excuses I've heard. Everyone has them. Here are just a few. They are real. I promise!

Excuse "A": What if I get anorexic? Un-excused: Sorry! Anorexia Nervosa is mental illness. Dieting doesn't cause mental illness. The mental illness comes first.

Excuse "B": I can't diet because I'm hypoglycemic or diabetic. Un-excused: Talk to your doctor. He or she will disagree. **You do have to be more careful than others,** but a good diet is what you need in order to be healthy. There are several books on how to reverse diabetes. They all have to do with eating healthy, losing weight, and avoiding certain foods.

Excuse C: "I don't care." Un-excused: Really? You would rather be fat, look ugly, and ruin your health? Come on. You can think of a better excuse than that. No one is going to believe that. Not even you.

Excuse D: "Diet food doesn't taste good." Un-excused: Maybe I should say "semi un-excused." If I make clam chowder with real cream and real butter, it tastes amazing! I can make the same soup with low-fat milk and herbs and it also tastes amazing, but let's be honest. High-fat soup tastes better, absolutely, beyond a doubt, but honestly, do I really need everything to taste like it just came out of a five-star restaurant 100% of the time? When I finally started eating low-cal foods, I had to stop acting like a big spoiled baby who cries, "My food has to taste amazing or I'm going to spit it out!" I knew if I wanted to lose weight, I had to make some sacrifices and stop whining. Instead, I chose to get creative and learn how to make low-cal food taste good.

Clearly, some diet foods taste terrible. I don't eat those. Pretty simple. But there are other diet foods that taste good. If I want it to taste good, I usually make my own. There are thousands of cookbooks filled with yummy low-cal recipes.

By the way, I can eat high-calorie, super tasty foods any time I want and still lose weight. I just have to count the calories.

Excuse E: I live with people who like unhealthy, high-fat food. Un-excused: but not totally. This one is rough if you are trying to diet, and if you live with someone who has a lot of garbage and junk food in the house.

If you are the mom or the one who does most of the cooking and shopping, you have power and some control. You get to buy the healthy foods and make the changes. Instead of letting others be a bad influence on you, why don't you be a good influence on them? Don't buy junk food. Don't bring it in the house. Buy vegetables, oats, rice cakes, peanut butter, and some of the other healthy foods mentioned in this book. If you live with roommates, ask them to work with you. Most people want to lose a few pounds anyway. Why not be a blessing to those you live with? (Read the chapter on Support.) If you aren't in charge of buying the food, you have options. Eat less. Count calories. Quite simple. You can do it!

Excuse F: My medication makes me fat. Might be excused. First of all, medication is often blamed for weight gain when it's just years of bad habits. IF you are convinced that your medicine is causing weight gain, talk to the pharmacists AND your doctor. Start by asking them, "What percentage of people gain weight on this?" You might be shocked to know it's only 2%. If it's 30 or 40% or more, see if you can do without it or make a change. If not, then I can only say this: Un-excused: Do you want to keep gaining more weight? Why not be the one who stays on this medication and does well? Be the one who inspires others who are having the same problems. Your choice.

Excuse G: So, what's your excuse? Whatever it is, you need to let it go. BE HONEST! Tell the truth. Do you want to know what the truth is? Dieting is hard. That's the truth. Remember what Jesus said. "The truth will set you free."

The Antidote: Self-Talk

We used to think that people who talked to themselves were mentally ill. Now we know it's a sign of self-awareness. Human beings are the only animals who do this, but what are we saying to ourselves? When self-talk turns into excuses, it's called "negative self-talk." Back in my fat days, I said them so much that I believed them. They became a part of me.

Here are a few of the things I say now to replace those damaging thoughts.

Negative self-talk (a.k.a. excuses)	Replaced with:
I'm the exception.	Nothing will stop me.
I'll start my diet tomorrow.	I'll cheat on my diet tomorrow.
I don't look that bad.	I don't look the way I want to look.
I don't eat that much.	I need to count calories. Then I will know.
It's hereditary.	My family history isn't the problem.

I'm too stressed.	Eating right relieves stress.
Diets don't work for me.	I will find the right diet and stick to it.
I get too hungry.	I can eat in an hour.
I don't have enough money.	If I eat less, I will save money.

Here are a few I say when I'm staring at some food that looks tempting. You can borrow mine or make up your own. I tend to say them a lot.

- I don't need that.
- Do you want to lose weight or not?
- I have to get on the scale tomorrow.
- That's poison!
- Get out of the kitchen!
- Go for a walk.
- Are you on a diet or not?
- Go do something.
- That's going to make you fat.
- I'm smart enough to stop eating.
- Is this the habit I want for life?
- What would Jennifer Aniston eat? (WWJAE)
- Turn on some music and dance.
- Just say no.
- Make a smoothie.
- Don't even think about it.
- You can do this!
- Devil, go away, in Jesus name!
- You haven't taken your vitamins.
- Lord God, Help me!

Hunger is another major problem, so I have some phrases I tell myself when I feel like I'm starving. Other times I want to indulge in something unhealthy. Here are some of my favorites:

- You can eat in an hour.
- You just ate.
- Are you crazy!?
- Drink some tea.
- Eat vegetables.
- Go read a book.
- Will this get me what I want?
- STOP!
- Dear Jesus! Help! Please!

You can make a copy of this and stick it on your refrigerator. You have my permission. Better yet, make up your own. I'm convinced that most people are smarter than they think they are. I hate to admit it, but most people are smarter than I am. Whatever you decide, tell yourself, "No more excuses."

PART III

Now for the Hard Part

(And You Thought the Last Part Stank!)

ONE

God Made Me Completely Unique, Just Like Everyone Else

When I was overweight, I used to go to the bookstore hoping to find the right book to help me lose weight. But I was overwhelmed with hundreds of diet books begging me to buy them and try them. As I scanned them, each author assured me they could help me lose weight. They were so convincing. Each one made sense in its own way, but when I picked a book and tried their ideas, it didn't work quite like they promised. In spite of all their claims, I sometimes gained weight. **Their methods may work them, but not for me.** Those books made me feel like a failure. That's because my body is different from the people who wrote the books. Yet I have friends who tried the same diet and lost weight.

One of my friends got into "juicing." She loved it, losing 35 pounds in three months. Then, for some strange reason, she gained it back. Other people swear by juicing.

So, what's the answer? What I discovered after years of dieting is this. There are hundreds of cut-and-dried dieting rules, like "Never skip breakfast," or "Follow the food pyramid." These rules may sound logical, but they don't work for 100% of the people, 100% of the time. Nothing does!

Consequently, I break several of those cut-and-dried dieting rules, because I'm completely unique, just like you. Here's a list of those rules that I've heard for years that didn't work for me.

Rule #1. Breakfast is the most important meal of the day.

For years, the experts told me, "breakfast will kick-start your metabolism." They told me that skipping breakfast causes weight gain and is bad for my health. Sounds logical, right?

What I discovered after years of dieting is this. **If I eat breakfast, I eat all day, nonstop.** It's like priming the pump. That means, I start eating and can't stop. I eat compulsively, so if I start popping food in my mouth five minutes after I wake up, I can't stop.

I made up my own rule: "Nothing Before Noon." (NBN) And I mean NOTHING! If I get hungry or thirsty, I get out my food journal and plan what I'm going to eat, AND what time I will eat it. Then I get busy with dishes or laundry. For the next few hours, I am setting the mood for the day: not putting food in my mouth. Am I hungry? Yes, but I've learned that it's okay to be hungry. When I finally eat, I enjoy each bite. For the rest of the day, I have the thought, *Wow! You did such a good job this morning. Don't mess it up now.* The tone is set.

For me, eating breakfast as soon as I wake up messes up my diet for the rest of the day. (Actually, I do eat breakfast. I eat it four hours after I get up.) It's one of those rules that kills my diet. Breakfast may be important for some people. Not for me.

Rule #2. Eat every two or three hours to keep up your metabolism.

There are two reasons this is supposed to work. First, if you wait too long to eat, you get too hungry. Then, you are likely to binge. Therefore, if you eat every two hours, you will never be hungry. This is another rule that sounds logical, but the trick is to eat **small amounts.** I don't know about you, but a carrot stick and a few crackers don't fill me up. I'm still hungry, really hungry, so it doesn't work for me.

The second theory is that if you eat every two or three hours, it tells your body there is plenty of food so your body doesn't store fat. Supposedly, eating more-often keeps your metabolism going, so you lose weight faster. Makes sense, right? And it works for some people.

But this is how I feel about it. **This is the stupidest rule I've ever heard.** Think about it. They tell me that I **have to** eat every two or three hours. Really? Does that make sense? What if I'm not hungry? What if I'm full? Am I supposed to keep stuffing myself just because some "expert" says that I'm supposed to? This rule does not and has not ever worked for me. I tend to eat too much anyway. This just makes me eat more.

When I feel like I'm being "forced" to eat, it changes how I think about food. I'm watching the clock so I can eat again. In addition to eating compulsively, now I have a rule that says I have to run to the cupboard and eat more often.

Here are my personal rules about how often to eat. After I eat a meal, I set my alarm or timer for three hours, and I don't permit myself to eat until it goes off, but no cheating no matter how hungry I am. But my second rule is this. If I'm not hungry when my alarm goes off, I don't eat. **I have a lifetime policy. If I'm not hungry, I don't eat.** If I eat when I'm not hungry, I gain weight. I know myself and have learned what works for me.

Rule # 3. Don't cut your calories too low:

Seriously? This one makes me crazy. They say if you cut your calories too low that your body will store fat. This translates as "Cutting calories makes you fat." Does that make sense? If that was true, people in foreign countries who are starving would all be fat.

I count calories, enough to keep me healthy, but the right amount for me. If I eat too many calories, I gain. If I cut back, I lose. Makes sense to me.

In the TV series, "My 600-Pound Life," the doctor tells his clients that they have to lose some weight before he will do the gastric-bypass surgery. (Most are too heavy for surgery.) Then he gives them all the same recommendation. "A thousand calories a day." Most doctors would say, "That's not enough!" But these obese people are desperate to get the surgery, so they cooperate with their surgeon. They cut their calories to 1,000 a day. The results? They lose about ten-pounds-a-week for a month.

I don't recommend going that low, but I'm making a point. Cutting calories works. I usually follow this rule: never go lower than 1,200 calories for women and 1,500 for guys. Sometimes I eat less, but I'm allowed to have unlimited green vegetables so it still adds up to 1,200 calories.

Rule # 4. Give up milk products:

Giving up milk has helped many people get healthy and lose weight. Mary Lou Henner, a beautiful actress said that she finally lost those last ten pounds when she gave up ALL milk products. Well, bully for her. Not me. (I think I was supposed to say, "Not I.") When I stop using milk products, I feel hungry. That leads to cheating. I love a little cheese on my salad or sour cream on my taco. Yogurt and berries is a quick snack that makes me feel full. Giving-up-milk or

A NEW PERSPECTIVE ON DIETING AND WEIGHT LOSS

milk products is another rule that doesn't work for me. If someone tells you to give up milk or some other food, try it and see.

Rule #5. Weigh yourself once a week:

This may work for some people, but not for me. I do something that the experts warn against. **I weigh every day.** Why? To be perfectly honest, I lie. My scale keeps me honest. It's like the mom who catches their kid with their hand in the cookie jar. The kid is dead meat. He's caught. He can't lie. If he tries, he looks like an idiot. His mom keeps him honest, and my scale keeps me honest.

When I used to weigh once-a-week, I told myself, "You are doing really well on your diet," but seven days later, my scale said, *No you aren't!*

If I weigh daily, and I'm up a little, I can go look at my food journal from the day before to see what I did wrong. It usually jumps out and slaps me in the face. Sometimes it's because I didn't eat any vegetables. Other times I didn't drink enough water. (I keep track of both.) Of course, there are times when there is no clear reason, so I don't sweat it. I just keep on keeping on. If I'm doing well, the pounds start coming off again, eventually.

If I my weight is up three days in a row, then I skip supper or fast for a day. Fasting gets me back on track. My mother, who weighs 135 pounds, does the same. If she's up a few pounds and can't get it off, she cuts back until she's back down again. Like my mom, I weigh every day. It keeps me honest. I don't care what the experts say.

The most important thing I can tell you is this. **The most weight I've ever gained in the smallest amount of time is when I stopped weighing myself.** When I finally got back on the scale, I was shocked to learn that I had gained seven pounds in three months. Here's the interesting part. I thought I was doing really well, being careful about what I ate, pushing aside dessert and refusing seconds. I needed a daily scale to help keep me on track.

In addition to weighing daily, I also have a weekly chart. Every Friday, I write down my weight because daily weight can fluctuate, but at the end of a week, I can see exactly how I did. Now I'm going to sound compulsive, but I chart my weight on the first of each month too. That way, it's very clear to me if I'm truly losing or not. A picture is worth a thousand word, but a chart is worth a million.

I have to weigh daily **AND** write it down, or I gain weight. Why? Because I am a cheater. Weighing daily keeps me honest. Maybe that's why the Bible says, "An honest scale is the Lord's delight." (Proverbs 11:1, loosely translated).

Rule #6: Never eat after 7:00 p.m.:

This sounds good, right? They say, "If you go to bed on an empty stomach, your food digests better and therefore, will lose weight." Makes sense, right?

Here's the **real** reason it why this rule works. Most of us have already had plenty to eat by the time we're finished eating supper. (Some of us have had enough by noon.) But in the evenings, we're tired. **When a person is tired, they naturally want to eat.** Worse yet, we flop out in front of the TV. The combination of being tired and watching TV compels us to eat mindlessly. At that point, we have no idea of how much we are eating. Consequently, we go over our calorie count as the day goes on.

Here's another way to look at it. Suppose you are burning 2,000 calories a day. By the time you are finished eating your supper, you've already consumed your 2,000 calories, but that bag of Doritos seems to be calling your name. So, you have a few, with some dip of course. Now you've gone over your limit. Anytime you eat more than you burn off, you will gain weight. A hundred extra calories-a-day (one small cookie) adds a pound-a-month, but when we eat mindlessly, we don't eat ONE cookie. We eat half-the-box. That's why we gain weight. It's not because of what time we ate. It's because we consume too many calories.

Here's what I learned about this "Don't-eat-after-7:00-pm-rule," and why it doesn't work. **When I count every calorie, it doesn't seem to matter what time I eat them.**

If I know I'm going out in the evening, I eat lightly all day. Then I consume the rest of my calories in the evening. It works. I don't gain weight as long as I continue eating the same number of calories every day. Try it for yourself. It makes sense.

All this being said, I rarely eat after 7:00. If I see something yummy in the fridge, I just plan to eat it the next day for lunch. In other words, **I've learned to postpone eating.** It works, at least for me.

Rule # 6: Take one-day-a-week off of your diet.

This one gives me too much "wiggle room." I occasionally take a day off, but it's planned and it's about once-a-month. When I know Thanksgiving is coming, or something special, I make a plan for that special day, but I NEVER just take a day off for no reason. However, I know others who swear by it. They say it gives them something to look forward to and helps them stick to their diet for six days. If you want to try it, good luck. We're all different.

The bottom line:

If you want to be successful in your diet and weight loss, you have to figure out what works for you. Just because Dr. Oz says it, doesn't mean it works. If you hear something new, try it for a while. If it works, continue to do it. If it doesn't, give it up.

I do a lot of praying. God created me. He can show me what's good and what isn't. I'm still learning. I'm always learning. The Bible says that God will give wisdom to ANYONE who asks for it. That promise is for everyone, even if you don't believe in God. You are totally unique. You and God can figure it out together.

TWO

If You Want to Win, You Absolutely Must Do This. No Choice.

I would bet 100-to-1 that everyone who is reading this has dieted at some time in their life. I would also bet that all those people lost weight. If that's true, you have to ask yourself, "What happened?" Most people just think it's a lack of will power, or some other excuse. Wrong.

Here's my personal reason why I used to fail. I always started out great. I'm on track, losing weight and sticking to my diet, but I get hungry, so I go to the refrigerator to get something on my diet. Unfortunately, the first thing I see is that yummy, leftover macaroni and cheese with extra cheese. I move it aside, looking for something low-cal, but all I see is a little lettuce that needs to be chopped up and I'm out of my favorite salad dressing. So, I look in the freezer. There's an unhealthy TV dinner and ice cream. I see some frozen chicken, but it would take too much time to thaw it out and cook it, and I'm **really** hungry, so what do I do? I choose the cheesy mac-and-cheese. Why? Because it's quick, easy and filling, and it tastes good, but that doesn't totally explain why I made that choice. **The real reason is poor planning.**

It doesn't matter which diet you choose, Atkins, Mediterranean, or Paleo Diet. They all require planning, every single one. How can I stick to my diet if I don't have the right foods in my house and I don't have a plan?

What if a coach didn't plan his football game ahead of time? "Come on men. Let's get out there and win this one! Sorry, but I have no idea how you can do it, but I know you can win!" Do you think this is a winning team? When it comes to dieting, we all want to be winners, but most of us don't plan. Or we plan at first and then quit planning.

Imagine sending your third-grader to school. You want the best, so you research his teacher. She has a Master's Degree in Education from a prestigious college with an amazing g.p.a. You meet her. She's warm and friendly. She seems perfect, except for one thing. She doesn't plan. She just shows up every day with a smile on her face and information in her head. She knows what she's required to teach, like multiplication tables and vocabulary, but she hasn't mapped out which direction to go or how she will accomplish what she needs to do. She flies by the seat of her pants. Every day, she makes speculations for these innocent little children. Would you want your child in her class? No matter how educated or intelligent she is, she will fail! A good teacher plans out her day **and** her week. Most teachers know what they have to accomplish before the school year starts. Then they make a plan for the entire school year.

Anything important requires planning. A wedding. A vacation. A baseball game, or any other sport. If you don't plan, you lose. The same is true with dieting. That's why *Jenny Craig* works. It's a diet program that is completely planned for you, everything. All your meals and all your food are perfectly planned, perfectly balanced. All you have to do is eat the food they prepare for you. However, it's a little expensive and also impractical especially if you eat with your family or roommates. Why? Because everyone in the house is chawing away on a pan of lasagna, dripping with four-types of cheese, while you sit there eating a preplanned, low-cal, diet meal by *Jenny Craig*. Not easy. **However, if you stick to their plan, you will lose weight.** Personally, I can't afford it and for me, it's impractical.

The other problem with *Jenny Craig* is that eventually, you may want to quit using their plan. When you do, they help you. They give you a common-sense, do-it-yourself eating plan, but most people have a hard time following the new plan. They've spent years leaning on others to do the work for them. Consequently, many gain back the weight when they try to go off on their own. Of course it's not 100%, but it would be interesting to check out the stats and find out what percent kept the weight off after leaving the program.

What if I'm not good at planning?

That's me. I am the total opposite of an organized, methodical, obsessive, type A, planner-type of person. It's not how I think. I hate planning and I'm not good at it. However, a lack of planning explains why all my diets failed, even the one I'm recommending to you. The "I'm-not-good-at-planning" was another excuse for me.

If you are not a planner-type-person, you have to turn yourself into one. You have to force yourself to change. I did. So can you. No matter who you are, you are smart enough to make a plan.

What if I don't have enough time?

PLANNING TAKES TIME. Sorry, but it's a fact. Most people don't have a lot of extra time. I don't either. Does anyone? We are all busy people. Do you really believe you don't have enough time? What if your rich uncle told you, "I will give you a million dollars if you will plan what you eat and count every calorie for the next six months." Wouldn't you make time? Your health is worth far more than a million dollars. Losing weight and look good makes me feel like a million bucks.

How much time does it take? More at first. As you get better, it's easier and faster. It's like tying your shoe. Have you ever seen a five-year-old trying to tie his shoe? Painful to watch, but you sit back and wait for the child to learn, but they do. When was the last time you had a hard time tying your shoes? The same is true for dieting, counting calories, and planning. It's hard at first, but after a while it's second nature. You just do it.

When I first started, I needed to set aside about fifteen minutes-a-day to plan my meals and about fifteen throughout the day to write down what I ate and count calories. That's all. Thirty-minutes-a-day to lose weight and feel great. Thirty-minutes-a-day to succeed. We are all busy people. When I made the time, I finally succeeded. "I don't have time," is a great excuse, but it's still an excuse. If it's important enough, there's no excuse.

My Skinny Cousin:

My cousin, Gina is thin and works on it. She plans ahead. One of her strategies is this: once-a-month, she spends about an hour making diet shakes for the entire month. (I have recipes later.) Then she fills her freezer with twenty individual cups with lids. Every morning before work, she grabs her healthy shake and it's ready to go. That's planning and it obviously works. She's in her fifties and has a smoking hot body. (It's so disgusting, but I still love her anyway.)

Getting the low-down on planning:

Here's what I do. When I started, I had to decide what type of diet to do. Since counting calories had been scientifically proven to work, and had worked for me in the past, that's what I chose. As time went on, I made some adjustments, some changes, and omitted certain food, but I ALWAYS counted calories. Still do.

You can use a different diet if you want, but counting calories has been proven over and over and over. I've tried dozens of diets. Counting calories works best for me. Consequently, choosing a diet was my first step.

The next thing was to buy the things I needed. Counting calories doesn't require a lot of money (another reason I like it). To start, I needed a calorie-counting book, a calculator, and a food scale. Many people count calories on their cell phone. Doesn't work for me, so I went to *Barnes and Nobel* and bought a little booklet *The T-Factor Fat-Gram Counter*. I like it because it's small. That means I can put it in my pocket or purse. Also, it has calories **AND** carbohydrates. (More about carbs later.) I also had to buy a food scale to weigh my food. You can pick one up at Walmart or Fred Meyer. I already had a pencil and paper. That's all I needed! Less than $20 to get started, the first part of my plan.

Next, I made a shopping list. **A teacher knows what to teach, but she needs to make sure she has all the necessary tools BEFORE she begins teaching.** Imagine getting to school and not having pencils or pens, or chalk, or markers. No books. No paper. Just show up and teach. You need tools to teach, and tools to diet. That requires planning.

When I first started, I often bought diet foods along with "failure foods," you know those foods that set you up to fail, chips and cookies and ... well, you know. I kept thinking that I would just control myself after I brought them home. DUMB! Over the years, I learned (and keep learning) how to shop and what to buy and what not to buy.

Now, when I shop, I avoid those unhealthy foods and read labels, especially yogurt. I used to look at the front, where it says "low fat" or "lite," but that's can be deceptive. Instead, I turn it around and read the back. There is one brand of yogurt that screams "healthy," on the

A NEW PERSPECTIVE ON DIETING AND WEIGHT LOSS

front, but it has nearly twice as many calories as other yogurts. Now, I try to buy yogurt that has 100 calories or less per cup. Another food that I'm careful with is granola bars. Some have way too many calories with too much sugar. **Read the label!** If I don't plan my shopping I fail.

Here are some things I buy every week. **I put a star by the foods that need the labels checked and compared.** Comparing is important. There is a HUGE difference on some foods. Here's my list:

Almond milk *	Fresh fruit	Frozen berries	Tuna
Fat-free yogurt *	Carrots	Granola bars *	Rice cakes *
Half & Half	Green veggies	Soup *	Rice crackers
Cottage Cheese 2%	Onions	Ground turkey*	Nuts and seeds
1% Milk	Romaine Lettuce	Olive oil	Almond butter
Eggs	Tomatoes	Coconut oil	Peanut butter

Those are just a few of the things I eat regularly, so they are usually on my weekly shopping list. There are other items that I keep stocked **tea, stevia, spices, rice, rice crackers, and oatmeal,** but this is just a general idea. I don't always plan 100% of every single thing, but when I'm shopping, I ask myself, "Would this be good for my diet?" Or, "Would Jennifer Aniston eat this?" No matter what's on the list, I've learned, **the better I plan, the better I diet.** Some people plan all their meals for the entire week. Good for them. I'm not there yet, but I have a lot of heathy diet foods in my cupboards and fridge.

Now that I've done my shopping, I start "cooking up a plan." Until I did this, I failed again. I would do well for a day-or-two, or maybe a week. Then, I would get really hungry, grab some chips and eat the whole bag. Hey! I was hungry.

Here's how I do it now. First, I always carry a pencil and paper folded in half the long way. Right after dinner (or supper as they call it in the Midwest), I start planning for tomorrow. This is a good time because after dinner, I usually want more of everything, especially dessert. I basically want to continue eating and I have a hard time stopping. Instead, of pigging out, I pick up my paper and pencil and look through the refrigerator and cupboards. Then, I plan what I'm going to eat the next day. It's best if I write down how many calories each item has, but I don't always get that part done. I can look it up later. I also use the other side of the page like a journal. I make notes about places I need to go and who I need to call. In other words, I plan what I am going to eat, but I also plan my day. It's best if I write down what time I'm going to eat. Sometimes I will put my plans for the day in numerical order. NO MATTER WHAT, I PLAN.

So, the left side of the page eventually looks something like this:
J -peg

Now I begin preparing the foods I'm going to eat the next day. That way, I don't do something stupid like wake up and eat a box of cookies. I put the soup in the crock pot, weigh my nuts and put them in a baggie. I put the ingredients for my smoothie in the blender and put it in the refrigerator. (If I'm using anything frozen, I add that in the morning just before blending.) I don't usually prepare my salad ahead of time because I like it fresh, but I check to see if I have what I need. Now everything is ready.

This may sound complicated, but I have to eat, so I may as well eat right and think about it before I do it. I have a choice. **I either plan my day or it plans me.** My day doesn't always go exactly as planned, but neither does anything else in life, so I just have to get over it, and do my best.

Now, for the right side of my paper. I wake up the next morning. I've got my day planned and my food planned. When I get ready to eat, I look at the list I made the night before and circle what I want. I like to have a healthy smoothie for my first meal, but before I eat it, I write it down. I also write down what time I eat and how many calories. Easy. (I count carbs too, but I don't want to get too complicated at this point.) At the end of the day, the right side of the page looks something like this:

J-peg # 2

You probably noticed that I didn't do it exactly how I planned, but I had healthy foods nearby so that I didn't fail. Planning helps me stay off those little bunny trails. It's harder to cheat when it's planned.

If you want, you can plan all this in the morning when you first wake up, but be sure to get up a few minutes earlier. I have learned if I plan it out the night before, my life and diet are so much easier. That way, if I wake up starving, I'm less likely to run in the kitchen, pig out, and ruin my day.

Super-simple planning:

If you are really busy, you need to plan three things. First, plan your vegetables. Most of us professional dieters forget the veggies. (More in the veggies chapter.) Next, have fresh fruit available, and frozen berries. Finally, get your water or flavored water ready. Those three simple things will help you stick to your diet.

If you want to be successful, you have to set aside a little time to plan. It's worth it. You're worth it. Everyone who is successful in life, plans, and a successful dieter, plans.

THREE

This Means War

Planning is good, but what is my attitude starting a new diet? Am I yawning or am I taking on my diet like a Marine drill Sargent preparing for combat? Am I saying, "Dieting is no big deal," or "Come on soldier. Let's do this." If I go at this as though it's smooth sailing, I lose. Dieting isn't easy. Neither is war. Both require planning, but both require an attitude of "I'm going to win and nothing is going to stop me."

Imagine General MacArthur saying, "Why don't you guys sleep in today? We're all tired of this war. We can work on the enemy later. No way! One of his notable quotes was, **"It is fatal to win a war without the will to win it."** He was a famous five-star general who knew about victory. It's all about attitude.

Robert E. Lee, another great war leader said, **"The devil's name is dullness."** Lee understood that dullness or apathy would not let you win.

Back in my "fat days," I would start a new diet with gusto and enthusiasm. Then hunger came along (or ice cream). My bubble burst. That gung-ho attitude was quickly replaced with one of those feeble excuses. **I went from warrior-to-wimp in a nanosecond.** (I hope I'm not the only one.) When I realized I had to continue my exuberance, it was a turning point. I finally figured out that I couldn't win a war without determination. Dieting is war. If I don't approach it that way, I lose *The Battle of the Bulge*.

FOUR

Counting Calories. It's Underrated.

I hate it. I hate it. I hate it. Counting calories is time-consuming, annoying, frustrating, and . . . just a minute . . . let me get my thesaurus . . . aggravating, unpleasant, dreadful, agonizing, yukkie, and well, you get the idea. Un-fun. However, counting calories works! It's proven. IF YOU WANT TO LOSE WEIGHT, DO NOT SKIP THIS CHAPTER. I wish I could make calorie-counting more interesting, fun or funny, but it's like learning your multiplication tables. It's time-consuming and irksome, but it's just part of life.

Think of all the things in life that are annoying, but necessary . . . like school. How many kids jump out of bed at six in the morning saying, "Oh boy! Thank you for waking me up at so early and dragging me out of my warm bed, so that I can go to school!" Instead, most kids whine and complain and can't wait for the weekend or summer. The adults force them to go because it's a necessary part of life, and the beginning of a healthy work ethic.

There are other things that are difficult but necessary. What about childbirth? If all women said, "It's just too hard," I wouldn't be writing this book because I would never have been born, and you wouldn't be reading it. (At least we wouldn't be fat.) Women chose childbirth because there is a reward at the end. The pain is worth it.

A NEW PERSPECTIVE ON DIETING AND WEIGHT LOSS

Counting calories is not nearly as difficult as twelve years of school and it's definitely easier than giving birth, yet most people don't want to be bothered with it. It requires time and effort. But when it comes to losing weight, counting calories is the easiest, cheapest, and most consistently proven method of weight loss, ever!

Counting calories is a little complicated, but it's worth learning. I remember in high school, there was a boy who was getting D's and F's in most of his classes. However, when he came in with his brand-new driver's license, he told everyone he got 96% on his driving test. When his buddy asked him how he managed to do so well, he said, "I really wanted a driver's license." He wanted it, so he worked for it. It worked. My question is this: how badly do you want to lose weight? **If you are motivated enough, you can do almost anything.** For you people who love your smarty-pants cell phones, you can figure out all this on your phone. For everyone else, here's what you need to know.

People often ask, "What's a calorie?" I discussed this in simple terms in the chapter, "I Don't Eat That Much." However, the dictionary defines a calorie as, "a unit of energy, often used in specifying the energy of value of foods, equal to the energy needed to raise the temperature of 1 kilogram of water through 1 C (4.1868 kilojoules)." What? I know. I don't get it either. Don't worry. In simpler terms, a calorie is a way of quantifying (or measuring) your food to help you understand how to lose weight. Let me see if I can make this a little clearer.

Suppose you didn't know about calories, but you wanted to lose weight, so you weighed your food on a food scale. You could see that a candy bar only weighs two ounces. Consequently, if you ate it, you should only gain two ounces, right. Wrong. Weighing food doesn't work, because you burn off some of it, but how much? You have to eat, right?

If I eat three pounds of food will I gain three pounds?" Maybe I will only gain one pound and burn off two. Don't panic. Once you understand calories, you can figure this out.

Studies show that the average women burns off about 1,500 calories a day, and men burn about 1,800, depending on how much they weigh and how much they exercise. Consequently, if you eat less calories than you burn, you will lose weight. If you eat more than you burn, you will gain weight.

Suppose you ate 1,200 calories in one day and burned off 1,500. You would lose weight, because there is a 300-calorie difference. It looks like this:

Burned	1500 calories
Ate	<u>1200</u> calories
Difference	- 300 calories burned off

Simple. If you did that every day, you would burn off ABOUT a pound-a-month, depending on your metabolism.

On the other hand, if you ate 1,500 calories one day, and only burned 1,200 that day (the opposite of the last one) you will gain weight because you ate more than you burned off. I need to repeat this to make sure you understand. **If you eat more than you burn, you will gain weight. If you eat less than you burn, you will lose weight.**

The rule of thumb is that 3,500 calories equals one pound. In other words, if you ate an extra 3,500 calories every month, you would gain one-pound per month. If you gave up 3,500 every month, you would lose one-pound per month. That's about 115 calories per day, or one cookie-a-day. In other words, if you ate an extra 115 calories every day for a month, you would gain one-pound per month. If you gave up 115 calories per day for a month, you would lose one- pound a month. Logical and scientific. Also, not complicated.

If it's not complicated, then why do people hate counting calories? There are two reasons (or excuses) that people give about why they dislike calorie counting. First, most people think counting calories is a pain in the neck or too difficult. Here's the truth. It's not easy, but not that hard either. Like anything else, the more you do it, the easier it gets, kind of like wiping after you poop. Most three-year-olds don't do it very well, while most adults don't struggle with it. Lots of practice. Just do it.

And remember, you probably have an app on your phone to count calories. (You don't need one for wiping.) I tried to use using the app on my phone to count calories, but found it frustrating and confusing, but you "phone geeks" and young people are probably jumping up and down for joy. No matter how you do it, it takes practice, but worth the effort.

The other reason (and probably the real reason) people don't like counting calories is that they don't want to limit their food intake. I don't. Let's be honest. None of us like it when someone or something tells us what to do, especially when it comes to eating. Counting calories is like having someone standing there, looking over your shoulder shouting, "STOP EATING OR YOU WILL GAIN WEIGHT!" **When we start counting calories, it forces us to stop eating even when we're still hungry. We don't want to stop.** Who wants that? Who wants to be hungry? I do! I do! NOT.

Food is the one domain that people don't want to sacrifice. Food is not illegal. It's not against the law to stuff yourself every day like a Thanksgiving turkey.

If I don't count calories, I eat too much, and then gain weight. For me, it's either count calories or get fat. Period. End of sentence. I choose to count calories, at least most of the time. However, it does take a little time and effort!

Portion Control:

Have you been beaten over the head with that phrase "portion control?" The experts insist that it works, but most of us don't have a clue how to "control our portions." Others think they do, but they are still gaining weight so they probably don't.

If I only eat one sandwich instead of two, isn't that portion control? Not for me! Before I learned to count calories, I made a bologna sandwich with more calories than three sandwiches. That's because I used ½ pound of cheese and a cup of mayo, guaranteed to make me fat. But not anymore. I have a choice. I can make a sandwich that will make me fat or I can control my portions. How do I do that? Count calories. One or two tablespoons of lite mayo is plenty, but if I don't measure it, how do I know how much to use? What if I'm using three or four tablespoons? When it comes to cheese, I just use one thin slice.

Without weighing, measuring, and counting calories, there is no portion control, even if it's just one sandwich.

Getting started:

Counting calories is like making a financial budget. You figure out how much is coming in and how much is going out, then plan accordingly. Start by figuring out how many calories you need. Men naturally have more muscle mass which burns off more calories so men can eat more than a woman. (Ladies, I know it's not fair, but we can't kill them.)

Every book has a different idea of how many calories we need, but in general, a woman should NEVER go less than 1,200 calories, and a man not less than 1,500 calories, ever. That's the absolute lowest. The more active you are and the more you exercise, the more calories you need in order to be healthy. If you are diabetic or hypoglycemic talk to your doctor. Also, **pregnant and nursing mothers, and growing children and teens need more calories. If you are in that category, please consult your doctor or family health care provider.** Let's just keep it simple. **Everyone needs to talk to their doctor before going on a diet.**

People who are morbidly obese, should not drop their calories too low. Here's why. If they are used to eating four-thousand calories every day, and suddenly cut it in half, they will get too hungry, way too hungry. That leads to starvation and discouragement, which brings the diet to a screeching halt. Here's the best advice I can give. When it comes to counting calories, PLEASE TALK TO YOUR HEALTH CARE PROVIDER BEFORE YOU START. Any advice I give about calories is just a suggestion. **I'm not a doctor!**

Counting calories is the cheapest way to diet, but there are a few things you will need to buy if you aren't using an app on your phone. I discussed this in the chapter, "I Don't Have Enough Money." You need a cheap calculator, pencil and paper, and a booklet that counts calories. These few items are quite a bit cheaper than *Nutrisystem* or *The Bowflex Tread Climber* or whatever else they advertise on TV. You also need a food scale and some measuring cups, something your phone probably doesn't do, but I wouldn't be surprised if it did.

How to:

To get started, you first need to figure out how many calories you need. The heavier you are, the more calories you get. There are dozens of ways to figure out how many calories you need, but this is the method I use to figure my calorie count for the day. Start by weighing yourself.

1. Weigh yourself — 250 pounds
2. Add a zero to your weight — 2,500
3. Your calorie count is — 2,500 calories a day

Quite simply, you just add a zero to your weight. It sounds like a lot. However, if you weigh 250 pounds, you are probably eating about 3,000 calories-a-day. In other words, you are probably eating **at least** 500 calories-a-day more than you need, probably more.

You may be looking at this thinking, 2,500-calories-a-day is a lot, but if you cut your calories too low, you will feel like you are starving. If you get too hungry, you will give up. The calculation I just gave is ONLY A SUGGESTION! There are dozens of other ideas! Using this particular method, you should lose at least a-pound-a-week probably more. In addition to your calories, you can have unlimited green vegetables, a cup of berries and one piece of fruit. (More about that later.)

Here's the next rule: Every time you lose ten pounds, you need to cut back another 100 calories until. In other words, if you get down to 240, you get 2,400 calories instead of 2,500. Keep subtracting 100 calories until you get down to the lowest possible: 1,500 for men and 1,200 for the ladies. If you are active, exercise a lot, or are still growing or a teenager, you will need more calories. **Children, teenagers, nursing and pregnant woman, and anyone with serious health problems need to talk to their doctor.** Actually, everyone needs to, but especially the ones just mentioned.

There are all kinds of rules about when to eat, like "Consume most of your calories in the morning." Bull! If my foster son eats in the morning, he barfs it up. No breakfast for him. He eats a good lunch and dinner and isn't fat. **What I've found is this: if I count calories, it doesn't matter when I eat them, nor how often. If I eat less than I burn, I lose weight no matter what time I eat them.** I just count calories and try not to gobble them all up before noon. (That's easy to do and it really sucks when you are hungry the rest of the day.)

Now it's time to learn exactly how to count calories. Here are four steps:

Step # 1:

Read the labels! (This is the easiest part.) Food in boxes, cans, and containers do all the work for you. The calorie count is right there on the side of cans or the back of packages. They all look similar. A box of cereal looks something like this:

Nutrition Facts
Serving size 3/4 cup
Servings Per Container about 14
Amount Per

Serving	Cereal	(With) Fat-free Milk
Calories	110	150

(There's a lot of other information, like vitamins and minerals, but don't worry about that for now. Calories are all you need to look at to get started.)

The first thing the cereal box tells you is that **you need to measure** 3/4 cup of cereal. That's one serving. It's at the top, under the word "Nutrition Facts," followed by the words "serving size." This particular cereal is 3/4-of-a-cup. Or on this one type of cereal, 3/4 of-a-cup equals 110 calories. The first time I measured out my cereal, I looked in my bowl and thought, *Where did my cereal go? This is all I'm getting? I'm going to starve!* I couldn't believe it was such a teensy-weensy amount. Before I counted calories, I put my cereal in a mixing bowl. When I finally started counted calories, I was shocked to see how little 3/4 of-a-cup of cereal is. It barely covered the bottom of the bowl. Someone should be arrested.

If you add ½ cup of nonfat milk to your cereal (which you also need to measure), you will have a total of 150 calories all together, because ½ cup of nonfat milk has forty calories. (40 + 110 = 150.) Simple. Boring, but simple. If you want 1% or 2% milk, you will have to read the side of the milk carton for the correct calorie count. I sweeten it with Stevia (or Truvia) which has zero calories, so my bowl of cereal about150 calories depending on what kind of milk I use and how much. If I want more, I can have it, but I have to weigh and measure. I also add a half-a-cup of berries. Tastes great and I don't count the berries because they are low cal and low carb.

For lunch, I decide to have soup. I like *Progesso Soup* because it's somewhat healthy, low in calories, easy to make, and reasonably priced. I pick up the can, and read the label. On the back it reads: "Calories 110." PLEASE NOTE! (THIS IS IMPORTANT.) 110 CALORIES DOES NOT MEAN THE WHOLE CAN HAS 110 CALORIES! You have to look at the wording above where it says, "Serving Size" (Store those two words in your brain for future reference.) A "serving size" is 1 cup for *Progresso Soup*. Underneath that, it says, "Servings per container, 2." What that means is that the whole can of soup has two servings. Each serving has 110 calories. Consequently, the whole can has 220 calories. Or 110 (calories) X 2 (servings) = 220 (total calories). Please watch the serving sizes carefully. If you feel confused, get a can of soup out and read it. It's clear.

One time, I was really hungry and stopped at a Minute-Mart looking for something to eat. I was on an I'm-going-to-be-thin-and-healthy kick, so I grabbed a little bag of trail mix (made up of nuts, seeds, and raisins). Healthy, right? When I glanced at the information, it said "180 calories." I thought, "That's a perfect afternoon snack." When I finished eating everything in the bag, I felt stuffed. What? How could I get full on 180 calories? I pulled my car over and looked again. The whole bag had three (3) servings! That meant my bag of trail mix didn't have 180 calories. It had 180 calories TIMES THREE! That's a total of 540 calories, a whole meal, plus some! The bottom line is this. When you look on a package or box for calories, be sure to look at the calories AND the number-of-servings. If the number-of-servings is greater than "1," then you need to or multiply the number of calories times the number of servings, but only if you want to eat the entire bag or box. Either that or just eat one serving. That requires measuring. If this sounds difficult, just start now. Walk out to your kitchen and look at a soup label. You can do this. They have done most of the math for you.

A NEW PERSPECTIVE ON DIETING AND WEIGHT LOSS

But what if you want to eat something that doesn't have the calories written on it, like an apple? That's where the next step comes in.

Step # 2:

This is pretty easy for people who want to count calories on their cell phones, but a little more difficult for the rest of us. If the calories are not written out for you on the side of the package (like an apple), then you have to find something that will help you. You can Google the food you are about to consume. I tried the techy route, but I prefer my simple little book, *The T-Factor Fat-Gram Counter*. To get started, look in the Table of Contents. It looks like this:

TABLE OF CONTENTS

BEVERAGES 14 -16
BREADS AND FLOURS 15-1931-61
CANDY, 19-21
CHEESES, 24-25
COMBINATION FOODS, 25-30
DESSERTS AND TOPPINGS, 31-36
EGGS, 36
FAST FOOD/RESTAURANTS, 36-61
FISH, 62-66
FRUIT, 66-68
FRUIT JUICES AND NECTARS, 68-69
GRAVIES, SAUCES, AND DIPS, 69-70
MEATS, 71-76
MILK AND YOGURT, 76-78
MISCELLANEOUS, 78-79
NUTS AND SEEDS, 79
PASTA NOODLES AND RICE, 80

POULTRY, 80-82
SALAD DRESSINGS, 82-83
SNACK FOODS, 84-87
SOUPS, 87-91
VEGETABLES, 87-91
VEGETABLE SALADS, 91-92

Now, are you ready to eat your apple? Look in the table of contents where it says "FRUIT." Turn to page 66. When you find "apple," you will see that you have a choice of "whole w/peel" or "dried." You want "whole w/peel." It looks like this:

	Total Fat	Sat Fat	Carbs	Calories	Fiber	Sodium
Fruit						
apple:						
whole w/peel	0.4	0.1	21	**81**	4	1

This may look overwhelming, but all you need to look at is the row in bold that has calories. Your apple is about 81 calories, as long as it's an average-sized apple. A large one has more calories and a small one, less. If you aren't sure, make a guess. **Guessing is always better than just stuffing food in your mouth.** If I have to guess, I always guess a little high or round up, but it's a free country. You can do it any way you want, but remember. The goal is to lose weight and be successful. Some calorie charts have everything by weight. Too much work for me. I don't want to weigh absolutely everything. I like simple.

What else? I buy a lot of my food in bulk, from a barrel. Most of these foods have a calorie count on the barrel, but if you don't want to

A New Perspective on Dieting and Weight Loss

stand around at the *Piggly Wiggly*, writing down how many calories in a tablespoon of craisins, just wait until you get home. Look it up in your book or you can Google it on your smart-phone. That works too.

My favorite on-the-go snack is almonds. I often grab a few if I'm hungry. That's when I look up NUTS, page 79. Twelve almonds have about a hundred calories, **but I have to count them out.** I can't just pop handfuls in your mouth, saying, "Close enough." I count the almonds, then count the calories. I like to put twelve in a little baggie. I make up six or eight bags. Then if I need to run out the door, I can just grab my nuts and go.

Get familiar with your calorie-counter book or whatever device you have. When you are standing in line at the store or waiting at the dentists' office, look through the different foods and their calories. Make plans. I like to get my booklet and circle the foods that I eat often. Not too hard so far, right? Well, it does get slightly harder, even for you techies. Sorry.

Step 3:

Suppose you want to make a big batch of spaghetti. How can you count calories? **The simplest way to do this is to have recipe books that have the calories in each recipe counted out for you.** Just look through the cook book before you buy them. The calorie count is usually at the bottom of each recipe. I pick up my cookbooks at garage sales or used book stores. It's cheaper. I love cheaper!

But, suppose you want to use your grandma's recipe for spaghetti. If so, get your calculator and your pencil and paper. Write down how many calories in each of the ingredients. Add them all up. Then divide. Like this:

½ pound of lean ground beef	250
1 14oz can of crushed tomatoes	120
1 26 oz. can pasta sauce (Ragu)	300

1 small can mushrooms	0
1 small onion	0
1 tablespoon crushed garlic	0
1 tablespoon Italian seasoning	0
1 teaspoon salt	0
½ teaspoon pepper	0
Total	670

Notice that I don't count the spices and healthy vegetables. That's because vegetables are low in calories, loaded with fiber, and don't cause weight gain. There aren't enough calories in the spices to bother with. I keep it as simple as I can.

Let's look at the can of tomatoes. To start, you need to know how many calories are in the entire can. To do this, look at two things. (1) calories, and (2) servings per container. That's all. Then you will multiply those two numbers in order to figure out how many calories in the whole can.

Here's how to do it. There are 35 calories per serving and 3.5 servings in the whole can. Get out your calculator. Now multiply. First put in 3.5, then X, then 35, then =. The total calories in the can is 122.5. I round down to 120 for the whole can. (Tomatoes are so good for you, so I round down instead of up.)

If you use pasta sauce (like *Ragu*) instead of tomato sauce, do the same as you just did. Multiply the number of servings, times the calories. So, the label says it has 50 calories per serving, times 6 servings per can, for a total of 300 calories (for the whole can).

Now for the beef: I use extra lean ground beef. But when I look it up in my book, it says that 3 ½ ounces of lean ground beef is 114 calories. But I'm using 8 ounces (half-a-pound). Now what do you do? Make a logical guess! Remember how to round off? (Third grade.) So instead of 3 ½ ounces, I round it off to 4 ounces. Close enough. I'm going to use 8 ounces of meat (½ pound). If 4 ounces has about 114 calories, then 8 ounces (the amount I'm using) would be double. So multiply 114 (calories) times 2, which is 228 calories. I round up to 240 calories. If you put it all this info into a smart phone, it will give you the exact amount. Your computer probably will too. Remember, it doesn't have to be perfect or exact. We only need a general idea of how many calories it has. But be reasonable. Don't spend all day counting calories. Keep it as simple as possible.

Now you know how many calories, a whole batch of sauce is, but you only want a little, so you measure the whole batch which is seven (7) cups of sauce, about 740 calories total. If you want one cup, get your calculator and divide 740 by 7 because there are seven cups in all. That comes out to 105 calories per cup (approximately). One cup of sauce is about the right amount to put over your pasta. **The good part is that you are writing this all down so next time, you will already have the calories counted. Consequently, calorie counting gets easier.**

You are going to put the sauce over something, probably pasta. Do you remember what to do first? Measure it. Two ounces is 220 calories. Please notice that the pasta has far more calories and less nutrition than the sauce, so **use more sauce and less pasta**. They recommend two ounces of pasta per person. I recommend about half that much. Whatever you decide, weigh your pasta and count the calories. If you cooked eight ounces for your family, then divide it up into four parts. Each part is equal to two ounces. (Or you can divide it into eight parts and each part is equal to one ounce.) When I divide it, I sometimes just look at it, make a guess, and round up. **A good guess is always better than eating without counting.**

I rarely eat wheat, so I usually put my sauce over green beans. Not quite as tasty, but great for my diet. Rice noodles are available in most stores in the Asian department.

Any time you make a large recipe, add up all the ingredients. Measure the whole thing; then divide it into parts. After that, do the division. Now you can eat that one part. This was the hardest part and you are done with it. Now what?

Step 4:

Here is the most important part of counting calories. **Something is better than nothing. If you aren't sure, make a guess.** Otherwise, you will eat without any boundaries. Make an intelligent approximation and round up. You can do it!

A few tips:

First of all, counting calories works best if you count them **before** you stick the food in your mouth. (Then you don't have to feel terrible about overeating and wrecking your diet before you start.) Second, you must weigh or measure **all** your food. (That's part of the annoyingness that I warned you about.) Now you are ready to count calories.

When I first started, I kept consuming too many calories. If you do that, don't worry! Instead, work on learning **how** to count calories. It's a huge shock when you realize how much you are eating and how much you have to give up. I always plan to eat 1,200 calories, but often end up eating 1,300 or 1,400. I still lose, but not as quickly. Whatever you do, don't get discouraged and don't quit. Consistency is so important. **Keep in mind that the longer you do this the easier it gets. I rarely have to look up anything anymore. Praise God.** Okay! That's it! You're on your way to a thinner you. Now, be honest. Isn't that easier than childbirth?

FIVE

Exercise: It's Overrated

When I say that exercise is overrated, I'm talking **specifically** in relationship to losing weight. Eating with boundaries is the best way to lose weight. Exercising is somewhat important to weight loss, but **controlling the portions of your food is more important. Far more**! According to Marie Osmond, weight-loss is 80% about food and 20% about exercise and she's gorgeous! Aren't you glad I told you that? Now you don't have to join a gym, or buy expensive exercise equipment, or run around and get all sweaty. Don't get me wrong. You still need to exercise, but don't do it thinking it's the best way to lose weight, or the only way. Counting calories (portion control) is best, but when a good exercise program is added, it enhances your weight loss.

Just a few of the amazing benefits of exercising:

1. Exercising is the most effective way to stave off the aging process. (Yes Virginia, there is a Santa Clause.)
2. Exercising is one of the best ways to combat depression. No drugs!

3. Exercise builds muscle and muscle protects our bones, preventing osteoporosis. (According to some doctors, it can even reverse it.)
4. Exercising builds muscle. **Muscle burns fat**, even when you are sleeping. The more muscle you have, the more fat gets burned. That means you can sit in front of the TV, with a cup of coffee and burn more calories than those who don't exercise.
5. Exercising helps prevent colds, flu, cancer, and numerous other diseases by pushing toxins out of the body.
6. Use it or lose it. Your muscles shrink and it's difficult to restore.

There are so many benefits of exercise that I can't name them all. These are just a few.

So please, **do NOT stop exercising.** It's good for you. However, DO NOT exercise thinking it's a great weight-loss secret. Too many people believe they can eat like an elephant as long as they exercise. No! No! No! It's simple math. If you eat more than you burn, you will gain weight.

Worse than that, people who exercise often fool themselves into thinking, "Hey, if I exercise, then I can eat more." So they do. Then they gain weight, and say, "Exercising doesn't work so I should just give up."

Here's another way to look at it. Can you say "Fat athlete"? Sorry, but they are overweight athletes in high school, colleges, and the pros. Professional football players exercise six hour-a-day or more. It's a grueling work out, but one-out-of-twenty are obese. Professional baseball players have weight problems too. Look at Babe Ruth.

In additions to the pros, have you ever been to a high-school baseball or football game? My kids and foster kids played sports and there were always two or three kids on the team who were obese, yet they do a backbreaking workout several-hours-a-day, five days a week. Why are they overweight? It's simple. They eat more than they burn. (You may have heard that before.)

The other problem with thinking that exercise helps you lose weight is that people form bad eating habits thinking that exercising is the answer. Many lose weight while exercising, but what happens if they get injured, or get sick, or tired of exercising? Most continue with their bad eating habits. Then they gain weight.

Look at some of the retired athletes like O.J. Simpson. He's fat! Just Google "fat athletes." There are hundreds of them. It's a serious problem. **Never count on exercise to totally save you from *The Blubber Demon*.**

Here's my personal testimony about exercising. My illness hit shortly after I turned fifty. I was basically and invalid who laid in bed all day. I started gaining weight. I thought it was because I couldn't exercise. I couldn't even walk across a room. But I discovered my weight-gain had nothing to do with my lack of movement.

Three years after I got sick, I got tired of gaining weight. I finally started counting calories. I was still flat on my back, but I lost weight slowly, but still lost. About eighteen months after dieting, I started seeing an "herbalist." Amazingly, my health began to return, but it made no difference with my weight. After another year of counting calories, I decided to start exercising. Most people wouldn't call it exercise, only about five-minutes-a-day to start. Gradually, I increased my time. Nothing strenuous. After another year or so, I joined a class at the Y, called "low impact." (That's a nice way of saying, "this class is for old people.") It didn't help with weight loss, but I knew the importance of exercise.

When I was in my 60's, I knew I wasn't 100% healthy, but I felt good enough to go back to work part-time. Guess what happened. Working made me tired, so I quit exercising. I didn't think exercising made any difference, because I continued to maintain my weight. I was wrong.

Four months after I went back to work, my clothes didn't fit. Well, they fit, but when I zipped my pants, I looked like a can of busted biscuits. I hadn't gained or lost one ounce, but when I stopped exercising, I gained inches. Here's another thing I noticed. When I exercise regularly, my stomach is flatter, my posture is better and my dance moves are more graceful, but I don't lose weight, just inches, and poise improves.

One last "exercising-won't-make-you-skinny" story. I met a man who was totally frustrated with on-line dating. He said that many of the women looked good in their picture, but much heavier in person. Sometimes their picture was outdated. Other times, they photo-shopped their picture. He said, "I finally thought I had found someone special when she told me she was an aerobics instructor, three hours a day, five days a week, but when I met her, I was shocked." Like the other women he had met, she also was overweight. He thought maybe she was lying about her profession, but he did some research and she was exactly what she said she was, a fitness instructor, fifteen-hours-a-week. He said, "She is the most physically fit fat lady I've ever met." He was rude, but he made a good point. You can exercise all you want. That doesn't mean you will be thin. I highly recommend exercising because exercising **enhances** weight loss, but it rarely works alone, unless your name is Michael Phelps or Dwayne Johnson.

Most of the people I know who are slender or fit are conscientious about what they eat, AND they exercise. "The sum of the parts is greater than the whole." That means that portion-control is about 70% of weight loss. Exercise is another 10%. However, the two together are more like 95% rather than 80%. (Those are my own made-up rules.) It also depends on how hard you exercise and how many hours. The harder and longer you exercise, the more fat you will burn, but portion control is still more important, especially for women.

I counted calories for several years before I started exercising. This is how I look at it. **Portion control helps you lose weight. Exercising**

firms you up and gives you a shape. If Arnold Schwartzenegger ate well, he could lose weight, but his body would not look the way it does if he didn't exercise.

Here is what is important. **Please exercise! But count calories (control portions) if you want to successfully lose weight.** There is one exception. Men have more muscle mass. Consequently, if they decide to exercise, they naturally loose faster than a woman. (I still like them anyway, a lot.) But most men have to change their eating habits too if they want to lose weight and keep it off.

The most important thing to remember about diet and exercise:

We all need to exercise to be healthy, but PLEASE DON'T START A DIET AND EXERCISE PROGRAM THE SAME DAY. It's too much to do all at the same time. I tried it several times and I thought my head would explode. Start with counting calories. Do that for at least a month, preferably two or three months or even a year. Then when you get the hang of it, start an exercise regimen. You don't want to change too many habits at one time. Starting a diet is hard work. So is exercising. Don't bite off more than you can chew, literally.

Which exercises do I do and why?

I am not *The Exercise Guru*. I'm more like *The Queen of Simple Exercise* or *The Duchess of Laziness*. If you really want to look like Arnold Schwarzenegger or Jillian Michaels, the fitness lady from *The Biggest Loser*, get some good books or a personal trainer. My book gives a few tips so you will be healthy or a little oned, but it's NOT *The Complete Guide to Getting Fit*. I'm just giving you a few tips.

When it comes to exercise, the most common excuse (and you know how I feel about excuses) is "I don't have enough time." I don't either, so I'm going to make this as simple as possible. If you have no exercise routine, I will give you a few suggestions, but there is something you need to do before starting.

Talk to your doctor or healthcare professional:

So many of us have bad knees, shoulder issues, heart disease, high blood pressure, or other illnesses. You need to have a physical, or talk to your doctor before you start exercising. Please!

The simplest way to get started, first and foremost: FIND YOUR PASSION

The easiest way to exercise is to find something you love. You might think that's not easy, but there are hundreds of sports and fun activities. How do you do find your passion? Start by thinking about something you loved to play or do as a kid. Your passions usually don't change much over the years. Did you like playing in the water? Why not go swimming or take a swimming class? Do you love music or moving to music? Dancing is great exercise, fun, and you no longer need a partner. Many night clubs have free line dancing lessons. (Of course, they want you to stay and have a few drinks, but you don't have to.) Most churches have baseball or softball teams. There are beautiful hiking trails all over the country. What do you love? Basketball, golf, bicycling, roller skating? Whatever seems fun, go do it (as long as it's legal).

I tried a lot of things. Running was one of them. I hated it! If you ever see me running, call 911. Someone is chasing me. I tried yoga too. YUK! Too slow and too mind-numbing for me. The instructor says, "Sit on the floor. Put the bottom of your feet together and lean forward. Now hold it for three minutes." Do you know how long three minutes is with your knees by ears? IT'S BORING! However, I know other people who love yoga. They look forward to it.

I need something a little faster. My passion is dancing. Nobody has to force me to dance. I love that feeling of moving to music. I don't have a lot of time or money, and I only get out once-a-week, but that doesn't stop me from dancing every day. When I'm home, I turn on my computer and play "Electric Slide" or "The Cupid Shuffle." These are fun, easy dances anyone can do because you don't need a partner. I turn on my computer and go to YouTube." I can line-dance with other people on the computer. Music and moving-to-music lifts my mood.

Sometimes, I turn on waltz music. I glide through the house, picking up laundry saying "right, two, three; left, two, three." When I feel an extra burst of energy, I wipe down counters to cha-cha music. If you don't know how to do specific dance steps, put on some marching music and just march through the house as you clean. *The 1812 Overture* is really fun! When the music goes "Boom," jump up. If you pick your knees up to the beat of the music, your kids will think you are nuts, however, you will be having fun, creeping them out, and exercising at the same time.

Another fun exercise to consider is a Wii. It hooks up to your TV. My friend does sports in her living room with her husband and kids. They play golf or go bowling and dozens of other activities. Her family is very competitive and keep score. They can't wait to get back to the games the next day so they can see who wins. Each family member has their own favorite activity. They have so much fun while exercising and spending quality time with each other.

Everyone has a passion. If you don't know yours, try different things. Go for a hike or run or a bike ride. Most places have beautiful hiking trails. Get some headphones and listen to music or your favorite radio talk-show host while walking and getting fresh air. Better yet, call a friend and see if she or he wants to go for a walk or hike with you. When you call, agree on a date and time. You can motivate each other. Start out twice-a-week and go from there. Getting out in the sun gives you vitamin D and elevates your mood. The air smells good and cleans your lungs. Most people don't go outside enough. Staying indoors can cause depression and disease. Mind your mother. Go outside and play. It's good for you.

If you haven't found your passion, join a gym, or the YMCA. The "Y" has numerous activities, like Zumba classes, yoga, basketball, swimming, etc. I prefer taking a class, because there's a specific day and time set aside. I know when I wake up on Monday and Wednesday, I have a class to go to. You can try different classes or activities until you find the one you enjoy the most. Find something you love, but understand, it's just a starting point.

Don't use money as an excuse. If you're low-income, most places have a sliding scale fee. *Planet Fitness* lets anyone join for $10.00/month. (Of course, that could change.) They also have classes and equipment. Fun for all.

Exercising while watching TV

Most of us sit down and watch TV because we are exhausted. Guess how we sit when we are tired? We do the *Couch-Slouch*. I'm guilty too. What do you think slouching does to your body? Try slouching. Just flop out. Now look down at your tummy. Do you think that is good for you or your digestion? When I do it, I look like The Pillsbury Dough Boy. My belly is sticking out like a rocket ship ready to launch. It won't launch, but it might explode. It is NOT healthy to slouch for hours and hours, but most of us do. Sitting-and-slouching is "the new smoking." Sitting is the opposite of exercise.

Here's how I get some exercise while watching TV. I exchange slouching for good posture. Yes, good posture is a simple form of exercise. Instead of slouching, I sit up straight, like someone is pulling my head toward the ceiling, chin parallel to the floor, and shoulders back. Then I skooch forward a little, leaving some space between me and the back of the chair or sofa, so that my back isn't touching anything. Then I tuck under my "bum" and tighten my muscles as tight as I can. If that isn't enough, I suck in my stomach. Hold for five full seconds. Then I relax and take a long, slow, deep breath and repeat, seeing how many times I can do it. Best of all, it strengthens my butt muscles (the biggest muscle in a person's body). When I build muscle, it burns calories. I burn fat in my sleep. Besides, sitting up feels better than slouching. I have a note on my TV that says, "SIT UP STRAIGHT! TUCK IT AND SUCK IT!"

Here's something else you can do while watching TV and it's easy. Breathing! It's not going to make you instantly thin, but it helps and we need all the help we can get. Here's how it works. The word "calorie" translates as "heat." When you breathe deeply, you burn calories. Think about it. When you start a fire and it looks like it's going to die, what do you do? You blow on it. You give it oxygen. Then what happens? The fire gets hot. It burns! Breathing deeply fires up your metabolism.

Deep breathing also improves your health. Do you know what a paramedic does when they help their victim? Give them oxygen, even if they just broke their little toe. Why? Because they know that oxygen immediately improves a person's health no matter what's wrong. 100% of all their patients get oxygen.

The problem is that most of us only use 50% of our lungs. That's why you yawn. Because every cell in your body screams for more oxygen. If you aren't breathing deeply, you deprive your cells. Let's get those puppies filled.

Start by sitting up straight. (Suck it and tuck it.) Slowly breathe in. Keep sucking in air. A little more. Then a little more until you don't think you can get any more air in your lungs. Hold for two seconds. Now slowly let it out, and out and out, slowly. Push it out until your lungs are completely empty. Just once. Now breathe normally. Every time a commercial starts, do one deep breath like this: in, in, in; hold it; and out, out, out. Breathe normally. Then do another one at the end of the commercial. Sucking in air feeds oxygen to your cells. Every cell in your body needs oxygen, just like every cell needs water. So, breathe deep. Drink water. Feed those cells. Your body will love you.

Want to strengthen your tummy muscles while watching *C.S.I*? Pick both of your feet off the floor about two inches with your feet directly under your knees. Hold your feet up for five seconds. Drop them back down. Relax. Breathe deep. Repeat. How many times can you do this? You can also tighten your tummy by stretching out your legs, then lifting them off the floor for five seconds. Both are simple TV exercises.

Another TV or desk exercise is to stand up and sit down. (Don't do this if you have bad knees. It hurts.) If you are watching TV, do this every time there's a commercial. Just stand up, and sit down ten times. **Use the commercials as a clue to tell you when to exercise.** If you are working at your desk, and stand up to take a break, stand up and sit down. Do it again. (I like the number ten.) If anyone asks you what you are doing, say, "I can't decide if I want to go to the bathroom or not."

Here's a simple TV or sit-at-your-desk exercise. Instead of sitting on a chair or sofa, sit on one of those huge exercise balls. You would not think that sitting on a ball (instead of a chair) would make that much of a difference, but it does because you constantly move to keep your balance. I met a lady who sits on one of these balls at work. She lost twenty-two pounds without doing anything else. She said she is more toned now than she was when she used to go to the gym five-days a week! She told me that it works all parts of your legs, abs, and buttocks. She had to start with fifteen minutes at a time, several times a day, gradually adding time to it. Now instead spending hours at the gym, she sits on the ball at work, then has all that extra time after work to do whatever she wants. This lady has a body that most of us would love to have (most of us ladies that is).

If you decide to do this, have the ball near your TV or desk. When you sit down, plop yourself on the ball. You will be fit and toned before you know it, and it didn't take any extra time out of your day. It's a great thing for the kids too, but they usually fight over it. Don't tell them it's healthy. They might quit.

One more sit-in-front-of-the-TV idea. For less than $100 you can replace your favorite recliner chair with the *Ab Lounger*. (I saw one at the Good Will for $10.00.) This lounger is a comfortable "chair" that you can sit in while watching TV and slowly do a few crunches to strengthen your tummy muscles. It's easy on your back and it works.

Get creative. Stop and ask yourself, *What exercises can I do while I sit here?* What about shoulder rolls forward and back. Ankle rolls clockwise and counter clock wise. Roll your wrists. Shake your hands. Wiggle your fingers and toes. These simple exercises help circulate your blood. If you ever watch TV, you can't use the excuse "I don't have time." As someone famous once said, "Just do it."

When I tell you that I like things easy, I really mean it. There is another simple thing you can do to exercise your arms and legs without taking any extra time at all. Buy some ankle weights and wrist weights. (Say that three-times real fast. Wrist weights, wrist weights, wrist weights.) **Something as simple as these weights will strengthen your arms and legs and takes no extra time.** Strap them around your ankles and wrists when you get up in the morning. They have different sizes and weights, from one-pound to ten-pounds. (I got mine at a second-hand store.) Start with the light ones and work your way up. I was amazed at how tired I was with just one-pound weights. I had to start with twenty-minutes-a-day. Don't overdo it or you will quit. When my health was poor, I couldn't even do the one-pound weights. These little weights are not as easy as it sounds, but simple, and it takes no extra time.

Now what? Everyone needs to stretch. Why not do it while watching TV? (It is even more effective if you wear your weights.) Stretch your legs out in front of you. Lean forward and touch your toes. Hold for five seconds. Relax. Then stretch your hands toward the ceiling. Hold for five seconds. Relax. Now lean forward and clasp your hands behind your back. Stretch. Hold for five seconds. Relax. Do each one of these five or ten times. Relax for a few minutes and do all of these over again.

Get creative. While watching TV, think of which parts of your body needs some exercise. Better yet, which part of your body do you want to improve? If you think of enough new exercises, you could put it in a book and call it, "The TV Exercise Guru."

Just walking around:

Most of us walk around all day without giving it much thought. We walk to the bathroom or kitchen. We jump up and walk around when our phone rings. We walk to our car and then from the car to the store. If you want to add some exercise, walk on your tiptoes. This strengthens your calves and thighs. This also tightens your buttocks when you tiptoe. While tiptoeing, you can clean the house, do laundry, or mow the lawn. If you want, you could tiptoe through the tulips. (Some of you will be too young to understand that.)

Standing in line at the store is a great time to exercise. Studies show that the average person stands in lines for twelve years out of their life. (Who does these studies?) In twelve years, you could really strengthen your legs. I often stand on my tiptoes while waiting in line at WinCo, my favorite store. Up for ten seconds. Down for two. Don't forget to tighten your buttocks. You are going to look and feel fabulous. Now hold on to the shopping cart, lean back and lift your toes, pointing them to the ceiling. This will stretch the back of your legs. Hold for ten seconds. Go back down for two. Continue doing this until the checker says, "May I help you." (And hope that it's not a long line.) You can also strengthen your legs by standing on one leg for a few minutes. Then stand on the other. You may look like a flamingo, but your legs will look great.

While standing in line, work on your posture. Just like before, suck in your stomach and stand up straight, shoulders back, chin parallel to the ground. Suck your stomach in as tightly as you can. Imagine sucking in so hard that your belly button touches your spine. Pull your naval in and up. Then tighten like you need to poop. Hold for ten seconds but breathe deep. Relax for five seconds. Do it again. Good posture opens up your digestive track, promotes healthy breathing, and improves the heart muscle. Sucking in also makes you look ten pounds thinner, and ten years younger, unless, of course, you are a teenager. Then good posture makes you look mature and confident. Do this exercise whether you are in the store or watching TV. Sucking in is so simple that I do it at stop lights.

One-minute exercises, two at the most:

So many people claim, "I don't have time to exercise. Not true. First, I'm going to give you three one-minute core exercises (upper, lower, and side core). What is the core and where is it located? Some call it "abs" or "tummy muscles." Actually, it's much more than that. It goes all the way up to your ribs, and surrounds your lungs. It also includes all the muscles surrounding your colon.

The core is most important part of the body. Why? Because this is where your body's center of gravity is located. Many trainers believe that strengthening your core is the most important exercise anyone can do. One of my profs at Portland State University said, "Don't come and complain to me if you have a bad back. I've told you over and over, 'if you strengthen your core, you won't ever have back problems'." Almost every move you make involves the core. **If you don't do any other exercises, do this.**

Florence Griffith Joyner, was considered "the fastest woman of all time," winning two Olympic gold medals. When someone asked her why she was so fast, she said, "I do 1,000 sit-ups-a-day." What? She was a runner. What do sit ups have to do with running? Like one of my aerobics instructors told me, "It's all about the core." That's why I did a parody of "All About the Bass." Goes like this.

> Because you know I'm all about the core,
> bout the core, not the elbow,
> I'm all about that core, bout that core, no elbow, no elbow,
> I'm all about that core, bout that core.

> Yeah, it's pretty clear, I ain't no size two,
> But I do crunches, like I'm supposed to
> Cuz I want to be healthy
> And not have back pain
> And all the right strength
> In all the right places.

Okay, you get the idea. The core is important. When I was sick, I forced myself to go for short walks in order to stay healthy. I did some obligatory stretching, but was so weak, I couldn't do much else. However, looking back, I could have done one or two "crunches" three-times-a-day. It's not a lot, but it would have made my life so much easier when I started getting healthy again. **My deepest regret about my health was that I didn't do anything to strengthen my core.** Well, now you know how I feel about the core. Work it hard and often (with your doctor's permission.)

<u>WARNING:</u> Do not work on your core and think that this will flatten your stomach! That's called "spot reducing." Spot reducing doesn't work. Covert Baily said, "If spot reducing worked, everyone who chewed gum would have skinny faces." Pretty clear. Work on your core for your health or maybe to have a "six pack," but that's it.

Sucking in your stomach or tightening your stomach is a great start, but you need more and it only takes one-minute a day for each of the three areas. Here it is.

(1) Shortly after I wake up, I get my watch with a second-hand because I want to know how many "crunches" I can do in one minute. (You can use the stop watch on your cell phone.) I also turn on some music with a good beat.

The first crunches I want to tell you about, works the upper and center abs. When I first heard about this, I thought how silly it was. Way too simple! If I can do it in one minute, it's worthless. Right? You will find out as soon as you try it. Here's how. Lay down, feet flat so that your knees point toward the ceiling. (You can do this laying on the floor, but I'm a pansy. I do it in bed.) Place your hands behind your head, **not clasped.** The tips of your middle fingers on each hand are barely touching, giving slight support to the head. Look at a spot on the ceiling straight above. The spot helps you to know how far to sit up. If you don't have one, put a cute sticker on the ceiling. (I have a picture of Jennifer Aniston, to encourage me. I may switch to a picture of Jesus, the Great Encourager.) When you start to sit up, do not take your eyes off the spot on the ceiling. As soon as the spot gets out of your eyesight, stop. Then go back down. That's one crunch and takes less than two seconds. Easy, right? You won't think so after you've done as many as you can in one minute. Ready? Set your timer. On your mark. Get set. Go! Do as many as you can in one minute. (I had to start with ten seconds!) If you want to have tight abs, work up to two or three minutes. You will be amazed how hard it is. I was. I was also surprised at how sore my tummy muscles were. It makes a huge difference and takes very little time. Sometimes I just do twenty. It's better than nothing and takes very little time.

(2) Now you are going to work on your lower abs. (Just as important as the upper abs.) Start by laying on the floor or bed. Pick up your legs and point your toes toward the ceiling. Drop your right leg a few inches and lift it back up. Then drop your left leg a few inches and lift it back up. Go back and forth as many times as you can in one minute.

(3) Let's work on those side abs (a.k.a. the obloquies). You have to get out of bed for this one. Stand up. Pick up your left knee and touch it to your right elbow. Don't bring your leg up too high. Bending forward is how you crunch your abs. After this you reverse it and touch your left elbow to your right knee. Tighten your tummy when you do this and be sure to twist to get those side abs. Do this for one minute.

If you don't do anything else, strengthen your abs. Now I have a one-minute exercises for the rest of your body, or most of it.

A pushup works the chest and arms, but there's a better pushup that works the legs too. I call them "wall ups." To start, put your nose and toes up to the wall. Then take one large step back. Now put your hands on the wall, and lean forward. Then push back. That's one. Look at the clock and see how many wall-ups you can do in one minute? Keep track. Watch the clock.

So you now have four exercises that each takes one minute. According to my calculations, that's four-minutes-a-day. If you move your way up to two minutes for each exercise, that's eight-minutes-a-day. Most of us have eight minutes. But wait! Here is the good news! You only have to do this three-days-a-week! Resting those muscles in between is good. I like to work these on Monday, Wednesday, and Friday and stretching (coming up next) on Tuesday, Thursday and Saturday. Why not make a plan right now? Decide which days you will exercise, then write it down. I'm not super organized, so I plan to do all of them every day. That way, I end up doing some of them three times a week. All the people out there who are disorganized like me are thinking, "What a great idea!" The rest of you organized people are scratching your heads and don't have a clue what I'm talking about. No matter who you are, just make a decision. Write it down and do it. Most important, be consistent, whether you are organized or not.

The 2-minute stretch:

You may think that stretching is silly or worthless. Let me tell you about a man who I counseled one time. He rode his bike about forty-miles-a-week to work and to run errands. His legs were great shape, but that was the ONLY thing in shape. When he came in to talk to me, he sat in a fetal position. His posture was poor and rode his bike hunched over. One time, I suggested that we stretch before we started. He thought it was ridiculous. Besides that he said that stretching made him cough. I gently tried to encourage him, but he became agitated. "You don't understand. I'm going to start coughing." I understood. His lungs were so scrunched up that he couldn't breathe. That's why he coughed. He made it clear that he was not willing to try. "Riding a bike 40-miles-a-week is more than enough," he said curled in a fetal position. After that session, I never saw him again.

Stretching opens up your lungs, heart and digestive system. It's vital to your physical **and** mental health. Best of all, stretching feels good and it's easy. But be careful! **If it hurts, stop. Consult your doctor.**

When you get up in the morning, get out of bed and set a timer for one minute or just watch the clock. Stand up and stretch your fingers toward the ceiling, as high as you possibly can reach. Stretch higher. Hold it five seconds. Relax. Take a long, slow deep cleansing breath in, then out. Now bend down and touch your toes or as close as you can without bending your knees. Stretch your back up like a cat. Hold for five seconds. Stand up. Deep cleansing breath, in and out. Then back up to the ceiling and down to your toes. Take a slow deep breath in and out between each one. Do this for one minute.

Now it's time for chest and back stretches. Clasp your hands behind your back. Lift your hands toward the ceiling. This will pull your shoulders back, chest out and chin up. Hold for ten seconds. Breathe deep. Now lock your fingers in front, pushing palms out.

Lean forward. Push hard. Then behind your back again and out front. Repeat until one minute is up.

Now for arm stretches. Grab your left elbow in your right hand. Pull your left arm close to your body. Closer. Hold for five seconds. Let go. Then try to scratch your left shoulder blade with your left hand. Take your right hand and gently push the left elbow back to give an extra stretch. Hold for five seconds. Now do the same to your right arm. Do arm stretches for one minute.

Now stretch out your sides for one minute. Put your left hand on your left hip. Reach your right arm up over your head, then lean to your left as far as you can without hurting yourself. Hold for five seconds. Take a slow deep breath in and out. Then bend left. Slowly, go back and forth until your one-minute is up.

Stretching gets your blood circulating and keeps you in good health. Stretching is a good time for morning prayer. I like to thank God that I'm healthy enough to stretch. I pray for my friends and family and of course I pray that I can eat well. Sometimes I turn on music. I like to start my day with some praise music, but do whatever appeals to you. Music keeps me motivated and activates my brain, and who doesn't want an activated brain?

The final exercise that you really have to do:

This one is the hardest for me. It's aerobics. This is the one that burns the most calories and staves off the aging process. The simplest definition of aerobic exercise is "exercise that increases the need for oxygen." In other words, "exercise that causes huffing and puffing." Technically, it has to get your heart rate up and keep it up for fifteen minutes to be called "aerobics." Then, in addition, you are supposed to do it three times a week in order to be heart healthy. If you play basketball or soccer regularly or run, you don't have to worry about it. You already are doing aerobics.

A NEW PERSPECTIVE ON DIETING AND WEIGHT LOSS

Over the years, as my health improved, I found a Zumba class called *Zumba Gold*. It's not expensive, and my passion is moving to music. *Zumba Gold* is for older people, but I can still get my heart rate up. Most classes encourage us to go at our own pace. Any kind of dancing is fun for me. Keep in mind that your goal is to be strong and healthy and stay that way. That includes some type of aerobics.

When it comes to exercise, please remember these five things: 1) Talk to your doctor first! 2) Find your passion. 3) Be consistent. 4) Don't depend on exercise alone to lose weight. 5) Unless you are totally neurotic, don't start an exercise program the same day you start your diet. Dieting is hard work. So is exercise. One or the other, not both. Learn to control your eating habits first. That's my opinion anyway.

SIX

Fats and Carbs. Carbs and Fats. I'm So Confused.

Fats first:

I've been trying different diets for forty years. I was like "The Children of Israel" who wandered around in the wilderness for forty years, trying to find the Promise Land. I experimented with nearly every diet that ever hit the market, trying to find the right one.

In the 70's, the "Low-Fat Diet" came on the scene. The experts made me believe that fat was my enemy. "Fat makes you fat," they told me. It made sense to me so of course, I tried it. No butter, no oils, nothing with fat. If something had one gram of fat, I didn't eat it. After three days of no fat, I was so weak, I could barely function. It took me two weeks to get my strength back. So much for that diet.

After much research, I found out that **fat gives you energy**. We all want and need energy. Also, our brains are made up of fat. Consequently, we don't function mentally without fat, but there is one problem. Fat is high in calories, even good fats. We need them, but we can't overdose on them if we want to lose weight.

I'm going to share with you what I've learned about fat. Are you ready? There are three types of fats. Good fats and bad fats and mediocre fats. **I don't count grams of fat. Instead, I avoid the bad fats, eat the good ones, and eat the mediocre ones in moderation.** Dieting is hard enough without having to worry about how much fat I'm consuming. I just count calories.

Bad fats:

Although there are a lot of names for fat, like "trans fats" and "saturated fats," and a bunch of other names, I want to keep this simple. I'm just going to give you a list of which fats are bad, unhealthy, and will ruin your diet. Here it is:

(1) Anything deep fried. Terrible. Spit it out.
(2) Most margarine.
(3) Fat from pork or beef (animal fat).
(4) Fat from processed foods like cookies, pies, and desserts.
(5) Most oils that are not cold pressed. (More about that later.)
(6) Corn or soy oil (I rarely eat anything with corn or soy.)
(7) Bologna (baloney), hot dogs, processed meat.

Bad fats are hard to digest, cause heart disease, cancer, skin problems, and weight gain. Sounds bad to me. I work hard to avoid the bad fats. It's not easy, but I like being healthy and I like losing weight. Isn't that the point?

<u>Oil</u>: There are healthy oils and unhealthy. When buying oil, I read the label, looking for the words "cold pressed." That means it hasn't gone through heat processing. It's healthy. The problem is that if it says "cold pressed," it's more expensive. Such a conundrum.

Important: Some oils like olive oil, are healthy when they are cold, but unhealthy when heated. It turns into a trans-fat, unhealthy. But there's one that retains its value even when heated, "Spectrum Organic All-Vegetable Shortening" (palm oil). Coconut oil also withstands the heat, but it adds a little bit of flavor. (I don't like coconut-flavored eggs.) Peanut oil bears the heat, but most peanuts are genetically altered, so I stay away from them. The good oils and fats cost a little more, but you won't use a lot anyway. Remember, when I first started dieting, I didn't have very much money. (Still don't.) I just ate less and bought what I could afford.

Another bad fat is margarine. It's cheap, but please, please be careful about buying this naughty fat! One article I read said "most margarines are one-molecule away from plastic." I don't know if that's true, but here's a clue that it's not healthy. If you leave margarine outside, the bugs won't touch it. Bugs prefer to eat dog poop. You might want to avoid food that's worse than dog poop. However, there is one margarine I like, *Brummel and Brown* made mostly from yogurt and salt, and tastes great. It's slightly more expensive than margarine but use less and it comes out the same. I also use real butter, but sparingly. It's tasty and healthy but loaded with calories. I don't worry about it too much. I just use less. In the long run, I save money. When I fry up onions or mushrooms or anything else, I use palm oil. It's a healthy oil that tolerates heat, but a little pricey. I don't use it that often, so it doesn't put a big dent in my food bill. I get it from Amazon.

Let's move on to two of the bad, unhealthy fats, animal fat and bacon. Most diet groups don't refer to bacon as "meat." My calorie-counter book organizes food in categories, and bacon is not under "meat." It's under "fats." That's because bacon is mostly fat.

In the Bible (Leviticus 3:16, NIV) it says, "All fat is the LORD's." (Love that verse.) That verse is specifically talking about animal fat. The priests were not allowed to touch it and never allowed to eat it because it belonged to God. It was to be burned on the alter. (Great way to start a fire too.) Even today, most Jewish people avoid animal fat. Studies show they are healthier, thinner, and live longer than the average population. To be healthy, avoid all fat from beef or pork (animal fat).

Good fats:

Now that I've ruined your day telling you to give up deep-fried foods and bacon, I'm going to tell you about good fats. Yeah! **To be healthy, you need good fats.** They are:

(1) Nuts and seeds
(2) Chia seeds and flax seeds
(3) Coconut oil
(4) Avocados
(5) Spectrum Organic All-Vegetable Shortening (or plain palm oil)

My favorite way to get my good fats are nuts and seeds. They not only contain fats that our bodies crave, but they are loaded with life-giving minerals. Cheap too. Dr. Oz said that the one food he carries in his satchel (man purse) is pumpkin seeds, because they are so nutrient-dense and give him a boost of energy when he's on the go. I eat nuts and seeds almost daily, but BE CAREFUL. Although nuts and seeds are an almost perfect food, they are also high in calories. I count them carefully. I like to combine ten almonds with two tablespoons of sunflower seeds and put them in a little baggie. It adds up to 180 calories, healthier than a man-made granola bar. If I don't count the calories, I will eat a whole container. (I'm making myself hungry.)

Flax seeds and chia seeds also have those amazing healthy fats. (Don't worry. Chia seeds won't grow hair all over your body.) Flax and chia have omega 3's that are guaranteed to lower inflammation, improve brain function and prevents heart attacks. These two seeds give me energy and help me to stay full longer. In addition, they are high in fiber, another one of those things most of us don't get enough of. (More about that later.) I add chia seeds and ground flax seeds to my oatmeal, smoothies, or yogurt.

My all-time favorite fat is an avocado. Oh yum! It contains protein, potassium, and lutein (for your eyes). Remember what good fat does for you? Gives energy and feeds the brain. How cool is that? If I'm running behind and hungry, I cut an avocado in half, salt it, and spoon it out. It's satisfying, and healthier than a bowl of cereal.

Another great breakfast with healthy fats is a scoop of coconut oil. You can spoon it out of the jar and eat it plain. Quick and delicious! The benefits of coconut oil are phenomenal. There are some studies that show that coconut oil can reverse Dementia and Alzheimer's because it feeds the brain. (I wonder if it works for ADHD?) However, you have to remember to add it to your calorie count.

Mediocre oils:

These are oils that aren't horrible and won't kill you. At the same time, they aren't healthy either. I just eat them and add them to my calorie count. Here it is:

(1) Most salad dressing
(2) Real butter
(3) Cream (milk fat)

<u>Salad dressing</u>: Most salad dressings are loaded with oil. Worse yet, it's the unhealthy oil. When I buy salad dressing, I buy the cheap stuff, usually **low** fat, but **never nonfat**. Here's why. Most foods that say "nonfat," take out the fat and put in sugar. Besides that, nonfat food tastes nasty. I don't like nasty food and I don't want sugar on my salad.

Because salad dressing isn't particularly healthy, I've found a way to improve it. I water it down with apple-cider vinegar. (Vinegar is healthy.) Shake well. When I water down my dressing, it cuts the calories and thins it out so that it covers my salad better. It also tastes better and lasts longer. When I'm feeling really ambitious, I make

A NEW PERSPECTIVE ON DIETING AND WEIGHT LOSS

my own dressing using cold pressed olive oil. Very healthy. (Recipe follows.)

Butter and cream: What about milk fat, like cream and butter? I get a different answer any time I ask. When I talk to naturopaths or doctors, they all have something different to say about the subject. So, here's what I do about milk fat.

- I use real butter occasionally, but usually *Brummel and Brown*, but I count the calories.
- I use non-fat yogurt and 2% cottage cheese. (I don't avoid milk fat, but I don't pig out on it either.)
- I use almond milk or coconut milk on my oatmeal, avoiding milk.
- When I buy milk, it's 1%, but I rarely ever drink it. I just use it for cooking.
- Whenever I use any milk products, I take a little pill called "lactaid." It helps milk products to digest.

Finally:

The experts tell us we are supposed to have about forty grams of fat a day. Others say that 25% of our calories s needs to come from fat. I could drive myself crazy reading labels, and trying to figure out how many fats I've had or how much I need. Counting calories is hard enough. If I have to figure out all this fat-stuff, I will get discouraged. I like to keep things simple so here are my seven simple fat rules.

Rule # 1: I don't eat anything deep fried, or rarely.
Rule # 2: I try to boil, broil, or bake rather than fry.
Rule # 3: If a label says "trans-fat," I avoid it (usually).
Rule # 4: I eat very little bacon or animal fat.
Rule # 5: I water down my salad dressing with apple-cider vinegar.
Rule # 6: I get most of my fat from nuts, seeds, coconut oil, avocados.

Rule # 7. **I don't keep track of how many grams of fat I'm consuming. I just count calories.**

Those are my rules. You can make up your own.

Carbohydrates:

IF YOU ARE DIABETIC, YOU NEED TO TALK TO YOUR DOCTOR BEFORE YOU START CUTTING CARBOHYDRATES OR CHANGING YOUR EATING HABITS. In fact, if you have diabetes, you have my permission to skip this chapter, HOWEVER, I also know that many people are diabetic because they spend their life overdosing on carbohydrates. My herbalist says, "You ate your way into this mess and you can eat your way out of it." Okay, I will get off my soap box and tell you what I've learned about carbs.

About twenty-five years ago, I went on a low carb diet. I almost died, literally. I ate tuna, lettuce, cream, eggs and cheese. After a few days, I was shaking so hard that I couldn't walk. The doctor me ". . . if you cut your carbohydrates too low, it messes up your ketones." I'm not a doctor, so I won't explain what ketones are, but I do know that low ketones kill people.

On the other hand, I have discovered, through trial and error, that if I eat too many carbohydrates I gain weight. **Learning about carbohydrates and figuring out how much I needed was an amazing turning point in my weight loss journey.**

The governments tell us that we need 300 grams of carbohydrates a day! **WOW**! That's like twenty-two slices of bread! If I ate that much, I could be the new "Pillsbury Dough Girl." However, that same government also tells us that raw milk will kill us and that milk injected with hormones is safe. Consequently, I don't pay much attention to what the government thinks about what I should or

A NEW PERSPECTIVE ON DIETING AND WEIGHT LOSS

shouldn't eat. My herbalist says, **"If you eat the way the government tells you, you are guaranteed to get sick."**

When it comes to carbohydrates, children and teens metabolize carbohydrates better, faster and more efficiently than us older people. My two sons were both athletes. The night before a big game or wrestling match, their coaches told them to eat a high-carb dinner so they would have energy the next day. It worked, but they are athletes! Their coach knew they would burn it off. I'm more of a slouch. I exercise some, but I'm not an athlete. What I've learned is that the older I get, the fewer carbohydrates I need. My body seems to turn those little boogers into fat. On the other hand, if I don't get enough, I don't feel good, or I get a headache.

You may be wondering, *What is a carbohydrate?* As you have probably figured out by now, my definitions are a little different from a doctor's or a dictionary. My definition of a carb is "it's a nice name for sugar." But, like fats, there are good ones and bad.

Beans are high in carbohydrates but very healthy and good for you. On the other hand, white bread and white sugar are both bad carbohydrates and unhealthy and cause weight gain. (If it's white, flee on sight.)

The best carbohydrate is "fiber." (In my opinion, it should not be considered as a carbohydrate because your body can't digest it or turn it to fat.)

So, there you have it. That was my carbohydrate lesson in a nutshell. I could go on and on, but here's how I do it:

- Because berries and vegetables are so healthy and our bodies need the nutrients, I don't count those carbohydrates. That's because half-of-those carbohydrates are fiber and you need fiber. I also allow myself one piece of fruit. (More about berries, fruit, vegetables, and fiber later.)
- **I try to keep my carbohydrates between under sixty-a-day, but I don't count the carbs from berries, one piece of**

- **fruit, and my vegetables.** (You will get about 40 to 80 from them.)
- In addition, I subtract any and all fiber from my total carbohydrates. **Your body doesn't absorb fiber, so it doesn't count.** Here's an example. Two tablespoons of peanut butter have eight grams of carbohydrates, but two grams of that is fiber. So I get my "Food Journal." Then I go to the column that says "carbs" and write 6, because 8 take-away 2 is six. Fiber is free.
- Carbohydrates from fruits, vegetables, beans, nuts and seed are healthy. Carbs from oats, brown rice, quinoa are mediocre.
- Carbs from sugar, processed foods, wheat, corn, and soy are bad. I avoid those.

I will show you more on keeping track of carbohydrates, but for now you need to know that **too many carbs will make you fat. Too few carbs will make you weak and unhealthy.** You have to figure out how many carbohydrates are right for you. Definitely talk to your doctor, especially if you are diabetic, still growing, pregnant, or nursing, or just a human being.

SEVEN

The Fatal Four, Plus a Few More

Have you ever said to yourself, *I keep dieting, but I just can't lose any weight,* then added, *What am I doing wrong?* I use to say that daily, sometime hourly. When I got desperate, I would call out, "God! What's wrong? Help me." If that sounds like you, don't give up. There is good news . . . and, well, bad news. The good news is that there are certain foods (four in particular) that most of us eat regularly that messes up our metabolism, and slows our weight loss even when we count calories. It's good news because it answers the question, "What am I doing wrong?"

The bad news is that these four foods are something that most of us eat every day and they are hard to give up. Sorry. I know how painful it is, but if you choose to give up these foods, it will greatly enhance your weight loss AND improve your health. When I tell people what these four foods are, they either love me or hate me, or choose not to believe me. In the end, if you are serious about losing weight, you will appreciate what I'm telling you.

Are you ready? Here's the painful information that nobody wants to hear, but like a spanking for a brat, this will give you something to think about and hopefully improve your weight loss.

FATAL FOOD NUMBER ONE: Wheat

The most common response I get to this is, "I don't like whole wheat." What? Did I say **whole** wheat? No. I said "wheat," ALL WHEAT! White wheat, whole wheat, anything with flour in it. That mean almost all breads, pastas, cake, pie crust, pizza crust, cookies, brownies, pretzels, most cereal, tortilla wraps, crackers, graham crackers, matzo, spelt, couscous, bulgur, wheat germ, farina, *Bisquick*, and hundreds of other foods we all eat every day. If it contains flour, it has wheat in it. Before you eat it, read it! If the label says, "wheat, flour (bleached or whole), durum, semolina, couscous, bulgur," it's wheat and it causes weight gain, absolutely 100% guaranteed. (Wheat explains why so many vegans are overweight.)

Of all the foods I have tried to eliminate from my diet, wheat is without a doubt the most difficult to give up, yet the one most likely one to cause weight gain. The problem with wheat is that we grew up on it. Our mothers gave it to us our whole life. Most of us eat wheat every day with almost every meal. **We've been brainwashed into believing that wheat is a normal part of our meals.** Think about it. What do you have for breakfast? Cereal, toast, French toast, waffles, or pancakes? What about lunch? A sandwich with two slices of bread, or a bowl of soup with noodles and crackers. For dinner we often have pasta, macaroni-and-cheese, and a roll to go with it. And what do we have for snacks or dessert? Cookie, pretzels, cake, pie . . . well you get the idea. We eat wheat all day long and never give it a second thought. It's time we do.

Consider this. What do you grab when you are running out the door and hungry? A piece of toast? A sandwich? When you stop at the Minute Mart for a quick snack, what do you buy? A cookie or one of those amazing muffins? (Darn, those things are good!) I used to grab a bran muffin, thinking I was doing something healthy. IT'S WHEAT! We are hooked. So was I. To be perfectly honest, I still struggle with it. But, like anything else, the more I resist, the easier it gets.

Six Reasons We Need to Stop Eating Wheat:

Reason #1: In the book *Eat Right for Your Type*, the cover says: *4 Blood Types, 4 Diets. The Individualized Diet Solution to Staying Healthy, Living Longer & Achieving Your Ideal Weight.* Look at that title, where it says **"Individualized"** The author, Doctor Peter D'Adamo (notice the word "doctor") believes that your blood type dictates what you should and shouldn't eat in order to be healthy and lose weight. He also tells us what foods cause weight gain for each blood type. I love this book because it clearly shows that we are all completely unique (just like everybody else). This book lists the foods to avoid for **each** blood type if you want to lose weight.

I focused on Type A, because that's what I am. It says that people with Type A blood (me) should be a vegan. People with my blood-type don't digest meat or milk products correctly. It also says to stay away from wheat (all wheat), white-wheat and whole-wheat, etc. I was quite surprised. I thought whole wheat was good for me. Not for blood type A. If I want to lose weight, no wheat of any kind, ever!

Each blood type diet is unique. For example, people with Type A blood gain weight from eating red meat. On the other hand, people with Type O blood **lose** weight when they eat red meat. That's because people with type O blood have a higher acid content in their blood. (They are also more likely to get ulcers.) My curiosity peaked so I started rummaging through this book for answers. **My goal was to figure out if there were any foods that caused weight gain for all four blood types.** I went to the weight-loss chart for each blood types. At first, it seemed there were no similarities. But after studying each blood type, I finally found it. There was only one food that caused weight gain for all four blood types. Guess what it was? Wheat! Here's what it says.

Blood Type A:
Wheat:
1. Inhibits insulin efficiency
2. Impairs calorie utilization

Blood Type O:
Wheat:
1. Interferes with insulin efficiency,
2. Slows metabolic rate

Blood Type B:
Wheat:
1. Slows the digestive and metabolic processes,
2. Causes food to be stored as fat, not burned as energy,
3. Inhibits insulin efficiency

Blood Type AB:
Wheat:
1. Decreases metabolism,
2. Inefficient use of calories,
3. Inhibits insulin efficiency

One lady said, "But I don't know my blood type." I almost said, "Unless you come from another planet . . ." Instead I said, "Pick one. They are all bad!" And unless you want to gain weight or be unhealthy, avoid wheat. (For you people who are diabetic, you might want to pay attention to what it says about insulin too. Ask your doctor, but don't be surprised if he doesn't have a clue what you are talking about.)

Reason #2: In 1999 I joined a weight-loss group, *Prism*. I had to document everything I ate and count every single calorie, agree to moderate exercise, and give up wheat and a few other foods. Guess what happened? I lost five pounds a week for six weeks! That's a rapid weight-loss! It was extremely difficult, partly because the calorie count was so low, but also because I couldn't have wheat. However, this diet worked better than anything else I ever did, and I tried just about everything else. Giving up wheat, plus counting calories proved the theory "the sum of the parts is greater than the whole." In other words, the two together (counting calories AND giving up wheat) made the weight loss more powerful than just counting calories. It was an interesting weight-loss group. Although this diet worked, there was no "wiggle room." It was too legalistic. I had to sign a contract promising, "I won't cheat." Twelve-hundred calories-a-day, no matter what. I thought I would starve to death! Too rigid, but it worked.

<u>Reason #3:</u> Celiac Disease! More and more people are being diagnosed with this disease. I've read the statistics on how many people have it. It's anywhere from 1% of the population to 8% (one-out-of-twelve), depending on which article you read.

What is Celiac's? A serious digestive disorder caused by something called "gluten." Wheat is loaded with gluten. (Gluten is also in rye and barley, but when was the last time you ate those?) Gluten clogs the tiny little hairs (villi) in the lining of the intestines. Those teensy-weensy hairs exist to absorb the nutrients from our food. When the villi get clogged with gluten, it prevents the body from absorbing necessary vitamins and minerals.

The symptoms of Celiac's are gas, bloating, diarrhea or constipation, digestive problems, abnormal stools, foul flatulence, weight loss or weight gain, fatigue, weakness, vomiting, depression, anxiety. You don't have to have all these symptoms, but digestive problems are the common denominator in Celiac's. Some doctors believe that Irritable Bowel Syndrome (IBS) and Crone's Disease may actually be Celiac's or a gluten allergy.

So, what happens if your body goes for several years without absorbing nutrients? Simple. Nutritional starvation. If your body doesn't absorb vitamins and minerals, you eventually end up with osteoporosis, mouth ulcers, dental disease, tooth decay, diabetes, migraine headaches, and anemia to name a few. In children it causes delayed puberty. Blood tests show things like a lack of the B vitamins, an iron deficiency, low vitamin D levels, or other low-levels of vitamins and minerals. Even if you eat the right foods and take vitamins, your body can't absorb them. Why? Because those little hairs in your intestines are clogged with gluten. Food goes right through your body. Just imagine all the health problems you will have if your body can't utilize the nutrients it needs. You are literally starving.

Some people with Celiac's might just have a general feeling of unwellness. If you haven't felt well or have a lot of digestive issues, get tested. You can start by testing yourself. Here's how. Stop eating all wheat (ALL) for a month and see if your digestion and bowels improve. (Technically, it takes six months to get the gluten out of your body, but one-month is a start.) While you are waiting to see if you will feel better, you should start losing weight and getting healthy. It's worth it. (If you are way too thin, you will probably start gaining weight.)

You can also ask your doctor to give you a simple blood test. The problem is that the test is not 100% accurate. If the first test is negative, ask for another. Don't be one of those people who walks around with Celiac's disease and doesn't have a clue what's wrong.

You might wonder why so many people have Celiac's now and not twenty years ago. Two reasons. First, our society overdoses on wheat. It's a major part of our diet, three or four times a day, seven days a week. Second, most bread and pasta today have three-times as much gluten as it used to. No one needs that much gluten! Our bodies don't know what to do with it, so we store it. Then we get sick.

By the way, if you don't have Celiac's now, just continue eating wheat three-times-a-day. You could eventually develop Celiac's or a wheat allergy. Your body can only take so much. It's your choice.

One time, I was watching a Seahawks game at *Applebees*. I asked my server if he had anything wheat-free. He made it clear that he could not guarantee that the food was 100% gluten free, but close. I was fine with that since I don't have Celiac's. (I just avoid it.) Then he told me he had Celiac's and couldn't have ANY wheat. I will never forget what he said next. He said, **"When I stopped eating wheat, I got my health back, and lost 70 pounds in four months."** Did you see that? (Of course you did. I put it in bold letters.) **He lost seventy pounds in four months!** I couldn't believe it. He told me giving-up-wheat was **the only thing** he changed. He also told me a year after he got well, he decided to have a few bites of bread. He was so sick that he missed two weeks of work. It was another two weeks after that before he was back to good health again. Two bites of bread sent his health reeling down a slippery slope for a month! I wonder how many sick people are wondering why they are sick and actually have Celiac's or a wheat allergy. They are sick and don't know why. How many people are obese and don't know why. Maybe it's wheat.

<u>Reason #4:</u> After two grueling years of losing weight at a snail's pace, I noticed an attractive, slender lady at *Taco Bell*. I couldn't resist the temptation to ask her, "How do you stay so thin and eat at *Taco Bell*." She smiled, then said, "Simple! I starting dating a guy who was allergic to wheat, so I gave it up along with him." I sat down with her, chatting for more than an hour. She told me that she had been dieting most of her life, and just couldn't get rid of those last twenty pounds. As soon as she met this guy and gave up wheat, those pounds disappeared. That was absolutely the ONLY change she made. Shocking! She said, "I think he's a keeper." I needed to hear what she said because it was helpful in my weight loss.

<u>Reason # 5:</u> During my ten-year illness, I started seeing an herbalist, Paul J. Rosen who tested me for food sensitivities. (His tests are different from a Western doctor's, but more accurate in my opinion.) After testing me from head to toe, he eliminated many foods from my diet, but one of them was wheat. After a few weeks, I started feeling better. As time went on, I took several of my foster kids to see him and he helped them too, but I noticed that he took us all off wheat, 100%. I also had some friends who saw him and they

also were taken off wheat. Finally, I asked him if he automatically took everyone off wheat.

He pointed his long, boney finger at me and said, "Barbara!" (Actually, he said "Baahbaahra") "I don't automatically do anything. I **test** the person, and then take them off wheat, because almost everyone I have ever tested has some sort of sensitive to wheat. In fifteen years, I've only tested two people who didn't show a sensitivity to wheat." He went on to explain that many years ago wheat was one of the healthiest foods on the face of the planet, but not anymore, especially in our country. He said, "It sits in storehouses too long and has been altered and cross bred so much that it's not even wheat any more." Most of his clients (patients) not only get healthier after giving up wheat. Many of them lose weight. Maybe that's what Jesus meant when He said, "Man does not live by bread alone."

<u>No Wheat. Now What?</u> I get more complaints about giving up wheat than any other food. One lady said, "Stop eating wheat? That's impossible!" No, it isn't! If you have Celiac's, you don't have a choice. You have to go cold turkey. But there's good news. There's hundreds of other foods you can substitute and ways you can minimize wheat. Here are a few things I do:

I turn my favorite sandwich into a salad. Want a turkey sandwich? Here's how. Put a small pile of chopped lettuce on a plate, topped with cubed leftover turkey, grated cheese and a tomato. Sometimes I add a couple of olives, a few slices of chopped cucumber, and a little salt and pepper. For the dressing, I mix some mayonnaise with a little horseradish, then thin it out with a teaspoon of vinegar. Then I pour the dressing over the top. Tah dah! A turkey sandwich without the bread. Delicious and healthy!

What about a peanut butter sandwich? I don't like peanut-butter salad. Instead, I spread the peanut butter on a rice cake with a little honey. It's so good. My grandkids will love it. Most grocery stores carry rice cakes. Not too expensive either. Peanut butter on a banana or celery is great too.

Would you like a tuna sandwich? Mix your tuna with some mayo and pickles or celery, or whatever you usually put in it. Instead of bread, use it as a dip. I love rice crackers. Amazingly different. Delicious too. They sell rice crackers at Walmart for $1.99 a box. If you don't have enough money for these crackers, put the tuna between two large lettuce leaves and eat it like a sandwich.

People ask me, "How do I give up wheat when eating out?" Easy. At restaurants, I ask the waitress to leave the croutons off the salad. If I order eggs or an omelet, I substitute vegetables or fruit for the toast. There is always something. I just have to think before I order. Many soups are wheat free like chicken and rice, and I NEVER put crackers in my soup. Why would I add a food that has unnecessary calories and guarantees weight gain? Because it makes the soup taste a little better? Another bad excuse.

Carl's Junior will wrap ANY of their sandwiches, or burgers in lettuce instead of a bun, no extra charge. They taste so good! Messy, but good. *Subway* will turn one of their wonderful subs into a salad. It's the best salad I've ever eaten. (Maybe other places will get a clue.)

If you are healthy and aren't ready to completely quit eating wheat, give it up little-by-little. Half-a-sandwich instead of a whole one or make an open-faced sandwich. That's a piece of bread on the bottom, meat and mayo next, but leave off the top. Both of these ideas will cut your wheat in half. My favorite bread is "Sandwich Skinnies." Two slices are equal to one slice of regular bread. They also have bread called "thin sliced." (My kids called it "cracker bread.")

If you make a sandwich with less bread and are still hungry, pour yourself a cup of tea and have a piece of fruit, to complete the meal. If you have pasta or spaghetti, do you really need a slice of bread too? Talk about overdose! If you have a potato, why do you need a dinner roll? You are supposed to be on a diet. You have to give up something. Start with wheat.

Get creative. Pretend like someone will give you a million dollars to figure out how to make a meal without wheat. You will be amazed how brilliant you are. Now that you know how bad wheat is, I need to tell you about another deadly food. (Hopefully I don't ruin your day.)

FATAL FOOD NUMBER TWO: Sugar

This one hurts me so bad. I love sugar. Love it. Love it. There! I said it! I'm a sugar-a-holic. I love sugar, but I'm working on giving it up. (Notice "working.") It's hard to let go of something you love so much. It's like letting go of an unhealthy relationship. You decide to let go, but it just keeps coming back, and it's never good.

And there is more bad news. Sugar is not just that white grainy or powdery stuff that comes in bags that say *C and H*. It also includes light brown, dark brown, and raw sugar. All of these are highly processed, unhealthy, unnatural, and make you fat. It should be called poison.

Dr. Bob Sklovsky, a well-known naturopath from Portland, Oregon is a popular guest on radio talk shows. One time I called and asked what his opinion was about sugar. He yelled at me, "IT'S A DRUG!" I was a little taken back so I asked him, "What about RAW sugar?" He yelled again, "IT'S A DRUG!" Sounds like it might be a drug.

There's a lot of interesting information about sugar, but my favorites come from the book, *Sugar Blues*. I read this book with my mouth gaping so wide that my kids thought I was catching flies. Like me, this author discovered the hard way that sugar causes weight gain, health problems, diabetes, cancer, and worst of all, zits (a nightmare for teenagers). If you hate hearing this or you don't believe me, you need to read this book. Let me reword that. If you want to be healthy and lose weight, this book is for you. It's loaded with facts, very depressing facts, but the truth hurts. However, it's not the book that makes you depressed. It's sugar, or maybe both, but whatever it is, it doesn't matter. One thing I have learned is that my health and my life are always better when I shun this chemical that the federal government calls "food."

The author of *Sugar Blues*, William Dufty tells countless stories, one after the other, page-after-page of people who gave up sugar and how it improved their life. The author starts by sharing his own personal testimony about his discovery that sugar caused his constant and repeated digestive problems that he seemed to have no control over. He also includes stories about his severe acne, even as an adult. It took him years to discover the culprit, but even when he had all the evidence that it was sugar, he refused to admit it. When he finally got tired of being sick and zitty, he had to be honest and acknowledge that it sugar was the cause. It took him several years, but when he let it go, he got healthy, lost weight, and his skin cleared. After he gives his personal testimony, he tells more stories. This one is amazing:

"During one of Christopher Columbus's early voyages to the New World, a group of his sailors fell desperately ill. Columbus was about to jettison the sick men to the fish when a green island came into view. When the sick men begged to be left on land to die, Columbus assented.

"When Columbus passed by the island months later on a return voyage to Europe, he was amazed when bearded, white men hailed the ship. Even more astonishing was the discovery that the sailors were alive and healthy. In honor of the event, the island was named Curacao, Portuguese for cure."

* * * * * * * * * ● * * * * * * * * *

Do you see what happened? While on the ship, the sailors ate food soaked in rum and sugar, nearly killing them. While on the island, they ate tropical fruit, plants, and fish. It saved their life and their health returned. The sad part is that no one made the connection for more than three-hundred years! Thousands of British sailors died of scurvy. A few doctors suggested that sugar depleted the body of vitamin C, but they were ignored, labeled as "addled." Hundreds of years later, when they finally figured out that the sailors needed vitamin C instead of sugar, they were given limes. Hence the name "limeys." That's when the sailors quit dying.

Sugar still kills, except now we have even MORE proof. We have thousands of studies that gives clear evidence that sugar is poison; it causes tooth decay, cancer, diabetes, and weight gain, but we chose to ignore it.

There's another story in *Sugar Blues* about a cargo-ship full of sugar that wrecked. The five surviving sailors survived on sugar and rum. They were found nine-days later, **nearly dead**. Most people can survive ten-or-more days quiet well on water alone, but these guys were dying of sugar poisoning.

In 1816, a famous French physiologist, Francois Magendie read about these poor sailors and decided to experiment with dogs and sugar. He fed them nothing but sugar water. He concluded, "they all wasted and died." (He should have been hanged.) Did you understand the connection? The sailors and the dogs were wasting away faster when they got sugar than someone who had water alone. This all proves that "nothing is better than sugar." That didn't come out right. Let me reword that. You are healthier and better off to eat nothing than to eat sugar. **If you get hungry, don't eat a candy bar.** Have a glass of water or a cup of hot tea instead. Those poor little dogs gave their lives so that we could save ours. (That wasn't meant to sound religious.)

The book *Sugar Blues* has hundreds of pages with more stories like this. In addition, there are thousands of studies that give clear evidence that sugar is unhealthy and causes weight gain, but we just keep eating it as though it was food. It's not. IT'S POISON! (I think I mentioned that.)

What's really sad is that the F.D.A. (Food and Drug Administration) calls it food. The Federal Government is supposed to protect us. They make decisions about what's food and what isn't.

Because of them, sugar is considered food. Consequently, people can buy it with food stamps. I'm not against food stamps and was a grateful recipient of them at one time, but why do hard-working, taxpaying citizens have to pay for poor people to consume something that is poison, and then have to pay for their dental and medical care too? Oooooopps. Let me step down from my soap box. Sorry. I need to stop ranting and write a letter to my congressman instead.

I had my own personal "sugar epiphany" a few years ago. Out of the blue, I started having intermittent stabbing pains in the back of my left calf, not a Charlie horse. There was no way to know when I would have an attack, but every day or two, I would just be walking along and suddenly, it felt like someone came up behind me, and stabbed me with a sharp knife in the back of my lower leg. I would scream in pain, fall to the floor, crying. The pain only lasted a minute, but frightening. I thought I might have cancer in my leg. When these pains kept happening, I finally decided to see a healthcare provider, but which one. I had my choice between my Western doctor and my herbalist. I knew my Western doctor would set me up for multiple tests and give me drugs to dull the pain. If nothing showed up on any of the tests, more drugs for pain. With Western medicine it would take several weeks or months to get an answer which probably would have been no answer. (Western doctors rarely come up with a quick answer, if any.) On the other hand, my herbalist would know immediately. I chose to see my herbalist who agreed to see me the next day.

I told him what was going on with the leg pain. He put his hand on the back of my leg and did his strange tests and said gruffly, "YOU'RE EATING SUGAR!" I nodded. He said, "STOP EATING SUGAR AND THAT PAIN WILL GO AWAY!" I did. It did. That simple. Since then, I've been more and more aware of my body. If I eat sugar, I often feel achy or unwell. I wonder how often I thought I had the flu, when I actually had a "sugar virus."

We keep telling ourselves, "A little sugar is not that bad. One little cookie isn't that bad." It sounds like a smoker who says, "A few cigarettes aren't that bad." They both think *That didn't hurt me.* But twenty years later it's the same result. The smoker and the sugar-consumer both have failing health. The only difference is that the one who smokes knows exactly why he's sick. Sadly, most doctors don't know enough about the dangers of sugar. They can't seem to make that connection. (That's the subject of my next book, about how dumb some doctors are.)

The Deadly Duo: Wheat and sugar. The worst part about wheat and sugar is that they often come in the same package. Think about it. Cookies, cake, and pie are obvious, but there are many others that we don't think about, like cereal and bread. And we have to have syrup on our pancakes, sugar on our cereal, and sugary jam on our toast.

This lethal combination (sugar and wheat) is guaranteed to mess up your diet, your metabolism, AND cause health problems, absolutely 100% guaranteed. If you choose to continue to eat them, don't complain if you can't lose weight. And twenty years from now don't complain about health problems, like arthritis, gout, diabetes, not to mention that your teeth will rot, your skin will age, and your hair will thin. Sugar and wheat together pack a deadly punch. You have been warned. You have a choice.

One More Thing: When I say, "Sugar is bad for you," there is something you need to know. Fake sugar or artificial sugar is bad too. True, it has no calories or carbohydrates, but very unhealthy!

What's a body to do? You want to lose weight and be healthy, but you also want something sweet. Some healthy choices are honey, molasses, coconut sugar, real 100% maple syrup, agave syrup, and *Whey Low*. All of these are considered healthy HOWEVER, they also have calories. *Whey Low* is the lowest in calories but still has some. You can have small amounts of any of these, but you have to add the calories. Also, these foods have carbohydrates. Too many carbs equal weight gain.

A NEW PERSPECTIVE ON DIETING AND WEIGHT LOSS

<u>Good News:</u> I can suggest three sweeteners. One is **"monk fruit,"** a plant 200 times sweeter than sugar. Supposed to be healthy, no calories, nor carbohydrates. I've tried it and liked it but haven't cooked with it. Most naturopaths allow you to have it, but I'm still researching it.

Another sweetener I can suggest: **"Stevia."** First of all, it's healthy. Some say that it lowers your blood pressure. Others say it reverses osteoporosis. Not sure about that, but the best news for dieters is that it has no calories, no carbohydrates, no fat and isn't poison. Amazing! I need to say it again. It's sweet, healthy, has no calories, no fat, and no carbohydrates. It's NOT artificial and NOT processed. Stevia is a plant.

However, there are a few problems. Too much Stevia is bitter. Too little and it's not sweet. It took several months to get it right, but now I love it. I'm learning to cook with it and I will share some my ideas with you in my recipe chapter. It's not hopeless. Just time-consuming.

Another small problem with Stevia is that food companies have come in and wrecked it by mixing it with other sweeteners like glucose, erythritol, and other chemicals. That way, it's cheaper to produce and they make more money. When I buy Stevia, I look for "100% pure Stevia." It costs a little more, but worth it. I want to be healthy. **However, Stevia blended with something else is still better than saccharin, aspartame,** or some of those others mixed with chemicals. Do your research. Decide for yourself.

The last sugar-substiture is called ***Whey-Low***. This is a new one for me, but so far, I'm pretty impressed. Whey is a byproduct of cheese. So it should be healthy. From my research, it sounds like a perfect substitute for sugar in recipes. I'm excited to try it and hoping it works.

My hope for you is that you will avoid sugar and start trying some healthier substitutes. Your body will appreciate it.

FATAL FOOD NUMBER THREE: Corn

Do you know what corn is used for? To fatten pigs. Guess what. It works! Do you know what else corn is used for? To fatten cows, and it works for them too. Have you ever seen a skinny cow or pig?

One day, back when I was fat, I walked past a mirror at the mall. I did a double take, shocked at my plump reflection. I pursed my lips tightly together fearing that I might oink or moo. Instead, I just hung my head and waddled away. I hated my fat, but I was eating foods that farmers use to fatten their livestock.

When I first heard that corn makes you fat, I thought, *That's okay. I rarely eat corn.* WRONG! I rarely ate **fresh corn** or **frozen corn**, but when I started reading the labels I discovered that corn is in almost everything in a box or a can. It's called "processed," corn. When humans alter corn, it turns into a product worse than fresh corn, like high fructose corn syrup (HFCS), one of the unhealthiest foods on earth. When corn is changed into HFCS, it becomes a chemical similar to gasoline. If you don't believe me, rent or buy the documentary *King Corn*. When you watch it, your eyes will pop open and your jaw will drop. I will sum up the entire movie in six words. "High-fructose corn syrup is dangerous." But wait! That's not all! HFCS is hidden in most ice cream, pop and candy, and not just a little bit. They are loaded. Read the labels.

You would expect a lot of sugar or corn syrup in candy, but what about "sugar-free" candy or other foods that say "sugar free." I used to buy those things, believing that it was a good diet food. After all, it proudly says "sugar free," right on the front of the package. I thought it had *Splenda* or some other no-cal sweetener, therefore it must be a good weight-loss food. Wrong. Many of these foods take out the sugar and put in corn syrup. Technically, it's sugar-free, just like the label says, but these "foods" often have just as many calories as the ones that contain sugar. Why? Because they take out the sugar and replace it with corn syrup. Corn syrup has calories. It's also high in carbohydrates. Too many carbs make you fat. So do calories.

There are other names for processed corn like, *corn starch, corn glutton, corn meal,* or *corn grits*. Some manufacturers come right out and say "this product contains corn." The more often you see the word "corn" in the list of ingredients, the more corn it contains. No wonder we have so many unexplained health issues in our country.

One of the most common foods loaded with corn is boxed cereal. Even the cereals that call themselves "healthy" sometimes contain 50% corn crap. Next time you buy cereal, read the ingredients. Many of the "healthy" breakfast bars contain corn syrup too.

And if that doesn't ruin your day, maybe this will. Fritos and Doritoes are fried, processed corn with a little salt. Corn chips and tortilla chips are corn too. These are perfect foods for anyone who wants to be fat and sick. One of the worst "foods" loaded with processed corn and corn syrup is those creamers that make coffee taste so delicious. Read the label.

Corn and corn syrup is also in canned soups, but we eat it because we have been told, "Soup is good for you." Homemade soup is, but much of the canned stuff isn't (with a few exceptions like *Progresso* soup). It's mostly vegetables, but I choose the soups that don't have noodles because noodles are mostly wheat. (Chicken-and-rice is great.) Bottom line . . . read the label. Some foods have less corn than others. Let's see what some of the "experts" say about corn, processed or otherwise.

<u>Eat Right for Your Type</u>: This book has a specific diet for each blood type. It tells you which foods cause weight-gain for each blood. In a nutshell, it says that **corn slows your metabolism, causes hypoglycemia, and messes up your insulin levels** for three-out-of-four blood types. If you are type O, B, or AB, corn will make you fat and sick and diabetic. If you don't know your blood type, stay away from corn!

<u>Another expert:</u> I suffered with chronic fatigue for years, until I saw an "herbalist," Paul Rosen. However, he does much more than give herbs. He tests each person and gives them a specific diet for their body and their needs. He took dozens of foods out of my diet. One of them was corn. When I asked him about it, he said that **every person he had ever tested showed a sensitivity to corn.** What does this mean? A sensitivity means it's "unhealthy," kind of like a cigarette. You can smoke if you want to. You can eat something you are "sensitive" to. Someday it catches up with you. Paul Rosen was the only person to help me get well after being sick for years. If you want to be healthy, no corn.

<u>My baby boy:</u> I had another "corn epiphany" one day when I was changing my son's diaper. The corn-on-the-cob he had eaten the night before, came out looking the same as it did going down (minus the cob). Later, I asked his pediatrician if there was something wrong with my son's digestive system. He said, "Don't worry about it. The same thing happens when adults eat corn." (How would he know that?) Sounds like our bodies don't digest it. If we can't digest it why would we eat it?

<u>Another story:</u> When I was a little girl, I was blessed to live in England. One summer day, my parents invited some of our English neighbors to an All-American backyard barbeque with all the trimmings, including corn-on-the-cob. Our English friends were mortified that we were serving and eating what they called "pig food," but the Brits are extremely polite. They felt obligated to try eating this crazy food (like Indiana Jones eating monkey brains). After we baptized the corn in butter and salt, they tried it, and surprisingly, they liked it. They were so excited that they wanted to know where they could buy this delicacy. My parents told them that the only place they could get corn-on-the-cob in England was either from the Americans or the nearest pig farmer. Hopefully, it didn't catch on. Don't want our British friends to get fat and sick.

<u>Warning:</u> **Watch out for anything that says "gluten free,"** like crackers, cookies and cereal. Corn does not contain gluten, so manufacturers take advantage of that. They take out the wheat (loaded with gluten) and put in corn or corn meal. BAD. BAD. BAD. Gluten makes some people sick. Corn makes everyone fat and sick.

Whether you're a cow, or a pig or a human, you need to give up corn if you want to lose weight and be healthy. It's just a fact. **Whoever thought that corn should be used to make gasoline was on the right track.**

FATAL FOOD NUMBER FOUR: Anything deep fried

I think I've covered this already, but I have to make it clear. Anything deep-fried, is unhealthy and fattening. Besides the grease, the food is usually unhealthy and fattening too. Look at French fries. A potato has some food value, but it's high in carbohydrates and calories. When you eat fries, you are getting bad fats, too many calories, and too many carbs. French fries are the perfect food for those who want to gain weight and be unhealthy. No thanks.

I used to order deep-fried green beans. I thought it was a great way to get my vegetables. The problem is that the green beans are "breaded." That means they are rolled in bread crumbs (wheat). By the time I get them, I've got a little bit of veggies along with bad fat and bad carbs. Most deep-fried foods are rolled in wheat. When I go out, I simply skip the deep-fried foods.

When I cook, I never deep-fry anything. I also avoid frying if I can bake or boil. I've forced myself to get creative. It's fun.

Bottom line: deep fried food is unhealthy and fattening. If you want to lose weight, avoid anything deep fried.

FATAL FOOD NUMBER FIVE: Potatoes

Whoops. I know I said four, but I have to include this one. I wasn't sure if I should throw in potatoes or not, because potatoes are different from wheat, sugar, corn and deep-fried foods. Those four are unhealthy. On the other hand, potatoes contain vitamins A and C, potassium, calcium, iron, and protein. They are a healthy food. That's the good news.

I'm picking on potatoes for several reasons. First, when people give up wheat, sugar, and corn, they crave carbohydrates, so they start pigging out on potatoes. Another reason I added potatoes is because they are high in calories, but the biggest problem is that they are a staple in our country. If we have eggs, they are accompanied by hash browns. A T-bone steak screams for a baked potato. When we go to a restaurant for dinner, the waitress says, "Would you like French fries, baked, mashed, or cottage fries?" They rarely give us a choice, just potatoes cooked a dozen different ways. **Everyone assumes we have to have a potato with our meal.** (And if you're like me, you cooperate.) I know I'm on a diet so I order a baked potato because it's so much better than French fries. When I was fat, it never occurred to me to say, "No, thank you." After all, I might hurt the waitress's feelings, and potatoes are good for me. They're a vegetable, loaded with vitamins and minerals. Right?

Potatoes are better than wheat or corn as far as my health goes, but potatoes are not good for weight loss. I had always been told that potatoes aren't the problem. It's all the butter and other toppings. I would like to believe that, but it's not entirely true. Definitely, most potato toppings are loaded with fat and calories, but potatoes by themselves are a poor diet food for two reasons. First, potatoes are high in calories. A medium sized potato has 190 calories! That's half my meal! The problem is that I don't eat a **medium-sized** baker. I eat huge ones! A large baked potato can have 300 calories or more, and that's without any toppings. French fries are worse because they are deep fried, dripping with fat.

Just when I thought it couldn't get any worse, there's more bad news. Potatoes are off-the-charts when it comes to the "high-glycemic index" (HGI). (If you don't know what this is, then it might explain some of your weight issues.) The simplest way I can describe HGI is like this. High glycemic is the enemy. Low glycemic is your friend. High glycemic spikes your blood sugar. The word glycemic is just a nice word for "sugar." If you get too much sugar, your liver turns it into fat. People who are diabetic have to watch their glycemic index. Sometimes it's called "simple carbohydrates."

Foods on the glycemic index are measured on a chart from one to a hundred. The lower the number, the less likely it will cause weight gain. (Healthier too.) If it's low glycemic, it won't spike your blood sugar. The higher the number on the glycemic index, the worse it is for you. **A baked potato is an eighty-five out of a hundred without anything on it!** There are a few foods higher, but it's things like sweetened cereals, candy bars, soda, and foods loaded with sugar and corn syrup.

Most people already know that junk food is bad. However, when it comes to the glycemic index, a potato has almost as much sugar as a cookie or candy bar. Many of us believe that if we use fat-free toppings, then a baked potato is a good diet food. Potatoes with or without toppings are an excellent food for those strange people who are trying to **gain** weight. For the rest of us, we need to avoid it or cut back on it.

You need to ask yourself, "Am I willing to eat a potato without anything on it? Mashed potatoes scream for butter or gravy. A baked potato calls for sour cream, butter, and bacon bits. The toppings that says, "nonfat" tastes terrible. Besides, most of those foods replace the fat with sugar. What about bacon bits? There are two types, real and fake. If it's real bacon, it's fat. If it's fake bacon bits, they are made of soy, usually genetically modified.

One last word about potatoes. **Potatoes are healthier than the other four fatal foods.** If you are out for nice dinner and you have your choice between a potato or corn, the potato is better. A choice between a potato or bread, chose the potato. If you are cooking at home, make scalloped potatoes or potatoes au gratin instead of mac and cheese. A horrible diet food, but healthier than mac-and-cheese. Sugar, wheat, corn and deep-friend foods are seriously unhealthy. A potato isn't, but all five cause weight gain.

Five More Foods You Might Want to Avoid (Someday):

When you start a new diet, you don't want something complicated, so I am going to share a few foods that you may want to think about giving up sometime in the future. Take the information I'm about to give you and save it for later. Right now, you probably have a bad case of TMI. Here's the list. Just something to consider.

(1) Soy: I really wanted to put this in "The Fatal Four," but this one is controversial. However, I have personal experience. When I was so sick, I kept reading about soy and how healthy it was, so I ate it almost every day. YUK! I didn't like it, but I kept eating it and continued to get sicker. My herbalist told me that I was allergic to it. He said, "soy is dangerous because it's genetically modified." When I stopped eating it, I felt better. He said if I went to China, I could probably find some healthy soy. It's here too, but you have to search for it.

The other thing I can tell you is that some dog foods contain soy. However, the healthy dog food (the expensive stuff) says right on the front, "Does not contain wheat, soy, or corn." Dogs are getting healthy when they stop eating soy.

Some soy is healthy if it's been "fermented," such as soy sauce or miso. It's up to you. I rarely eat anything with soy in it.

(2) Diet food: That's right. We see that word "Diet" or "Lite" or "Fat Free" on a label and we automatically think, *Oh boy! This will be*

great for my diet! NOT, for several reasons. Most foods labeled "Diet Foods" contain several of the Fatal Four, especially corn syrup. Then they put in a bunch of artificial crap making it even more unhealthy.

Many take out the fat and sugar and load it with white salt. Too much salt causes water retention which causes weight gain, bloating, high blood pressure and other health problems. In other words, **most diet foods contain poison.**

If I made you a big batch of delicious brownies and told you that there was only one teaspoon of dog poop in it, would you eat it? It's only a spoonful in a large batch of delicious brownies. Does that sound good? That's how you need to look at the unhealthy ingredients in foods called "diet food." The only diet food I know about that's healthy is vegetables, but manufactures don't call them that. They call them vegetables. Go figure.

Remember my friend who said, "I never eat anything packaged that has more than five ingredients"? If you read the ingredients on the label of things called "diet food," most have at-least twenty ingredients.

Another important fact is that diet food is not always low in calories. If you buy something that says, "Diet Cheesecake," it may have slightly fewer calories than regular cheesecake, but it can still make you fat. Whenever you see the word "lite" on something, it usually means they took out the fat and added more sugar. On the other hand, when you see the phrase "sugar free," it usually means that they substitute fat for sugar. In other diet foods, they take out the sugar and put in a bunch of crap, like corn syrup and fake sugar, but not 100% of the time. Thank God, it's only 99%.

Also, sugar-free usually means that they put in artificial sugar. Do you know how most artificial sugar is made? They start with sugar (which is already bad). Then they mix the sugar with formaldehyde. Do you know what that is used for? Formaldehyde is used to embalm a dead person so that their body doesn't rot. That means we are going to be embalmed before we die. Next, they take this sugar, laden with formaldehyde, and add chlorine. Chlorine is what we use to bleach our clothes to make them white. I don't need my guts bleached. That's why I carry Stevia with me, a healthy no-calorie sweetener. When I go to a restaurant, and ask for ice tea, they bring me "little packets of poison." No thanks. I don't want to be a human Zombie with sparkling clean guts.

There are a few "lite" foods I buy that aren't totally unhealthy, like lite mayo. It seems to have the same ingredients as regular mayo, but less fat. I also buy plain, fat-free yogurt. Most of the time it's just yogurt with no fat and no other ingredients. The plain yogurt allows me to add my own fruit and a healthy sweetener. I don't do it perfectly all the time, but I'm learning and willing to make changes. All I can say is, "Read the labels before you eat." Better yet, read the label before you buy. Don't bring home something that would make you fat or sick. When I do bring home that bad stuff, I feel obligated to eat it.

Finally, most diet desserts taste good, but Jack LaLane, a pioneer in health and fitness firmly states, **"If it tastes good, spit it out!"** Personally, I can't agree with that one, but it's always good to know there are people out there nuttier than I am.

(3) Anything you can't pronounce: This is a good motto to live by: "Read the label. If it has ingredients you can't pronounce, don't buy it. Don't eat it." On the front of the Jell-O pudding box, in bright, yellow letters, it says, "Sugar Free - Fat Free." Sounds good, right? But turn it over and look at the ingredients. Read each one and see if you can pronounce it.

Modified food starch, maltodextrin, tetrasosium, pyrophosphate and disodium phosphate (for thickening), contains less than 2% of nonfat milk, artificial flavor, salt, calcium sulfate, zanthan gum, nono- and diglycerides (prevents foaming), aspartame+ and acesulfame potassium, dipotassium phosphate, yellow 6, yellow 5, artificial color. +phenylketonurics: contains phenylalanne dandylion.

Does that sound like something you want to put in your body? My computer doesn't even recognize most of those words. Remember,

"You are what you eat." If I eat that, I'm either a garbage can or a toxic-waste dump. No wonder I had so many health problems.

(4) Kidney Beans and Lima Beans: In the book "Eat Right for Your Type," 90% of all people gain weight on either kidney beans or lima beans. If you don't know your blood type, stay away from them because they cause a spike in blood sugar and slow your metabolism, both counterproductive to weight loss. **Black beans and pinto beans are the best.**

Also, many people are losing weight and getting healthy on the Paleo Diet. I've talked to several people who are on that diet and they are losing weight. This diet is based on what our ancestors ate and thrived on. Interestingly, no grains, no sugar, no soy, and NO BEANS. (There's more to it, but that a general idea.) We all think of beans as healthy, but kidney beans and lima beans can slow your metabolism. People are losing a lot of weight with the Paleo Diet. By the way, I was going to try the Paleo Diet, but I couldn't find any free-range mastodon.

(5) Pop (a.k.a. soda) is bad for everyone and everything that breaths. When I told this to one friend, he said, "Mine is sugar-free, and caffeine-free." That's even worse! They use unhealthy chemicals to turn real sugar into "fake sugar," and even more chemicals to get rid of the caffeine. When it comes to pop, it's not the sugar, nor the caffeine that makes it unhealthy, although that's part of it. The worst part is the carbonation. Do you really want all those gas bubbles inside your body? **I know three people who gave up pop and their skin totally cleared up.** The carbonation causes skin eruptions in some people. In addition, have you ever read all the horrible ingredients in pop? Here's a list.

Water
High fructose corn syrup
Citric acid
Sodium benzoate

Modified food starch
Caffeine
Ester gum
Yellow 6 (food coloring)
Red 40 (more food coloring)

Corn is in there twice, and yellow food coloring has been banned in Europe because they know it causes health problems. If you don't mind putting garbage in your body, then don't complain when you get sick.

Fill in the blank. There's a food that you know is bad for you, probably more than one. You get to fill in the blank. For me it's coffee but not black coffee. Mine is bad because of the extra ingredients I use. I put so many extra ingredients that my dad calls it "soup." Black coffee is okay, or coffee with a little milk, but too many additives are a killer. This is how I discovered how bad additives are. Once, I stopped at a little Minute Mart and got some of that coffee that comes out of the machine, with all the sweeteners and cream. (So yummy!) It was late, so I brought it home, left it in the fridge, planning on heating it up and drinking it later. The next morning, I looked at it in horror! (You won't believe this.) My coffee was the consistency of snot. It looked like brown slime. Yuk! I wondered what they put in it to make it thick like that. I was afraid to pour it down the sink because it might clog the sink. I had been drinking that stuff for years and had no clue what was in it. Still, don't. I won't be drinking it again. I never feel good after I drink one of those. I need to either stay away from coffee or drink it black.

Each of us has a fairly good idea what is bad for us. If you really don't know, start listening to your body and your common sense. If you feel unhealthy or guilty after you eat or drink something, give it up. Do you want feel sick? Do you want to lose weight or not? You have to start somewhere. Give up that food that you know is making you sick.

EIGHT

The Truth About Fruit

Do you want to know the truth? There are so many books on fruit that no one really knows the truth. Here are some of the things I've learned that might be helpful.

Several books I've read on "food combining," explain **in detail** why fruit should **always** be eaten on an empty stomach, all by itself. Why? Because fruit is digested in the lower intestines rather than the stomach. Therefore, if you eat fruit with other foods, it will sit in your stomach and rot. (That's what the food-combining experts say.) They also say that eating fruit alone helps with constipation. Then they say, " . . . eating fruit alone is the ONLY way to get all the nutrients and benefits."

When I told this to my daughter, it made sense to her, so she tried it. The next morning when she woke up, she ate a large apple on an empty stomach. Then, she went to work and fainted. Why? Because she was hypoglycemic. It was a bad rule for her, because she had low blood sugar, but all these people who wrote the books on fruit swear by it. That's a perfect example of a truth that isn't always true.

Let's look at some of the benefits of fruit. To start with, if you want a powerful antioxidant, fruit is packed full. What is an antioxidant? It's a substance that protects your body against cancer, lowers cholesterol, and builds your immune system. Clearly, you need antioxidants to be healthy, therefore you need fruit to be healthy.

If you ever watch *Sesame Street,* then you know you are supposed to eat "... all the colors of the rainbow." Fruit is the best way to get those colors. Think about it. Blueberries, apples, apricots, cherries, pomegranates, grapefruit, grapes, oranges, peaches, pears, cantaloupe, and on and on, an amazing display of colors. Fruit is so beautiful that artists have spent centuries painting pictures of it. Each and every piece of fruit has their own unique qualities.

If you look at an apple, it has fiber, but did you know it has three different types of fiber and your bodies need all three. One type of fiber in apples is pectin. It's hard to find pectin in anything else. It helps the bowels move and lowers cholesterol. Apples also have vitamin C and traces of calcium and iron. The old adage, "An apple a day..." is so true.

Apricots have vitamin A, something most of us don't get enough of. Grapes are known to prevent heart disease, help the respiratory system, improve skin, help with night blindness. I could easily write several pages on each fruit, but follow Big Bird's advice. "Eat all the colors of the rainbow."

Do not be deceived (or stupid):

I used to think that a big glass of orange juice was a great alternative to an orange. Wrong! Fruit juice is a poor substitute for fruit. They aren't the same thing. Repeat after me: "FRUIT JUICE IS NOT FRUIT!" Most fruit juice has sugar and corn syrup. (Read the label.) Fruit juice is cheaper than fresh fruit, but fruit juice causes weight gain because it has TOO MANY CARBOHYDRATES, way too many! Too many calories too! Maybe this will make it clearer:

1 orange: 62 calories 12 grams of carbohydrates
1 cup orange juice: 125 calories 30 grams of carbohydrate

Look at that! The calories are double and carbs are almost triple. **(If I ever get too thin, I'm going to start drinking orange juice.)** Besides, a glass of o.j. doesn't have as much fiber as an orange. HOWEVER, if you make your own, by squeezing an orange into a glass, that's okay, but why not eat the whole orange. Then you get everything including the fiber.

When I occasionally drink fruit juice, I water it down and add Stevia (my favorite sweetener). If you get your juice from the health-food stores (fresh squeezed), it **might** be okay, but read the label, and make sure it has no additives. Just fruit. If so, it's an okay substitute for fruit, but count the calories. Keep in mind that fresh fruit juice from the health food store can be very expensive. You are much better off to just eat fresh or frozen fruit.

Dried fruit like raisins and craisins taste good, but I don't count them as fruit. It's too high in sugar, carbs and calories, a quick way to gain weight. Raisins are shriveled up grapes. Here it is again.

1 cup grapes:	62 calories	16 carbohydrates
1 cup raisins (dried grapes)	434 calories	115 carbohydrates

That's why you should never use dried fruit as a substitute for fresh fruit. If you really want to substitute raisins for grapes, you could measure out two tablespoons of grapes. That has the same number of calories per cup, but I would rather have a whole cup of cold, juicy grapes, than a few tablespoons of raisins. Wouldn't you?

There's even more deception when it comes to canned fruit. If you think it's because it has too much sugar, you would be right. If it says, "lite" then it has less sugar, but it still has sugar. The only exception is canned pineapple "packed in its own juice." But pineapple is high in calories and carbohydrates all by itself. Be sure to weigh and measure your canned pineapple. In spite of it, pineapple is good for you. (I love pineapple, canned or fresh!)

One important note about canned fruit; the cans are aluminum. There is some evidence that the aluminum seeps into the fruit. The higher the acid content, the more aluminum, something you don't want in your body. One of the theories about Alzheimer's is that it is caused by aluminum deposits in the brain. Just something to think about.

Finally, canned fruit and fruit juice are not a good substitute because it strips the fruit of its peeling, where much of the fiber and vitamins are. Fruit juice or canned fruit is cheaper, but you can't get the nutrients you need.

Watch for the specials. Last summer, I got fresh pears for nineteen-cents-a-pound. Good deals are out there if you watch for it. The three cheapest fruits are usually bananas, apples and frozen strawberries. Of course, that can change at any time. Talk to your friends who shop carefully (a.k.a. tight wads). They can tell you who has fruit on sale (vegetables too).

How Much?

There seems to be some controversy about how much fruit to eat. It depends on whom you talk to. Most weight-loss groups tell you to eat three servings a day. That's what most doctors tell you also. Another diet group says you need five servings. Another, seven! Sounds like a little too much to me. (I would be in the bathroom all day.)

My cousin, Lisa who is a member of *Weight Watchers* is allowed to have unlimited fruit! Let me reword that. Fruit does not count as part of their point system. Zero points. I was shocked! That would NEVER work for me. Not enough boundaries and too many carbs. Carbohydrates without limits cause weight gain. A small banana has 100 calories and 24 carbohydrates. If I ate five bananas a day (and I could easily do that), that's 500 calories and 120 carbohydrates! I love bananas. I would get fat if I followed the *Weight Watchers* diet.

A NEW PERSPECTIVE ON DIETING AND WEIGHT LOSS

But my cousin who has a lot of self-control said, "Sometimes when I get hungry, I just grab a handful of grapes, and I'm satisfied." Good for her. I would eat the whole bag. All that being said, my cousin is thin, trim, and healthy. *Weight Watchers* works for her. **(BTW, *Weight Watchers* tells you not to overdo the fruit, but I have to have firmer boundaries.)**

My herbalist has helped thousands with their health. After testing his diabetic clients, he takes them off **all** fruit, 100%. It must work because most are able to eventually stop taking their diabetic medication and shots after following his diet for a few months. He believes "fruit in moderation." When I went to see him, I was taken off all fruit except strawberries, blueberries, and raspberries. Not sure why, but I didn't care because he helped with my health more than any Western doctor, ever did. Berries are lower in carbohydrates and higher in antioxidants than almost any other fruits. (I personally think that berries should be in their own category, but the FDA disagrees with me.)

The rule-of-thumb is three servings of fruit a day. For some of you, this sounds expensive, but a "serving" is small, only fifty or sixty calories. If you are trying to save money, a cup of strawberries is the cheapest of all the berries, about sixty-cents-a cup. Most apples are large enough to be counted as three fruit servings, less-than a dollar. If you are counting every penny, get an 18-ounce can of pineapple on sale for a dollar a can. It has four servings. That's only twenty-five-cents-a-serving. Again, be sure to weigh and measure everything, even your fruit.

If you want to know how much fruit to eat, I would say between 100 to 150 calories-a-day.

<u>When it comes to fruit, here's what I do:</u> I eat one cup of berries every day. They are low in calories and carbohydrates, high in vitamins, minerals, fiber, and antioxidants. It's one of the best foods in the world for losing weight and best of all, it tastes good! **That's why I don't include them in my calorie count. They are "free."** I like

to eat blueberries one day and strawberries the next, then something else the next. The bigger the variety, the healthier I am.

I use berries to make smoothies or mix it with plain yogurt and some sweetener. Sometimes, I put blackberries in a bowl with some Stevia. Then I heat them up and add two tablespoons of half-and-half. It's almost as good as hot blackberry pie and ice cream. YUM! Berries are awesome. It's the one area that I spend a little more money on instead of going to *Starbucks*.

In addition to the berries, I eat one piece of fresh fruit each day. That is also a free food for me. I don't add it to my calories. I try to eat a variety, but whatever I buy on sale is what I munch on. So that's two fruits per day. Also, if I make a drink with lemons or limes, I don't count the calories on those. They are so low in calories and carbohydrates that they aren't worth adding in, but they are healthy and they are considered fruit.

Finally (and this is important) fruit is a healthy snack. If you get hungry, choose an apple instead of a cookie. Eat an orange instead of potato chips, even if you've been eating fruit all day. Even though bananas are high in carbohydrates, it's better than a candy bar. Cheaper too. If you want to be healthy, make healthy choices. Quite simple.

I allow myself one piece of fruit and one cup of berries, unlimited lemons or limes per-day without counting the calories. Any fruit after that counts.

NINE

Mama Was Right
Eat Your Vegetables

Would you like to know how I got so fat? I ate too much lettuce and way too many cucumbers. I'm not serious, as you probably know. **Unlike fruit, it's impossible to gain weight on green vegetables because they are mostly water and fiber.** It's different than fruit because fruit has a lot of sugary carbohydrates. It's healthy sugar, but too much can cause weight gain.

I used to wonder why some of my vegan friends were overweight. How can they gain weight if they are eating vegetables? After much observations, I figured out three reasons why vegans gain weight. First, some of them rarely eat vegetables. You would think people who called themselves "vegans" would eat vegetables, but if you ask them, "What is a vegan," they usually say, "I don't eat meat or anything from an animal," but that doesn't mean they eat vegetables! They just stopped eating meat.

Second, vegans often eat too much wheat, sugar, and corn. (Three of the Fatal Four). Instead of meat and milk, they eat too many carbohydrates, often unhealthy carbs. They give other vegans a bad name. Finally, vegans are often overweight because they eat a lot of nuts and seeds; healthy but high in calories. I love nuts and seeds. I eat them often, but I weigh them first and count the calories. Otherwise, I eat too much. I don't want to look like a chipmunk storing food for the winter.

Here's one of the best pieces of information I can give you about vegetables: **non-starchy vegetables are the only food that has no fat, few carbohydrates, and almost no calories.** On top of that, vegetables are packed with vitamins and minerals. In addition, they are mostly water and fiber. Water has zero calories, and fiber isn't absorbed into the body. It just goes through you, scrubbing your guts and making healthy poop. (More about awesome poop later.)

Fiber is that stuff that our doctors tell us to get more of. Why? Because fiber lowers cholesterol, protects against cancer and heart disease, helps control diabetes, and a dozen other things. Better yet, our bodies cannot digest fiber. It doesn't cause weight-gain. Fiber's purpose is to clean, not absorb.

According to the dictionary, fiber is ". . . dietary material containing substances that are resistant to the action of digestive enzymes." In other words, it doesn't digest, impossible. This means you can eat fiber all day long and it won't make you fat. In addition to all that, fiber makes you feel full. **Because green vegetables are mostly water and fiber, most diet groups allow you to eat unlimited green vegetables in addition to their other recommended foods.** Me too. (More about fiber later.)

Don't believe it? Have you ever heard anyone say, "I got fat from eating too many celery sticks"? (I've heard some bad excuses, but not that one.) When was the last time you saw a fat person chowing down on alfalfa sprouts while everyone else was eating cake and ice-cream? That's usually the skinny lady.

Ask yourself, *Would I get fat if I ate lettuce all day?* Impossible. Lettuce has so much fiber and water that your body can't possibly absorb it. Instead, it goes through your body, cleaning your stomach and colon, then eliminated. Eating vegetables is like eating water-

A NEW PERSPECTIVE ON DIETING AND WEIGHT LOSS

soaked sandpaper. Besides, you get your daily supply of minerals when you eat vegetables.

Here is a list of vegetables that you can eat all day and never gain weight:

green beans	broccoli	spinach	alfalfa sprouts
lettuce (all types)	cauliflower	onions	asparagus
peppers (all colors)	Sauerkraut	celery	artichokes
cabbage (cooked)	mushrooms	cabbage	bamboo shoots
Brussel sprouts	kale (yuk)	leeks	mustard greens
parsley	radishes	rhubarb	summer squash
watercress	wax beans	zucchini	fresh tomatoes
<u>½ cup per day of one:</u>			
carrots	acorn squash	winter squash	
pumpkin	butternut squash	tomato sauce	

The second group has some calories and carbohydrates and a lot of vitamin A, something you can get too much of. Therefore, I allow myself one serving-a-day of those.

Green vegetables are the most perfect weight-loss food that most of us ignore or forget even. Why? Because it's easier to grab a candy bar or a cookie, than toss a salad. Vegetables take more time to prepare, but do you know the real reason I don't eat my veggies? There's several.

First: habit. When I get hungry, I just do what I've always done, grabbing whatever I feel like, something easy, something unhealthy, like cookies or chips, gobbling them down, then filled with regret, partly because I know it causes weight gain, but also because I feel nauseated afterwards, wishing I had made better choices.

Another reason I don't eat vegetables is because vegetables don't taste as good as a *Snickers* or a bag of *Doritios*. Be honest. What tastes better, a stick of celery, or a chocolate chip cookie? A bagel with cream cheese or a bowl of broccoli? I would much rather eat a batch of brownies than a bunch of carrots.

We're programmed to believe that our food has to satisfy our sweet tooth. **Vegetables never satisfy a sweet tooth.** We want to eat what we FEEL like eating. I interpret this as *I'm a bratty, spoiled baby*, like a toddler in a high chair who wants a cookie. When Mommy puts strained spinach in my mouth, I spit it out. Then I pound my fist on my little tray and shout, "I want a cookie!" Am I the only one?

The other problem is that we've spent our whole lives centering our meals around carbohydrates, instead of vegetables. If we have a chicken dinner, we have mashed potatoes and gravy, a roll, and a teeny-tiny helping of green beans. Then we top off our meal with dessert made from wheat, sugar, and corn syrup. Some people wash it down with a can of pop or a tall lemonade. Worse yet, when we go back for seconds, we don't go for the broccoli. We grab another deep-fried chicken leg or a heaping helping of mashed potatoes with half-a-stick-of-butter or a tub of gravy. If we are having a spaghetti dinner, we take seconds on the spaghetti and bread sticks, instead of the salad. Why? I do it because it tastes good and I'm a big spoiled baby with a lot of bad habits. When was the last time you took seconds on salad when cheesy lasagna was available? It's a hard choice for a spoiled baby like me.

Some people can give up meat, but not carbohydrates. Why? Because carbs taste good! However, I have to say this. I'M NOT AGAINST CARBOHYDRATES. I'm not even against processed, unhealthy carbs, occasionally. We need carbohydrates in order to be healthy, but people in our country build their meals around bread, pasta, and sugar. It explains a lot of our weight issues **and** health problems.

One last reason I don't eat vegetables: too many vegetables give me a stomachache. That's because vegetables have a lot of fiber and **fiber can be hard to digest if you aren't used to it.** When I first started eating more veggies, I cooked or steamed them. That makes them easier to digest. Now I eat a lot of veggies, but I had to step it up slowly.

Another reason we eat too many carbs is because of the food pyramid. They encourage a lot of carbs. The old food pyramid from 1992 is atrocious. It has grains on the bottom! They think grains are more important than fruits or vegetables. It looks something like this:

Jpeg #3

Look at all those grains and carbohydrates! They recommend 6 - 11 servings-a-day! Imagine eating eleven bowls of cereal! No wonder we're struggling with our weight. Besides grains, the pyramid has way too much fruit and milk for me, both loaded with carbohydrates. And where are the healthy fats like nuts and seeds, coconut oil, and avocados? Who puts out these things?

Here's one of the newer pyramids.

Jpeg #4

This one is a big improvement, but they put fruit and vegetables in the same class. WRONG! Vegetables are low in calories and carbs. Most fruit isn't. A serving of green beans has 15 calories and 3 carbs. A banana has 100 calories and 27 carbohydrates. People look at the food pyramid and think they can skip the veggies and load up on fruit.

My herbalist says, "If you follow the food pyramid, you are guaranteed to get sick." He believes the food pyramid was put out by the cereal companies. Another study said that the food pyramid was made by a bunch of attorneys. I wonder if they were fat?

That's why I had to make my own pyramid. Mine makes more sense (at least to me). **Jpeg #5**

Our meals need to center around vegetables instead of everything else. Here's the formula: veggies first and foremost, everything else needs to be considered, the opposite of what we usually eat or are told to eat. The federal government probably hates me as do the cereal companies.

I like to make a vegetarian dinner once or twice a week. One of my favorites is a big batch of steamed broccoli, cauliflower, and carrots, topped off with some melted butter or *Brummel and Brown* (a healthy, low-cal margarine). This vegetable mix is also delicious sprinkled with fresh Parmesan cheese. (Notice the word "fresh".) This dish is filling and my family loves it. Steamed vegetables with mixed herbs are fun too. Some herbs come already mixed together.

Salad topped with a little chicken also makes a tasty dinner. Sandwiches can be turned into a salad by substituting lettuce for the bread. It's mostly vegetables and meat. You get protein, fiber, and very few calories.

Spaghetti sauce is a great place to hide vegetables and it makes your sauce thicker with more texture. Add fried onions and green peppers or mushrooms. If your family doesn't like crunching into vegetables, pour the spaghetti sauce in the blender with some cooked broccoli, carrots, and celery. With all those vegetables, you can cut back on the meat and your family will love it. When you can't see the vegetables, but you can taste them, your friends will bite into it and ask, "What is in here?" Ask them to guess. Makes an interesting conversation, and they are usually wrong.

Anything that calls for tomato sauce can be substituted with vegetable juice or V8. (Then you don't have to hit yourself on the forehead and say, "I should have had a V8.") Better yet, use fresh tomatoes instead of that canned stuff. Oh my gosh! Too darn good!

Another way to get more vegetables in your spaghetti is to put your sauce over green beans or steamed bean sprouts instead of pasta.

Some people think this is too complicated, but ask yourself, *If someone gave me a million dollars to increase my vegetables and decrease my carbs,* how would I do that? You will be amazed at how many of your own ideas you can come up with. (Darn. I ended that sentence with two prepositions.)

More vegetables, means more water, more fiber, more vitamins and minerals, while absorbing fewer calories, less fat, and fewer carbohydrates. If our meals were 50% to 60% vegetables, we would all be thinner and healthier. Isn't that the goal?

Vegetables should be the most important part of your meal. Remember. I'm not a nutritionist or doctor, just a former fat lady and also a former sick person. When I stick to my own food pyramid, I'm not only thinner. I'm healthier.

Other veggie ideas:

Pancakes are not healthy, but if you want to make your pancakes somewhat healthy, use carrot juice and instead of water, or put the batter in the blender and blend in some cooked carrots or canned pumpkin. Then add cinnamon and ginger. Top with high-grade maple syrup. Yummy! Carrots and pumpkin are two of the healthiest foods on the planet, loaded with vitamin A (one of those vitamins we don't get enough of). Carrots have beta carotene, a powerful antioxidant vital for healthy skin, hair, and eyes. They are so sweet that I often add carrot juice to *True Lime* drink mix. People wonder what that flavor is, but nobody ever guesses correctly or complains.

Whenever I make an omelet, I put in fried mushrooms, broccoli, onions, and green peppers. Omelets make a great lunch or dinner and a fun place to hide a variety of vegetables. A veggie omelet is a whole meal for me. Eggs are one of those-almost-perfect foods.

My herbalist eats twelve to fourteen eggs a week. He's very healthy! Skinny too!

For the world's easiest Chinese stir-fry, get a bag of frozen vegetables. Simply fry them in some sesame-seed oil with some drained Chinese bean sprouts and sliced water chestnuts. When it's heated through, add lite soy sauce. My vegan friends flavor it with *Bragg's Amino Acids*. If you want some protein, add leftover chicken or shrimp. It's an entire dinner, extremely healthy, and your family will love it. Ooh! I'm making myself hungry!

Another way to get your vegetables is to put them in gravy. Throw the gravy and cooked vegetables into a blender. Vegetables actually enhances the flavor! Gravy with cooked carrots and onions is so good that your guests will say, "This is delicious. Could I have your recipe?"

My all-time favorite way to get my vegetables is soup. You can make homemade, or semi-homemade. When I'm in a hurry, I take canned vegetable soup, follow the directions, but add some leftover green beans or broccoli. Look at my recipes in this book or get creative. Use your imagination. You can do it. If you come up with enough recipes, you can make your own cookbook and be rich and famous, oh yes and thin.

If you aren't the creative type, read *Deceptively Delicious*, a fun cookbook that teaches you how to hide veggies in your child's favorite foods. Adults too. Now eat your veggies. Eat lots, while getting healthy and thin. Yummy! Fun! Losing weight can be tasty!

TEN

It Doesn't Take a Rocket Scientist to Flush a Toilet

Flushing a toilet is a no-brainer. You need two things: a working toilet and a lot of water. Imagine trying to flush a toilet with a tablespoon of water. What if you increased it to a cup of cup? You would have a hard time pushing the "crap" through the toilet. You need a lot of water to make the toilet work, right? When the toilet is plugged, you need a plunger and MORE water to get it moving again.

The problem is that we are nicer to our toilets than we are to our bodies. We fill ourselves up with food, snack-after-snack, meal-after-meal, and then have a few sips of water, wondering why we feel bloated, constipated, fat, and unhealthy.

There are rumors that John Wayne died with a forty-pound colon. IT'S NOT TRUE. However, there was a man who died with a twenty-pound colon, filled with fecal matter. The poor guy didn't understand that his body was begging for water, the most important nutrient to life besides air. It explains why some people have a beer belly.

There is one person who understands the importance of drinking. Tom Brady (one of the greatest football players who ever lived) believes that his "athletic excellence" is due to drinking a lot of water. He claims to drink 37 glasses-a-day. That's more than two-gallons-a-day. But remember, he's an athlete. Do not do that!

If you've ever been on a diet, you've already been nagged to death about drinking eight glasses of water, and I could give you a whole slew of information about the importance of water, but you've already heard it five-hundred times. I'll keep it short and just give you the important parts. Here's what I've learned:

First of all, when I'm drinking a lot of water or fluids, I lose weight faster, feel better, and my skin is clearer. I've observed this phenomenon in my weight-loss group, T.O.P.S. After we weigh in, we ask the "loser of the week" how she managed to lose so much weight that week. At least a third of the time our biggest loser answers, "I drank a lot of water." One time, one of our fellow-dieters lost 3 ½ pounds in one week! Our leader asked her, "What did you do this week to lose so much?" She got a big smile on her face and said, "I peed and peed!" She obviously drank a lot of water.

When it comes to drinking water, you can read all the books and get all the information on why it works (and you probably have), but from someone who has been a chronic dieter, I can attest to the fact that it's a simple weight-loss trick that works. When I'm drinking a lot of water, I lose faster. More importantly, I'm healthier, but I still have to count calories.

How much do you need?

First, you can get too much. You can't think, *The more water I drink, the more weight I'll lose, so I'll drink a gallon a day.* Yes, I'll lose a lot of weight, because dead people lose weight quite rapidly. **People have died from drinking too much water.**

How much? Well, I've learned that I need at least a quart of water to get my toilet to flush. (A quart is four cups.) And we need about a quart of water, twice a day in order to flush all that food through our bodies, and get our systems clean and running right. Two quarts is eight cups. Simple. But is everyone on the face of the earth supposed to drink exactly eight glasses of water? If you're an athlete, or sweat a lot, wouldn't you need more? Wouldn't someone who weighed 400-pounds need more water than someone who weighed 150?

The "experts" have created a new formula like this: Take you current weight and divide by sixteen. (Use a calculator.) That number is how many cups of water you are supposed to drink in ounces. For example, if you weigh 160 pounds, divide that number by sixteen. That equals ten. That means you need ten cups of water a day. However, **I don't agree with this formula**. If you weighed four-hundred pounds, you would have to drink twenty-five glasses of water a day! That person would drown. **Ask your doctor.** Most doctors will tell you eight-glasses-a-day is a great place to start.

Three simple ways to find out if you are drinking enough:

The first way to know if you are drinking enough water is that your urine (pee) should be almost colorless. The darker it is, the more you water you need. If your pee is clear or almost clear, you're probably drinking enough water. Dr. Oz says that your pee should be clear enough to read the newspaper through it. What? I refuse to pee on my newspaper. I can just look at my pee and make a guess. Pale yellow or almost clear is good.

Second, if you are not drinking enough water, your urine will smell. If you are drinking eight glasses of water and your urine is clear (or almost clear), it shouldn't have an odor. If it does, ask your doctor. You either need more water, or could have an infection.

Finally, if you are not drinking enough water, you will be constipated. One time, when I was in for a physical, my doctor asked me those routine questions including, "Are you constipated?" I said, "Sometimes." The first question he asked was, "How much water are you drinking?" I was surprised, yet glad that he didn't want to write me a prescription. (I have an awesome doctor.)

Usually, the world's answer to constipation is laxatives. Either that or "more fiber." Wrong! Start by drinking eight glasses of water a day, or more if you sweat a lot, or are extremely obese. Eight glasses is a starting point. You need water to flush the poop out of your body, because poop is poison. Constipation can be a sign that you are not getting enough water. If you are still constipated after drinking your eight glasses, talk to your doctor. He will probably tell you to eat more fiber, then write you a prescription.

Another reason for constipation is too much calcium and not enough magnesium. More about that in the chapter on vitamins.

Most people think that constipated means they don't go very often. There's more to it than that. Here's how to know if you are plugged up.

- If you are sitting on the toilet, grunting and groaning for more than two or three minutes, you are constipated.
- If your poop floats, you are constipated.
- If your poop looks like brown marbles or golf balls, you're constipated. (It should look more-like a fat, S-shaped snake.)
- If your poop is hard and dry, you are constipated. (Poop should be the consistency of pumpkin pie.)
- If you aren't going every day (or maybe every other day), you are probably constipated.

A lack of water is only one cause of constipation. There are other causes, but this is the most common one. The bottom line (no pun intended) is this: if you aren't drinking enough water, you will not be regular.

Can I substitute water with other drinks?

My number one rule is this: never substitute poison for water. You probably think you don't drink poison, but I call pop, alcohol, or anything with a lot of sugar or diet sugar "poison." If you've been substituting pop, diet drinks, or other garbage for water, you need to give yourself a spanking or bang your head against the wall, because you're killing yourself.

You drink water to lose weight, but also to be healthy. Water helps transport nutrients throughout the body. If your water is poison, it will transport poison throughout your body. These poisons kill nutrients. Pop depletes your body of calcium causing brittle bones.

Everyone wants to know if they can use coffee for water. Although black coffee is not poison, it absolutely cannot be a substitute for water, ever, because coffee causes dehydration. That means **it takes water out of your body.** That's why you have to pee so much after you drink coffee. In fact, one article I read said that if you drink coffee or pop, you need to drink two glasses of water to wash away each cup Then, in addition to that, you have to drink eight glasses of water. Seems like an overkill. If we all did that, we would have to build an arc because the sewers would erupt.

Milk is NEVER a substitute for water. When you can take a drink, and make it into a solid food (like cheese and yogurt) it's not a drink. It's food. Milk and milk products are healthy for most people, but it's not a substitute for water.

Making Water Taste Good:

Do you like the taste of water? I don't. One of the reasons I don't like water is because most tap water tastes bad. That's because it often contains chlorine, fluoride, bacteria and parasites. My body is telling me to spit it out. Besides that, some tap water contains lead. That's why water, straight from the faucet, doesn't taste good. It's not healthy. In order to keep it simple, I boil mine. I have one of those pots that you fill up, plug in and it heats in five minutes. (You can buy those pots for about $15.00.) Water that has been frozen is okay, and is better than straight tap water. Parasites and bacteria can't survive in a frozen environment.

Before I boil it, I filter it with a *Brita* water filter. I have one that hooks on my faucet. Very simple, but they have Brita water pitchers and water bottles too. You can either filter it or boil or freeze your water, but the best water is FILTERED AND BOILED. Clean water tastes sooooo much better. Water from a well is usually good too. I wouldn't filter it because it's loaded with minerals, but I would definitely boil it.

Some people buy water from the store. I don't, unless I know for sure it's clean. Some store-bought water is just tap-water in a bottle. Also, bottled water often absorbs chemicals from the plastic. You would be better off to boil your own tap water.

Flavored water:

Even when I boil and filter my water, it's still boring. Right? I have some ideas to make water taste good. If you want to substitute something else for water, I recommend *Healthiest Lemonade*. (The recipe is in the chapter "The Joy of Fasting.") It's so healthy and so low in calories that I don't count the calories.

Here's another idea. I substitute herbal tea or green tea with a little **Stevia** for my water, but be careful. There is the store-bought powdered tea with sugar, corn syrup, or fake sugar. Poison!

Here's another substitute. Juice can be watered down. After I filter and boil my water, I do the *Three-Times-Three Drink*. Simply take three cups of juice; then mix it with three cups of water, then add three packets of Stevia. This idea works with pineapple juice, carrot, cranberry, apple or orange juice. It also saves money! I serve it to my family and friends. No one knows and no one ever complains and believe me, my grandkids aren't afraid to complain. My "water-juice" tastes delicious, cuts the calories, saves money, and gives my body the water it desperately needs. However, I count the calories from the juice. If I drink two cups, one cup is counted as juice. The other is water.

When I make it for myself, I make it with one cup of juice and four cups of water with a little sweetener, but I still count the calories. It tastes so much better than plain water. Just remember to **add the calories to your daily calorie count.**

Finally, *Barb's Favorite Tea* is a perfect way to get your water. Tastes delicious hot or cold. Drink up!

Finally:

Picture your stomach and intestines as a human toilet that needs to be flushed regularly throughout the day. Your colon builds up all the foods that you've been putting in it during the day. Your body miraculously turns the stuff you don't use into waste or poop. Don't you want to get rid of it? Do you leave poop in your toilet?

Picture yourself drinking lots of water to flush out your poop. Get rid of it. Get healthy. You don't want to die with a thirty-pound colon. It doesn't take a rocket scientist to flush a toilet.

ELEVEN

Scrub the Toilet

What would happen if you always flushed the toilet, but never scrubbed it? Try it for three months. Flush regularly, but don't scrub. Eeeeeeeuuuwwww! Besides all the germs and bacteria, there's an ugly brownish residue that builds up. If you wait too long, it could leave a permanent ring, impossible to remove. And what about the odor? Pew! Stinky! Well, guess what? Your stomach, colon, and intestines are like that too. Water alone doesn't clean it thoroughly. You flush down the food down with water, but **you also have to scrub your guts**. Why? Because you have millions of little, tiny hairs (called villi) that gets caked with poop. Those little hairs are there to absorb nutrients. If they are plugged, you will be nutritionally starved. If you don't clean them, you will get poop stuck in your gut hairs. Who wants poopie gut-hairs? Imagine trying to wash poop out of your hair with without shampoo? Water isn't enough.

When you wash your hair, you want the best products, and when you clean your toilet, you want to make it to be as clean as possible. When you clean your guts, you want to scrub those little hairs and get rid of the poop that the water doesn't wash away.

A NEW PERSPECTIVE ON DIETING AND WEIGHT LOSS

Want to guess how to wash your gut hairs? There's only one product for that: **fiber**. It's the stuff that your doctor keeps telling you to get more of. (Oops. Ended that sentence with a preposition.) Fiber is the part of food that can't be digested. Eating fiber is a bit like eating a *Brillo Pad* or *Scotch Bright*. It scrubs your insides, then goes right through you. It's found in fruits and vegetables, nuts and seeds, beans, oat bran, and rice bran. It's also found in whole grains, but remember. You can live without grains!

Rarely do any of us get our recommended daily amount of fiber! Women need at least twenty-five grams-a-day. Men need about thirty. (Some doctors recommend more, but it's a start.) Unfortunately, most of us get about half of the RDA (recommended daily allowance) but good news! It's not hard to get what you need. However, there are a few things you should know about this important part of your diet.

The first thing you need to know is that fiber makes you healthy. But more importantly, a lack of fiber makes you unhealthy. It also causes you to have a big belly. **Instead of a "beer belly," they should call it a "pooh belly."**

Remember, the guy in the last chapter, who died with a twenty-pound colon? He probably didn't eat a lot of fiber. More like triple-beef cheese burgers on white bread. (Zero fiber in that.) Part of his problem was not-enough water, but another problem was probably a lack of fiber. Just think. If he had been drinking water and eating his fiber, he could have died twenty-pounds thinner!

I wonder how many of us are carrying around twenty pounds of fecal matter in our gut? We could get rid of most of it if we just drank more water AND ate more fiber.

Your doctor and your mother constantly tell you, "Eat fiber," but do they ever tell you what types of fiber? Nobody ever told me either. When I took a health class at Portland State University, I was shocked to discover there was more than one type of fiber. Here's what I learned.

To start with, fiber is divided into two categories: soluble and insoluble. My doctor told me to get more fiber but didn't tell me which type. Neither did my mom. They didn't even tell me there was more than one type. Maybe they didn't know. Here's a little more information about the two types.

1. <u>Insoluble fiber</u> **does not dissolve in water.** It removes and pushes toxic waste through the colon in less time which helps with constipation and allows regular bowel movements. **Insoluble fiber works mostly in the intestines.** Brown rice, legumes, carrots, cucumbers and tomatoes contain insoluble fiber.
2. <u>Soluble fiber</u> **dissolves in water**. It helps lower blood glucose levels (important for diabetics). It also lowers the bad cholesterol, slows digestion so that sugar is released more slowly, making you feel full longer. **Soluble fiber works mostly in the stomach.** Oatmeal, oat bran, nuts, beans, lentils, apples, and blueberries contain soluble fiber.

But that's not all! Under each one of those categories, there are sub categories. They all do something different and all very important. For example, pectin (a soluble fiber) is in apples, pears, strawberries. Pectin helps form healthy stools. (I don't want unshapely stools.)

If your doctor recommends *Metamucil* so that you can get your fiber, you should know that ***Metamucil* has no pectin. Zero. It has no insoluble fiber either.** It's made of psyllium husks, a soluble fiber. It's not complete.

A subcategory under insoluble fibers is something called "lignin." This one is found in green beans, Brazil nuts, peas, and carrots. **Lignin is not in *Metamucil* either**. Lignin lowers cholesterol, balances blood sugar, and may prevent colon cancer. You need this type of fiber too.

Other types of fiber (that I can't pronounce) slow the food through the digestive system. Some enhance the immune system. Others increase the good bacteria. Some types of fiber help with diabetes because sugar is released more slowly. Still others absorb water to form healthy poop, and helps move the poop through the intestines. Some fiber helps to move the poop faster.

Beans are a fibrous food, but they are high in carbohydrates and fairly high in calories. (Be sure to weigh and measure.) Also, beans don't have pectin or lignin. If you ate beans, you would get plenty of fiber, but you wouldn't get the assorted types of fibers you need.

I used to think I was getting all my fiber because I ate a lot of broccoli, the most fibrous, low-calorie food on the earth. Three cups gave me my minimum daily requirements, but it only has one type of fiber. The "experts" told me I was getting what I needed. They were wrong.

Green beans and apples have four different types of fiber, but they don't have the necessary twenty-five to thirty grams that your body needs. **But don't stress out. I'm going to make it simple.** Here's the answer to getting all types of fiber and the right amount.

1. Eat a variety of berries, fruits, and vegetables, but especially vegetables.
2. Eat oats with oat bran twice a week.
3. Eat beans once or twice a week.
4. Eat two or three tablespoons of nuts and seeds every day or almost every day.
5. Count your calories.

<u>DANGER:</u> If you've only been eating ten grams of fiber a-day, and suddenly eat thirty, you will get a terrible tummy ache! Your body isn't used to it. **Increase your fiber slowly and talk to your doctor.**

TWELVE

Vitamins, Minerals, Herbs, Food Supplements, and Whatever the Heck Else You Want to Call Them

I'm not a doctor, but I'm a big fan of vitamins. Let me explain how my "vitamin journey" began.

When my son was seven-years-old, he had suffered with strep throat for more than a year, NONSTOP! Strep is a serious disease. If not cured, it turns into scarlet fever, then to rheumatic fever, then death. His doctor was stumped. I found a new pediatrician who tried several different antibiotics. He even tried vitamin B shots. Nothing worked.

Out of desperation, I called Dr. Lendon Smith, a renowned pediatrician and author who believed that most children's health problems were caused by diet. Although he was world-famous, his home phone number was listed. When I called him, he answered the phone, like he was my next-door neighbor! After I caught my breath, I told him about my son, this is what he said. "Take your son off ALL milk products. That includes cheese, yogurt, butter, and ice cream. In addition, give him 5,000 milligrams of vitamin C an hour." I gasped. He was only seven-years old. I asked, "For how long?" He told me, "Until he is well." I didn't think it would work, but I had no choice. My son was dying. I took my son to my mom's, then went to the store and got some chewable vitamin C. I couldn't bring myself to give him 5,000 milligrams-an-hour. Instead, I gave him 2,000-an-hour. The results were bizarre and instantaneous! In three hours, my little boy had color in his face for the first time in more than a year. The next morning, I took him to his pediatrician who took one look at him and couldn't believe the change. The black circles under his eyes were gone, replaced by rosy, pink cheeks. On top of that, his strep test was negative. Thirteen months of antibiotics did nothing. Vitamin C plus the antibiotics and a diet-change worked! That happened thirty years ago, a turning point for me. My eyes were opened to the value of vitamins. (My son's pediatrician made some major changes too, a story for my next book.)

A more recent vitamin story: When I was 62, I "shattered" my left ring finger (the emergency-room doctor's exact word). They x-rayed it and gave me a temporary cast. Then they told me to see an orthopedic surgeon (a bone doctor) in one week. They also told me I would need surgery. A week later, I saw the specialist who took a second x-ray to compare to the first. He said something like this. "I was quite surprised when I compared the two x-rays. You won't be needing any surgery. Your bones are healing nicely." When a bone surgeon tells you that you have good bones and you're in your sixties, then you know you are doing something right. I also have great teeth. I go to the dentist every ten years and rarely have a cavity. My healthy teeth and bones are because of my supplements, especially the magnesium I take from *Abundant Living Nutrition Center* combined with vitamin D and MSM. (More about that later.)

If you've ever watched Dr. Oz, you have been educated-to-death about which vitamins and minerals and herbs and a-thousand-other-things you are supposed to pop in your mouth in order to be healthy or lose weight. I love Dr. Oz and I think he's got some great ideas, but it can be rather overwhelming, and I disagree with him on a few things.

Most importantly, THERE IS NO MAGIC PILL FOR WEIGHT LOSS. Although Dr. Oz doesn't say there is one, it's sometimes implied, but here's the good news. If you are missing a vital nutrient in your diet, you may feel hungry and overeat. When I feel hungry, I stop and think, "Have I taken my food supplements (vitamins) today?" Taking the right nutrients MIGHT curb your appetite, but keep in mind, there is no instant weight-loss pill.

To start with, most doctors (including Dr. Oz) will tell you to make sure to take a multiple vitamin. NOT ME. Do you honestly believe that a tiny pill, the size of a dime has every vitamin and mineral you need in order to be healthy? It may contain all those vitamins, but how is that possible? It doesn't come from fresh fruits and vegetables. My guess is that it's a bunch of chemicals squished into a pill. Most are neither healthy nor absorbable.

In addition to all that, the vitamin industry is not well regulated. That's probably why *Web MD* gives three separate studies that show that vitamins are useless and don't improve your health. They all agree that we are wasting our money, **especially when it comes to multiple vitamins**. Of course, those don't work! In fact, they are bad for you. (That's my opinion anyway.) Yet, doctors and other healthcare professionals will tell you that you need to take a multiple vitamin every day to be healthy. Go ahead and take them. I refuse. It's chemicals. I try not to put chemicals in my body.

How do I get my vitamins? I eat healthily most of the time so I get a lot of vitamins and mineral from my food. Here are a few of the nutrient-dense foods that I try to incorporate in my diet. Daily or almost daily, I eat **assorted berries, a little fruit, nuts and seeds, a variety of vegetables, carrot juice, eggs, and fish**. That covers dozens of the necessary vitamins and minerals my body needs. I also eat beans and oatmeal once or twice a week for extra fiber.

However, I've learned that I don't get everything I need from my food, even it's healthy and organic. I've researched vitamins and minerals for years and there's a few I take regularly to stay healthy, but I'm picky where I buy them, and who I get them from. The supplements I need are.

vitamin A and D	turmeric	chromium picolinate
MSM	hawthorn	magnesium
probiotics	vitamin C	

It sounds like a lot, but here's why each one is important and why I take them.

<u>Vitamin A</u> is one of those vitamins that most of us don't get enough of. It's also one of the vitamins that you can take once-or-twice-a-week. That's because vitamin A is considered "non-soluble" or "fat-soluble." That means your body stores it (the same way a camel stores water), but **I don't take vitamin A in the form of a pill**. Why should I take a pill when God gave me carrots? I drink two-tablespoons of carrot juice a-day, or a cup-a-week. Carrot juice is far superior to raw carrots because your body absorbs the nutrients better when carrots are juiced. Since I'm not crazy about carrot juice, I add it to my smoothie or orange juice or *Healthiest Lemonade*. Carrot juice blends in because of its sweetness. I get my carrot juice from the health food store. It lasts for six to eight weeks in the refrigerator.

Vitamin A is important for several reasons. I have a friend who used to have severe night blindness. When she started drinking carrot juice, it went away. Completely! It's great for your skin too. If you drink carrot juice, your shingles, eczema, psoriasis and acne might disappear. Carrots give your skin a healthy glow too. Don't worry. The glow isn't orange.

If you really don't like carrot juice, you can get vitamin A from "orange vegetables" like pumpkin, yams, or sweet potatoes.

One important thing! **Too much vitamin A is toxic.** Two or three servings of orange vegetables per week is plenty.

Vitamin D is another one most of us don't get enough of. Harvard University believes that at least one billion people on the face of the earth are deficient in vitamin D. Most doctors agree. That's why a good doctor checks your vitamin D levels when you go in for a routine physical. It's usually low.

Vitamin D is actually a vitamin AND a hormone. Technically, it's D3 that your body screams for. This unique vitamin has the ability to cross the blood-brain barrier in order to feed the brain. Consequently, it often helps with mental issues, especially Season Affective Disorder (S.A.D.) and mood swings. That's why some people call it the "happy hormone." Children who are not growing often need Vitamin D. It also protects against muscle weakness and regulates the heartbeat. Finally, it enhances the immune system. **Without vitamin D, your body won't heal.** If you don't believe me, Google 'Symptoms of vitamin D deficiency'.

Vitamin D is fat-soluble like vitamin A. That means you don't have to take it every day. Your body has a reservoir designed specifically to store vitamin D. If your doctor says your vitamin D levels are low, that means your reservoir is empty and your body desperately needs D. One of my friends takes 50,000 IU of vitamin D **once a month**. Doctor's orders. The recommended daily allowance is 600 IU per day or 4,000 IU per week, more if your reservoir is empty. Ask your doctor.

There are three healthy ways to get vitamin D:

- Twenty minutes of sun twice-a-week **without** sun screen. However, most oncologists (cancer doctors) advise sun screen, but you don't get any vitamin D when you do that.
- Fish oil and fatty fish like salmon, sardines, or tuna, contain D.

- Take a food supplement or pill. The best one is Sunshine Plus from *Abundant Living Nutrition Center*, but just be sure to take something if you don't get enough sun or fish.

Some foods, like milk say "fortified with vitamin D." Since most vitamin D comes from fish oil, I'm guessing that "fortified" means chemicals. (After all, my milk doesn't taste fishy.) I don't trust foods that say "fortified." There are other, more natural foods that contain vitamin D like egg yolks and oatmeal, but it's only in small amounts. You can also get Vitamin D through caviar or tofu, but YUK!

Warning: too much vitamin D can be toxic. It's rare, but possible. I get my vitamin D levels checked one-a-year. Even though I take more than the recommend amount, my levels are always on the lowest end of normal. I'm working on getting it up closer to the other end, because I understand the value and power of vitamin D. Without D, I know I would not be healthy. PLEASE, talk to your doctor.

Vitamin D needs calcium in order to maximize absorption. I take it with plant-based calcium.

<u>Calcium</u> is vital for healthy teeth, bones, and gums, besides helping your body to absorb vitamin D. Calcium and D together are amazing.

However, I'M VERY CAREFUL ABOUT WHICH CALCIUM SUPPLEMENTS I TAKE for two reasons. First, most calcium supplements are not absorbable. If they don't absorb, they can cause calcium deposits in your arteries, kidneys, tendons, joints, brain, breasts. Kidney stones and gall stones are partially calcium. Here is a list of calcification issues:

- Artery calcification
- Pericardial calcification (heart)
- Kidney calcification
- Joint and tendon calcification

- Brain calcification (dementia and Alzheimer's)
- Breast calcification

Although it is not clear about the link between oral calcium and calcium deposits, I'm not willing to take that chance.

One time I bought some expensive calcium from a health-food store. Afterwards, I read an article that said to put your vitamins in water with a little vinegar, and see how long before it dissolves. Three months later, my calcium was still sitting in the water in its original shape. It looked like it was laughing at me.

Some people take TUMS to get their calcium. Here's the problem. TUMS absorb acid. You need acid to absorb calcium. TUMS are great for acid indigestion and heartburn, but it doesn't sound like a good way to get your daily intake of calcium.

Another problem with calcium is that it can interfere with the absorption of prescription medication and some vitamins. Ask your doctor or pharmacists. It is often written on the label.

Besides all that, **too much calcium causes constipation**. But your body screams for calcium. So how do you get your calcium? I get my calcium from my food. Milk products such as cheese, yogurt, and cottage cheese are loaded with calcium. Other foods high in calcium are eggs, broccoli, kale, spinach, kelp (seaweed), sardines, beans, almonds, and soy products. I also take plant-based calcium, because I know it's completely digestible.

When buying calcium, go to your local health-food store and get either plant-based calcium, liquid calcium, or powdered. I use the plant-based. The only other calcium I recommend is "Life Cal" from www.AbundantLivingNutrition.com. You can get it online, but it is so popular that they are often sold out. All of these are easily digested and absorbed.

Magnesium is a miracle mineral. A lack of magnesium can cause muscle cramps, muscle twitching, pain, anxiety, hyperactivity, high blood pressure, diabetes, stress, confusion, and insomnia. According to Natural Society, "**Magnesium is involved with more than 300 metabolic processes in our bodies, leading to the mineral being called "the master mineral."** In fact, when I Googled "benefits of magnesium," the first five-out-of-six websites also confirmed "300 different processes." Three-hundred! Sounds like you need this mineral to be healthy.

The most important reason to take magnesium is because your body needs it to transport calcium to your bones and teeth. Calcium without magnesium causes calcium deposits because the calcium has nowhere to go. Without magnesium, calcium can cause hardening of the arteries or arterial plaque leading to heart failure. Worse yet, too much calcium (without magnesium) can cause calcium deposits in a man's private parts, making him impotent. **Calcium can't do its job without magnesium.**

In addition to all that, you could get seriously constipated if you take calcium without magnesium. If you are constipated, you may be getting too much calcium and not enough magnesium. However, too much magnesium gives you diarrhea.

<u>Chromium picolinate</u> is an essential mineral that most Americans don't get enough of. It's one of the most effective natural supplements to prevent or control blood-sugar issues like diabetes and hypoglycemia. Technically, chromium picolinate is two different substances. Chromium is a mineral known to enhance and improve insulin activity. "Picolinate" is a substance that allows the body to absorb the chromium. The two together (chromium and picolinate) are a powerful way to balance blood sugar. Studies show that most type-2 diabetics are low in chromium. Chromium is found in some foods, but it's poorly absorbed. In addition, chromium decreases with age. According to Stephanie Briggs, PhD., "Obesity often accompanies Type 2 diabetes, but chromium may overcome insulin resistance and help diabetics lose weight."

When I Googled "diabetes/chromium" thousands of articles came up. **CAUTION:** If you are diabetic or on medication for diabetes, consult with your physician before taking this!

I'm not diabetic and my blood sugar is always normal, but maybe that's because I take chromium picolinate every day, 200 mcg-a-day. The maximum allowance is 400, however, some people take 800 mcg-per day! Sounds like too much, but if I ever have a serious problem with my blood sugar, I will take more. I prefer to do everything in moderation and naturally whenever possible.

Turmeric is a plant or herb in the ginger family. You can sprinkle it on your food, but I choose to take it in a tablet. Turmeric makes a lot of claims, but I take it for one main reason. **It is a powerful anti-inflammatory.** Inflammation is the cause of hundreds, maybe thousands of diseases, many fatal. I chose life and health. I take two tablets a day so I can avoid those diseases. It's may not prevent everything, but it's a start.

Probiotics are neither a vitamin nor a mineral. They are called "friendly bacteria." The word "biotic" means "life." When a person takes an **anti**biotic, it kills the bad bacteria along with the good bacteria. **If you've ever taken an antibiotic, you probably need to replace all that good bacteria that you killed.** Probiotics do exactly that. It supplies the gut with beneficial bacteria and stimulates digestive juices. It's found in yogurt, but usually not enough. It's also found in sauerkraut, but how often do you eat that? Other foods that contain probiotics are kefir, miso, kimchi, or kombucha tea. I don't eat or drink those things often enough and some don't have enough probiotics to be beneficial. Consequently, I get my probiotics from a local health-food store, usually in the refrigerated section.

MSM: I first started taking MSM when I saw an old friend who had turned her health around. She had been bitten by a Lyme tick thirty-years earlier. Her health had deteriorated year-after-year. The last time I talked to her, she told me she would be in a wheelchair within a year. But now she was back to work and had joined a gym.

When I asked her what had happened and why she was so healthy, she said one word. "MSM." Her before-and-after appearance made a believer out of me.

MSM stands for "methylsulfomylmethane" a compound that every cell in our body needs in order to be healthy. The claims for this substance are unending, from healing arthritis to reversing diverticulosis. MSM is mostly sulfur (a mineral). **Without sulfur, we would all die.** It's as important to life as water. Sulfur disinfects the blood and helps the body to resist bacteria. Some studies show that it slows the aging process.

MSM is an organic sulfur compound that use to be in our food, but our soil is so depleted now, that we can't get enough. MSM fights inflammation, arthritis, joint pain, chronic pain, headaches, p.m.s., scleroderma, t.m.j., and about ninety-five other things. There's a book called, "The Miracle of MSM: The Natural Solution for Pain." My friend who should be in a wheelchair would totally agree. She's running and doing palates. MSM is a miracle.

There are foods that are high in MSM like onions and garlic. It's a great way to get it, but I don't eat those foods every day. I get my MSM from a powder. I used to get it from Swanson's in a pill form, and it's a good place to start. However, the MSM I use now is pharmaceutical grade and the best on the market. I get it from "Norm's OptiMSM Products," 541-746-5272. The problem is that there is no recommended daily allowance, so you are on your own there. I put my MSM in a salt shaker and sprinkle it in all my drinks and most of my food.

Ask your doctor. I started small and added some. Beware! In rare circumstances, some people are allergic to sulfur. More about MSM in the chapter on fasting.

CoQ-10 a.k.a. Coenzyme Q-10 or Ubiquinol is a vitamin-like substance similar to vitamin E and a powerful antioxidant. CoQ-10 aids in circulation and, like sulfur, all of our cells demand it. It increases tissue oxidation so it stimulates the immune system, fights gum disease, improves allergies, and asthma. It's used to fight candida, multiple sclerosis, and diabetes.

The University of Texas did a six-year study for those being treated for congestive heart failure. People who took MSM had a 75% higher survival rate compared to those who didn't. Those who didn't take it only had a 25% survival rate.

We all have a certain amount of coenzyme Q-10 in our bodies, but as we age, it declines. **Therefore, we need to take a supplement as we get older.** Ubiquinol is a more powerful form of CoQ-10, but either one is vital to good health. CoQ-10 works better when taken with vitamin E or fish oil. Fifty milligrams of CoQ-10 is the recommended amount. I take 100. Ask your doctor.

Fish oil or krill oil helps your body to assimilate CoQ10. Since CoQ10 is one of the most important nutrients in a person's body, we want to make sure it gets absorbed. Fish oil helps with absorption.

Fish-oil also crosses the blood-brain barrier! That means it feeds the brain. Some studies show that it helps brain disorders such as depression, ADHD, and Alzheimer's. Best of all, fish oil lowers inflammation, the root cause of thousands of diseases. The list goes on and on, but I know that Jesus ate fish regularly. If it's good enough for Him, it's good enough for me.

Vitamin C: So many of us are opting to skip the flu shot and take vitamins instead. Vitamin C builds your immune system to fight colds and flu. That's why "AirBorn" is so popular. It's mostly vitamin C. I have several friends who swear by it.

If you get the cheap vitamin C, it doesn't work. All it does is give you a bad case of "the trots," (running to the bathroom). I trust the vitamin C from Abundant Living Nutrition Center. It's the best!

Once-a-year: I do a parasite cleanse with something called "Parasmart Cleanse" by ReNew Life. (I get it from Amazon.com.) Parasmart is just herbs squished into pills, so it's safe for most people, unless you are allergic to one of the spices. **The first time I did this cleanse, my health began to improve after being seriously ill for**

years. I discovered that some of our foods and most of our water has parasites. I'm a huge fan of a parasite cleanse. Ask your doctor. He or she will probably say, "She's nuts." Maybe, but I'm a healthy nut.

That's it: Those are the ones I take, but there is one more thing I need to tell you. I make a healthy drink by adding powdered greens (from Swanson's Vitamins or *Nature's Way Alive*), two tablespoons of carrot juice, MSM granules and a packet of *True Lime* to a glass of clean water. When I add those first three ingredients to anything, I call it my **Healthy Drink (HD)** and highly recommend it if you aren't feeling well.

I don't do flu shots and I rarely go to the doctor. Personally, I don't think shots are safe, but in addition to that, it's usually expensive, even with health insurance. I prefer to take herbs or supplements.

Where I buy my vitamins:

- Calcium and magnesium and vitamin D: *Abundant Living Nutrition Center* AbundantLivingNutrition.com
- MSM: *Kala Health MSM* www.EarthTurns.com
- Greens or vitamin C: SwansonsVitamins.com or Amazon
- All others: SwansonsVitamins.com
- Your local health-food store has high-quality products and their employees are a wealth of knowledge.

If you get your vitamins someplace besides the ones that I mentioned, be sure they are ones that your body can absorb. **Remember, many vitamins are made of rocks or chemicals.** (By the way, I don't get any extra credit for pushing any of these products.)

Honorable mentions:

There are a few others that I take occasionally. I need to point them out because they have helped me in so many ways.

Lysine: an amino acid that prevents or heals herpes, mouth sores, or shingles. If I take it once-a-week, it seems to be enough. If I ever get shingles, I will take it every day.

Digestive Enzymes: helps food to digest; especially helpful as we age.

Dairy Digest: Helps digest milk products including cheese and yogurt.

Garcinia Cambogia: helps to feel full.

Hawthorn: This is highly recommended by Peter J. D'Adamo *Eat Right for Your Type*. He believes that hawthorn is so important that he says, **"If I had my way, extracts of hawthorn would be used to fortify cereal, just as vitamins are."** According to him, he said that it is used in Germany for heart patients with NO SIDE EFFECTS! Pretty good stuff.

I gave this to my neighbor who said, "I don't have much time left. I have a bad heart. My ankles are swollen, and my chest hurts." I gave her two hawthorn tablets. Four hours later, all the swelling was gone and her chest pains stopped." Amazing, but DO NOT take this if you have low blood pressure. It could be dangerous. Ask your doctor and do the research.

These herbs do NOT help me to lose weight. THERE IS NO MAGIC BULLET. I take herbs to improve my health, avoid doctors, and revive my energy. I'm also SLIGHTLY less hungry when I take my herbs. If you are thinking about taking some of these, please talk to your doctor or health-care provider first.

THIRTEEN

The Only Book Better Than Mine

I get a lot of my ideas about food, dieting and weight loss from this amazing book. I've read it over and over and I am always learning something new. This extraordinary book is the Bible. Do you think the Bible is boring? Can't understand it? Don't believe it? No matter how you feel about the Bible, there are yummy nuggets of wisdom and delicious morsels of truth. We can all glean new ideas, especially about dieting and weight-loss.

The Bible has two different types of dieting advice. First, there are foods named specifically in the Bible like the bread, honey, almonds, grapes, olives, fish, eggs, and locust. (I don't think I'll skip the bugs.)

Here's some fun info about food in the Bible. Did you know that the bread Jesus served the 5,000 wasn't made with wheat or flour? It was barley bread! When was the last time you ate that? The Bible could have just said "bread," but it's clear that it was barley bread, NOT wheat. Interesting.

There are also dozens of Scriptures about honey and how healthy it is. How about a slice of barley bread with some raw honey? Local honey is known to fight allergies. Then there's almonds, one of the healthiest foods in the world. The list goes on and on.

The other thing I love about the Bible is that there is a lot of great suggestions. There are Scriptures about guidance, direction, and common sense to help people who are struggling and don't know what to do, or why they aren't losing weight, like this: "There is a way that seems right to a man, but its end is the way of death." (Proverbs 14:12, NKJV) This makes me think of all those fad diets and diet pills. Everyone thought they were going to suddenly get skinny by popping a pill that was invented by someone who just wanted to make money. People thought "it seemed right." Instead, they were getting chemicals or drugs which often lead to death, just like this verse says. We need wisdom from God to know what's right. We want to lose weight and be healthy. God knows us better than we know ourselves. He created us. Then He gave us a book to live by. It has all the answers.

There's another verse in Hebrews 12:11 that says, "For the moment, all discipline seems painful, rather than pleasant, but later it yields the peaceful fruits of righteousness (ESV)." Did you notice that phrase, "**ALL discipline seems painful?**" That's the "No pain. No gain" theory. It's in the Bible! Notice that it's followed with a happily-ever-after verse. It says that **"LATER" (after the pain) you will have peace.** You just have to get through the painful part first. When I stick to my diet, I get hungry and feel denied. It's painful, but **LATER** when I get on the scale, or my pants are falling off, I feel peace and joy. Of course I do! It's in the Bible.

My favorite Scripture about dieting is, "All fat is the Lord's" (Leviticus 3:16b ESV). Who says God doesn't have a sense of humor? Let's all grab our fat and say, "Here God. Take it." That's what I said the first time I read this, while I was laughing. Thousands of years ago God knew there would be a nation full of fat people. He put that verse in there for people like us.

One of the best "food stories" is the tale (tail) of Adam and Eve. According to the Bible, there was no sin in their perfect world. Adam and Eve had the best life of anyone, ever. All their needs were met.

They had food and shelter, never too hot or too cold. They could cuddle with lions and romp with lambs. They had a warm, loving relationship with each other and talked to God throughout the day. There was no sickness, pain nor death. They didn't have to worry about getting old or achy. They didn't even have to worry about getting fat. They could have anything they wanted in the entire world, except for one thing, one specific food. It was the only thing they couldn't have, but they kept looking at it, wanting it, desiring it. No matter how hard they tried, they just couldn't stay away from it. In Genesis 2:17b, God told said this about the tree: "If you eat it's fruit, you are sure to die," (NLT). Obviously, Adam and Eve didn't believe Him.

One day, when Eve was staring at the delicious-looking fruit, longing for it, Satan (disguised as a snake) came for a visit. " 'You will not certainly die,' said the serpent said to the woman. For God knows when you eat from it, your eyes will be opened and you will be like God, knowing good from evil' " (Genesis 3:4-5 NIV). Interestingly, part of what the devil told her was true. Eve's eyes were open when she ate it, but it wasn't good. **One bite of the wrong food brought sin and death to the whole world!**

I used to look at Eve and think, *What is wrong with that woman?* Her life was perfect, but it just wasn't good enough. Now I have to ask, am I any different from her? I can have fish with 1Instead, I grab cookies filled with processed sugar, flour, corn syrup, and bad fat. Why do I do it? Because, just like Eve, I can't seem to resist. It's like the cartoon with a devil on one shoulder and an angel on the other. One of them says "Eat the cookie. It's not going to kill you." The other says, "That stuff is poison. Go for the salad." Which one wins? The one who I cooperate with.

The sad part about Eve is that she only understood the truth **after** she ate the wrong food. There's nothing sadder than standing in front of your doctor and hear him say, "You have diabetes." Most of us eat our way into bad health and obesity. We think, *One little bite won't* *hurt.* But one leads to two, and two to three and eventually we gain weight, ruin our health, and work our way to an early death.

Notice this: **Eve's sin was not eating. It was eating the wrong food.** She made a poor food choice. Does any of this sound familiar? Can you relate? Please tell me I'm not the only one. All day long we are constantly tempted. It seems like one bite of the wrong food isn't a big deal, but poison is still poison, and our society offers us a lot of processed foods, that are toxic to our health and causes weight gain. It makes us feel terrible. I'm sure there's an angel telling us not to eat it, but we slap him around or put duct tape over his mouth. We prefer to listen to the other voice. Instead of "we," maybe I should say that **"I"** prefer to listen to that naughty voice. Why? Because I like cake better than celery.

There's more to the story of Adam and Eve, but it's just a small sample of what the Bible says about food. Here are some of my other favorites.

> John 21:12
> ***Jesus said to them*** (his disciples), ***"Come and have breakfast."***

Jesus wanted them to eat breakfast, but this wasn't a typical American breakfast. Jesus served fish, one of the healthiest foods on earth, and fresh baked barley bread. No fruits or vegetables. Just fish and bread. Interesting way to start the day. Healthy protein. Healthy carbs, but if you read the whole story, his disciples had been out fishing all morning. Breakfast was actually served after working for a few hours. I'm guessing they were well-hydrated during those hours, but no food. I'm not trying to change your mind about breakfast, but just giving a different viewpoint.

Proverbs 25:16

If you find honey, eat just enough – too much of it and you will vomit (NIV).

This one is self-explanatory. It's okay to have a few sweets occasionally, but moderation is key. Besides, honey is healthy. Sugar isn't. Too much of anything isn't good for you.

Mark 14:38

Jesus said to Peter, *"Keep watching and praying that you may not enter into temptation. For the spirit is willing, but the flesh is weak."* (NAS)

Wow! Isn't that the truth! In my spirit, I'm willing to diet. Way down inside, I'm more than willing to give up my favorite foods and be a little hungry, but my flesh won't cooperate. So frustrating! However, there's good news in this Bible verse. I can get help. It says I can pray. Prayer strengthens me.

There are other verses that can help you, like the ones about patience. We all want to be more patient especially when it comes to dieting, but the correct translation for the "patience" is "long suffering." You might ask for patience, but when was the last time you asked God, "Please help me to suffer for a long time"? However, when you diet, you have to be patient. That means you have to suffer for a long time.

Even Paul, the man who wrote a large part of the Bible said, *"For I do not do the good I want to do, but the evil I do not want to do – this I keep on doing."* (Romans 7:19. NIV). This sounds like me when I'm trying to lose weight. I know what I want to do, but I can't seem to do it. Paul may have failed, but he didn't quit. Later, he wrote these words. *"I have fought the good fight. I have finished the race."* (II Timothy 4:7 NLT). This means he overcame whatever he was struggling with. It's comforting to know that the great people of the Bible failed. They struggled like I do, like we all do. At the same time, we can learn from their mistakes and feed on their wisdom. Better yet, they finally overcame.

If the Bible seems hard to understand, try *The Living Bible*. It was written by a man who had twelve children. He wanted them to learn God's word, but the only Bible he had was the *King James* version with all the "Thee's" and "Thou's." He knew they would have a hard time understanding it. That motivated him to rewrite the Bible on the level of a ten-year-old, so he could read it to his children. That's how *The Living Bible* came into being. I like it too. I have a master's degree, but this simple version is my favorite, fun and easy to read. Please know that *The Living Bible* is not a word-for-word translation, but it's a great interpretation of what God wants to share with us.

If you want to know where to start, go to the middle of the Bible and read Proverbs filled with wisdom It was written by King Solomon, the wisest man who ever lived. Proverbs has hundreds of wise sayings, common sense, and a lot of humor. The neat thing about Proverbs is that there are thirty-one short chapters, one for each day of the month. If it's the fourth-day of the month, I read the fourth chapter of Proverbs. If it's the fifth day, then I read Proverbs five. It only takes about ten minutes to read one of these chapter, but I get so much wisdom and insight that I read it over and over.

Finally, to get them most out of my Bible, I say a short prayer before I read, asking God for understanding. God promises to give wisdom to those who ask for it. It's in the Bible.

FOURTEEN

When All Else Fails

On January 11, 2005, just before bed, I stepped on the bathroom scale. 199.99 pounds! I couldn't believe it! How was it possible? I had been so careful, making one sacrifice after another. I had been trying so hard, but I just kept gaining. No big gains, but a pound here, a pound there. No matter what I did, the weight continued to creep up.

I threw myself on my bed, erupting tears. I didn't want to be a fat lady, but now, at nearly 200 pounds, I was. *Why, God? Why?* Tears ran down my cheeks, onto my pillow. *God, help me. I don't know what to do. I keep trying, but nothing works.* My tears and heartfelt prayer continued. I tried to pull myself together, but whenever that number popped back into my mind, the tears resurfaced. Two-hundred pounds! How? I had given up red meat, sugar, and junk food, not to mention bad fats and bad carbohydrates, but clearly it wasn't enough. I had been gaining a pound-a-month for nearly four years and nothing worked! I called out to God again, but did He really care?

I kept wondering, how? My tears turned to anger. Why wasn't God doing something, anything? I did my part. He needed to do His. I began to moan, complain, and cry again when all of a sudden, it dawned on me. **I had been talking to God, but wasn't allowing**

God to talk to me. Although I've never heard Him audibly, I knew He spoke to my heart or some would say to "my conscience." Either way, I decided to be still, stop complaining, and ask. *God, I don't know what to do. Tell me what to do. I'll do anything.* I expected to lie on my bed for several hours, begging, waiting for a reply. I was wrong. The thought came quickly and clearly. **Count calories.**

My mind raced. I remembered back to my "thin years," when I was a teenager. That's exactly what I did. I wouldn't dream of putting anything in my mouth unless I weighed it, measured it, wrote it down, and counted every calorie. It was work, but I was thin.

I snapped back to reality. My tears vanished, replaced by hope. I fell asleep thanking God for His answer and His love for me.

The next morning, when I opened my eyes, those two words "count calories," were foremost on my mind. Instead of dragging myself out of bed like I usually did, I sat up straight, ready to start a new day. I was still struggling with chronic fatigue, but forced myself to dress quickly. After my girls left for school, I started a load of laundry, then climbed in my car and headed to my favorite book store to pick up a calorie-counter book. When I got there, I knew I wanted a booklet small enough to fit in my purse. I chose *The T-Factor Gram Counter.* Besides the size, I liked that it counted calories, carbohydrates, and fat. Unlike the other booklets, it also included fast-food places. Six bucks!

After picking up my booklet, I drove to the local one-stop shopping center and picked up a purse-sized tablet of paper to keep track of my calories, a food scale to weigh my food, and last of all, a cheap calculator. That was it. Less than $20.00. I had everything I needed to get started. It was a turning point, finally!

That year, I diligently counted every calorie and lost eight pounds. Most people say, "That's not very much!" Yes, but that's the size of a healthy newborn! I was losing my belly. Slow but steady, just like the turtle in *The Tortoise and the Hare*, a little here, a little there, and don't quit. The tortoise wins by a hair.

Then next year, I lost seven pounds. I was down fifteen pounds. That's a bowling ball. The third year, I lost another eight pounds. That's twenty-three pounds altogether, the size of a two-year-old.

The next two years I maintained. No losses. No gains. In some ways, it was frustrating, but my common sense told me, that's victory! Since then it's just been one-or-two-pounds-a-year, but I finally stopped gaining! God heard my prayer and answered. All I had to do was obey.

Part of my problem was that I had been looking for an easy answer. "Pop a pill," said the skinny lady on TV. And Dr. Oz often gave simple techniques that made it sound like I could lose a lot of weight if I took his advice.

In Proverbs 9:6 it says, "Leave your simple ways and live." Counting calories is not simple. Not that hard, but definitely not as easy as popping a pill. It takes time and effort. I've tried all those "simple" ways. Whenever I go back to them and quit counting calories, I gradually start gaining.

Counting calories works. It's affordable, and scientifically proven. Here's a fact: if you eat more than you burn off, you gain. If you eat less than you burn off, you lose. God had it all figured out.

Since that night many years ago, I learned a few things about dieting. First, I learned that it's okay to pray about my weight. Even though I had prayed regularly about "important things," it seemed silly to bother the God-of-the-Universe with something as trivial as my pot belly or pudgy thighs. Since that night, I've learned that God wants me to talk to Him about everything. If it's important to me, it's important to Him.

Second, I've learned that when I talk to God, I need to stop talking and start listening, a two-way conversation, not a gripe session. In Matthew 6:10 (*The Lord's Prayer*), Jesus told us to pray, "Thy will be done." How can I know His will if I don't stop and listen? Asking is good. Listening is better, but He isn't going to butt-in and talk to me while I'm rambling on and on. He's a gentleman. My motto is "Why bother asking, if I don't want to hear what He has to say?"

All those years, He wanted to talk to me, but I wasn't open to hearing Him, or maybe I was so busy complaining that I couldn't hear what He had to say.

Picture yourself going to the doctor with a fever and sore throat. Then you decide to leave before he gives you a diagnosis or a prescription. Imagine the look on the doctor's face as you walk out the door. I can almost hear him saying, "Excuse me," following you out of his office. "Excuse me. I need to talk to you." The doctor would be confused, and you would still be sick.

Sounds crazy, but I used to do that to God. Whining and complaining was so much easier than listening and cooperating. When I complained, I played the victim. I got to act like a baby.

I'm still learning. Sometimes, I don't want to hear what God is telling me. When He does, I have to ask myself, "Do I want to respond?" I get to choose. When God tells me something, I have to stop playing the victim. God often tells me something I don't want to hear, but I try to cooperate. It's for my own benefit. I'm learning to trust Him and His wisdom.

My Daily Walk:

Every day, I get to choose if I want to talk to Him or not. I get to decide if I want to listen or not. God doesn't force His will on me or anyone, but here is what I've noticed. When I get up in the morning, get busy, and forget to pray, I eat more, and usually unhealthy, fattening foods. In addition, I can't seem to stop eating once I start. I feel out-of-control, like I'm falling off a cliff with nothing to stop my fall.

However, if I pray and ask God for His help, I notice two things. First, I usually make better choices, like a piece of fruit instead of a cookie. I eat more vegetables too. I've also noticed that I have more

A NEW PERSPECTIVE ON DIETING AND WEIGHT LOSS

will power. If I start to pick up a cookie, or I start to go for seconds, resisting is easier, but only if I'm "prayed up."

The interesting part about prayer is that I don't always remember to do it. How stupid is that? Praying is so simple, but I still space it. **If someone gave me a pill that helped me lose weight, I know I would remember to take it, but I don't always remember to pray.** However, I've learned the hard way that prayer works. It's not mind-over-matter. It's a loving God, helping me with my needs. He cares.

Doesn't it make sense, that the God who created you, would want to spend time with you? Wouldn't someone who loves you want to talk to you, and help you, the way a loving father would? It also makes sense that He wants to stretch us, and show us how to grow, change, and mature. If He's our Father, He wants to help us, just like a good earthly father would.

Prayer is the best-kept secret of weight-loss. It's the one thing I still forget, but it works. Best of all, it's free, designed specifically for my individual needs.

For me, I will always have that night when I cried out to God, and a very gradual weight-loss to remind me that God cares about every detail of my life, including my weight. He really does answer prayer. I used to say, "When all else fails, pray." Now I say, "Pray first, so I don't fail." A heart-felt prayer was the turning point in my weight loss.

FIFTEEN

The Joy of Fasting

Before beginning any fast or change in your diet, check with your physician or health-care provider. To fast, simply means "to abstain from food". There are so many benefits of fasting that I can't begin to list them all. Originally, people fasted for religious purposes, skipping meals in order to spend time with God. They fast as a sacrifice to show their love and devotion for Him. However, modern medicine has proven that fasting has incredible healthy benefits. Best of all, it's a quick weight-loss trick, and there's a way you can do it without falling over dead.

The benefits.

<u>Medically</u>: Have you ever noticed what doctors do when you go to the hospital emergency room? They start by telling you that you can have nothing by mouth (N.B.M.). In other words, they force fasting. Then they give you an I.V. That means they stick a needle in your veins that fills you with water, sugar and salt. This combination is similar to your blood make-up, but NO FOOD. Emergency-room doctors understand that fasting is the quickest way to turn a person's

health around. A lack of food gives a body complete rest. Within hours, the doctors often send you home.

Digesting food is hard work. Many of us need to give our digestive system a complete break. I know I do, but I didn't want to wait until I was in the emergency room, half dead. Besides, hospital visits are expensive, and disrobing in front of a hot doctor isn't fun either.

One of my favorite books, *Prescription for Nutritional Healing* states, "Fasting is recommended for any illness, as it gives the body the rest it needs to recover." Did you see the phrase "any illness" and "gives the body a rest"? This book also says that fasting is ". . . an effective and safe method of helping the body detoxify itself." So, if you've been sick or unhealthy, and nothing has worked, ask your doctor about fasting.

Weight loss: *The Columbian Newspaper* (Vancouver. WA) carried an article about fasting on February 13, 2009. They interviewed a guy named Dennis Brooks who at age 60 had been struggling with his weight. He noticed that when he skipped breakfast, he started losing weight. (So much for the-most-important-meal-of-the-day theory.) After a while, he started skipping lunch. Now he fasts on alternate days, one day on, one day off. He's lost 50 pounds, gained energy, and says that his blood pressure and cholesterol levels are down. He recently published a book "The Skip-a-Day Diet System." Right now, your doctor is stamping his foot and throwing a fit. Most doctors would disagree, but read on.

The National Institutes of Health is now supporting calorie-restriction research at three medical centers. Dr. Luigi Fontana studies show that " . . . **people who fast are not malnourished and have excellent cardiovascular health.**"

A food writer from Seattle, Kathleen Flinn recently started a once-a-week fast. She said, "I tried to diet and exercise, but I felt I was missing a piece of the puzzle." She said that fasting helped make her aware of what she was eating. I agree! Whenever I stop eating, I realize that I'm eating almost all day, nonstop. Fasting gives me a new perspective, painful but good.

Clearly, fasting has numerous benefits, but like all other dietary changes, please CONSULT YOUR PRIMARY HEALTH CARE PROVIDER OR PHYSICIAN BEFORE FASTING.

How to fast without dying:

A true fast means no food at all. I don't recommend doing that for obvious reasons. Even when they put you in the hospital, they inject you with salty, sugar-water. However, most of the modern fasts encourage people to either drink fresh squeezed juice or eat something that I call "Horrible Soup." Yuk! It has cabbage, tomatoes, carrots, rutabagas, onions, garlic, celery, and water. The word "horrible" doesn't do it justice, but if you want to fast and not faint, **and** lose weight quickly, I have a recipe for Horrible Soup in my recipe chapter, but I'm warning you, you'll gag.

I do have some good news. When I fast, I make something I call *Healthiest Lemonade*. It's yummy, has nine simple ingredients. Each one is extremely healthy and important. Here it is.

Ingredient # 1 and 2 - Lemons and Limes: (I guess it wouldn't be lemonade without the lemons.) Lemons and limes are so healthy that I could write another book on it, but I will give you just a few of the basics. You already know that they're loaded with vitamin C, but they also have something called 'bioflavonoids". This is an important antioxidant more powerful than vitamins C, E, or beta-carotene. Bioflavonoids help prevent cancer.

These two lovely citrus fruits also have potassium which relieves water retention. (Smile ladies.) People who retain water are often told to give up salt, but the real problem is usually a lack of potassium. A healthy balance of potassium helps the body make the correct use of salt, so water retention is relieved. Potassium is also important for a healthy nervous system, regular heart rhythm, prevents stroke, and aids in muscle contraction. Lemons and limes lower histamines which control allergies naturally. They also are known to lower cholesterol levels, and cleanse the liver. If that's not enough these little sour babies contain (are you ready?) Vitamins A, C, E, K, thiamin, riboflavin, niacin, vitamin B6, K, folate, pantothenic acid, and that's just the vitamins. They also contain the following minerals: calcium, iron, magnesium, phosphorus, zinc, copper, and selenium. Whew! Quite simply, they are extremely good for you.

Lemons and limes also have a cleansing effect on the digestive system, cleaning out your stomach, liver, colon, kidneys, and other organs. Dr. Stanley Burroughs, creator of *The Lemonade Diet* recommends his lemonade diet to his patients who have ulcers. That's right. **Dr. Burroughs believes ulcers are caused from excess mucous, not acid.** According to him, lemons actually heal ulcers. Exactly the opposite of what most doctors tell you. (By the way, my recipe is much different than his.) These two citrus fruits are so cleansing that beauty queens and movie stars drink lemon-lime water to give their skin a healthy glow.

You may wonder, "Why lemons **and** limes, both? Because lemons have vitamins and minerals that limes don't have and vice-a-versa. The combination of the two loads you with dozens of nutrients your body desperately needs.

There are several ways you can get lemon or lime juice. I like to buy *Santa Cruz* 100% organic juice in glass bottles at the health food store. They are about $5.00 a bottle, but two bottles last several months. When I have the bottles sitting in my house, it's easy to add them to almost anything my family drinks. I want them to be healthy too.

If I want to squeeze it myself, I use a plastic lemon juicer I got from Walmart for about $8.00. This is a cute little device has a plastic bowl on the bottom with a pour-spout, and a little pointy thing with slits on the top. All I do is cut the lemon in half and push it down on the pointy part and twist back and forth. In my head, I sing, *Come* on Baby. Let's Do the Twist. (Now I'm going to have that song stuck in my head.) Anyway, the juice slides down through the slits into the bowl. Then, I push the pulp through the slits for extra fiber. Finally, I pour the juice in the pitcher. My grandkids love this little contraption. Cheap and entertaining. Whatever you do, DO NOT buy that cheap, artificial crap that comes in a plastic lemon. Get the real thing.

My friend buys organic lemons and limes and puts the whole thing (peelings too) in a juicer. You can also put it in all in a blender with two cups of clean water. Whiz on high. When done, pour it through a sieve or strainer, but some people have a hard time digesting the peelings. I get a stomach ache when I eat the peelings, even when it's strained. Don't forget. If you want to use the lemon peels, buy organic. If it's not organic, the peelings absorb toxic chemicals.

Ingredient #3 - 100% Real Maple Syrup: It's hard to believe that something so sweet and delicious can be healthy, but it is. Like lemons and limes, it's laden with vitamins and minerals, but especially **calcium and iron, two minerals most of us don't get enough of.** It also contains vitamins A, B5, B2, niacin, pantothenic acid, biotin, potassium, magnesium, and manganese. Each one of these vitamins and minerals do something different, but all are important to maintaining good health. The good news is that biotin together with pantothenic acid helps boost your metabolism and gives you energy too. Better yet, maple syrup doesn't cause spikes in your blood sugar like most other sweeteners do. (There is some controversy about this, so if you're diabetic or hypoglycemic, **please ask your doctor.**)

Just to clarify, the maple syrup I'm referring to is the **100%, pure maple syrup.** (The other stuff is mostly sugar and corn syrup. Do NOT use that.) However, there are two small problems with real maple syrup. First, it does have some calories, about 50 per tablespoon, but in my recipe, it works out to 25 calories per ten-ounce glass. Not a lot, but not calorie-free either.

The other problem is that real maple syrup is expensive. But if you only use it when you fast (which should be rare) it's not that expensive. (If you stop buying potato chips, candy, cookies, and other junk food, you come out ahead.) In addition, you will be healthier and have fewer doctor bills. Praise God. If you are really struggling financially, you can substitute black-strap molasses for the syrup. It's not as tasty, but it has multiple minerals such as iron, calcium, manganese, and magnesium. It also has B6. Some studies say that molasses prevents cancer and heart attacks, give energy, cleans the colon, builds strong bones, soothes the stomach, and aids in weight loss. All that is wonderful, but be sure you get the molasses that says "Black Strap." Plain old molasses has less minerals. Molasses are not expensive and lasts for a year or more if kept in the refrigerator.

Ingredient # 4 - Stevia: This is a no-calorie, no carb, healthy sweetener. (Actually, the Federal Government said that we aren't allowed to call a sweetener, but I don't know what else to call it since that's what it is, and that's what it does, but what do you expect from the Feds?) If you want to know more about Stevia, go to the chapter "The Fatal Five". (Stevia's not fatal. It's a healthy substitute for sugar.) I use Stevia in this lemonade recipe to make it taste good. Also, I can use less maple syrup. This helps cut calories and cost.

Ingredient # 5, MSM powder: MSM is a natural food supplement. MSM stands for Methyl-Sulfonyl-Methane. (Now don't you feel enlightened?) It is an odorless, crystal-white powder, that looks a lot like cocaine, so I've been told. For now, ignore the words Methyl and Methane and notice the word between the two 'M's, "sulphur." Every cell in your body screams for sulfur. MSM is the absolute best way to get the greatly needed mineral, sulphur. Sulphur is the most important mineral that anyone and everyone should take, at least in my never-to-be-humble opinion, but please ask your doctor. In rare cases, some people are allergic to it.

Natural sulphur is found in the tissues and fluids of all living organisms, and is essential for life! It is one of the few food-supplements that goes all the way down to the cellular level. It disinfects the blood and helps resist bacteria. In addition, MSM nourishes the hair, skin and nails, relieves pain and inflammation, reduces allergies and cleanses the bowels. Sulfur is the key ingredient in garlic that makes it so healthy, but sulphur doesn't cause bad breath.

Many years ago, we got all of our necessary sulfur from fresh fruits and vegetables, meats, and some grains. Unfortunately, storing and cooking, and growing food in chemicals destroys most of this life-giving nutrient, making us seriously deficient.

MSM is particularly good for older people because as we age, our cells become hardened, which block nutrients from entering. MSM softens cells to accept more nutrients. Sulfur is one of the best ways to stave off the aging process.

I have a friend whose life and health turned around when she started taking MSM. It's a miracle mineral. You can take MSM in tablet form, but the powder is more absorbable.

If the government passed a law saying that we could only take one food supplement or mineral, I would choose this miracle mineral. It is almost as important as water, yet none of us get enough of it. The recommended daily allowance is not clear, but I take 2,000 mg. However, I started SLOWLY with 500 milligrams-a-day because it detoxifies. Whenever I detox, I do it slowly. Also, some people are allergic, another reason to go slow. You can buy it in a pill form if you want, but the powdered form the best. I take the pharmaceutical grade MSM from *Kala Healthy MSM Organic Crystals*. It's not bitter like some of the others. I get it from www.EarthTurns.com. It's probably on Amazon too, but I prefer to support the smaller companies.

Ingredient #6 - Carrot Juice: Yukkie! Is that what you're thinking? Don't worry. Carrot juice is quite sweet and hides well other juices. It adds an interesting flavor that's really not "yukkie." Besides, when you mix it with lemons, limes, water, Stevia, and maple syrup they cover up the taste. I've given it to my grandkids when they think they're drinking pure orange juice. They never say a word. I add it to spaghetti sauce too. No one knows it's in there.

Carrot juice has beta carotene which your body converts into vitamin A. Two tablespoons of carrot juice contain enough beta carotene and vitamin A to last all day. Only 10% of us get the recommended daily allowance of vitamin A. This vitamin usually comes from yellow vegetables. How often do you eat a carrot or squash? Vitamin A contains a powerful antioxidant that helps prevent cancer, heart disease, and stroke. Vitamin A is a natural healer too. If you're unhealthy, vitamin A improves your health especially shingles, herpes, and skin diseases. It can also help with night blindness.

Vitamin A doesn't wear off quickly like other vitamins. You can either take two tablespoons of carrot juice-a-day or one-cup-a-week. That's plenty to get you through the week. If you don't want to drink carrot juice, plan to eat a few carrots or other yellow vegetables like cantaloupe, pumpkin, or yams, but carrot juice is the best. You need your vitamin A.

<u>Ingredient # 7, Vitamin C powder or crystals:</u> I use vitamin C instead of flu shots or to prevent colds. If I'm taking it regularly, I rarely get sick. Why do you think that "Cold-Eeze" works so well? It's mostly vitamin C. The lady who invented it knew how effective vitamin C was, so she squished it into a pill and made ten-million dollars. (Darn! Wish I would have done that!) She has followers all over the world who swear by her product. They have tried it and have proven how effective it is.

I get my vitamin C powder from Swanson's Vitamin company or *Nature's Way Alive* from Amazon is high quality, but most pharmacies and drug stores carry some form of vitamin C. The recommended daily allowance (RDA) is 60 milligrams. WOW! That's just enough to prevent scurvy. I take 2,000 mg. per day, but never worry about getting too much. The best thing about vitamin C is that your body will tell you if you are getting too much. You will get diarrhea. I take 400 times the RDA, and have never had the trots. Here's a hint about how much to use. A naturopath once told me to gradually increase my vitamin C until I got diarrhea. Then cut back slightly. Ask your doctor. (Of course, he will tell you it's not necessary, but I have to say it anyway.)

Ingredient # 8 - Chia seeds: One of the biggest problems with fasting is a lack of fats. Fat gives you energy, and chia seeds are healthy way to get your fats. The best thing about these seeds is that they have those healthy omega 3's that Dr. Oz is always talking about.

This is one ingredient you need to add need to add right before you drink it. Chia seeds are like little sponges. They thicken your drink.

Ingredient # 9 – Clean water: I already discussed clean water, but it's so important. To make sure my drinking water is clean, I run it through a *Brita* water filter. Then I boil it and cool it. Please don't use plain tap water. Most of the time, it's unhealthy. If you want to keep it simple, just boil your water before bed. It will be safe to drink the next morning.

Just for taste, I sometimes add a packet of *True Lime*, little packets of flavoring similar to *Kool-Aid* except healthier. I add it to my healthy lemonade to make it taste good. My theory is "If it tastes bad, I won't drink it." *Healthiest Lemonade* tastes fairly good, but the *True Lime* makes it a pleasure. I usually use one or two small, **single-serving** packets. That's plenty. Please understand that this one ingredient is NOT particularly healthy, but it adds a lot of flavor.

So, here's the part you've been waiting for, my recipe. Makes about two quarts. I also included a recipe for one cup.

Healthiest Lemonade
3 tbls. lemon juice (more if you want)
3 tbls lime juice (more if you want)
½ cup 100% Maple Syrup
½ - 1 ½ teaspoons powdered MSM (start low)
1/3 cup carrot juice
2 - 6 packets Stevia (to taste)
2 teaspoon vitamin C powder (it's sour)

2 tablespoons Chia Seeds
1 scoop fruit/vegetable powder
1 or 2 packets of *True Lime* single-serving (totally optional)
7 cups clean water
Mix together all ingredients.
3 tablespoons chia seeds (add just before serving)
Serve over ice. Keep refrigerated.
(It's delicious hot, but I add the MSM **after** I heat it.)

Mix all ingredients except the chia seeds.
Add 1 teaspoon of seeds to each cup just before drinking.
If you want to try a thick drink, add the seeds ahead of time. It's interesting.

Makes 8 cups, about 40-calories-a-cup, with some healthy fats and about three carbohydrates.
If I'm fasting, I don't worry about the calories or carbs.

Making this will seem time-consuming to start, but now I rarely measure anything. I just dump everything together. It just takes a few minutes and it's worth it!

I love this drink because I know I'm getting dozens of nutrients without the calories. It also has a cleansing effect and I want my insides to shine like Tyler Perry's teeth after visiting the dentist. More importantly, I'm always trying to get healthy. *Healthiest Lemonade* is healthy, extremely healthy, especially if you leave out the *True Lime*.

Sometimes, I like to start my day with a healthy cleanse and don't have any made up, so I just squeeze a teaspoon or two in a glass of clean water. Then I add two packets of Stevia, a tablespoon of carrot juice, and a sprinkle of MSM, Finally, a teaspoon of vitamin C. Sometimes I add a small packet of *True Lime*. I don't measure any of it. I just throw it together. It's a great way to start my day especially when I don't eat breakfast. Sometimes, I like to make a pitcher of this amazing drink and keep it handy in case I get hungry. It's a handy-dandy, healthy drink to fill in between meals.

Now here's the important part. When I'm fasting, I get hungry. That's okay. It's normal. Most of the time, I ignore it or just pray. However, if I get shaky, I add a little bit of food, usually five or six nuts and a tablespoon of sunflower seeds or pumpkin seeds. I do this because I'm a very busy woman and I don't want to faint. Nuts, seeds give me some energy and are two of the healthiest foods in the world. They also have beneficial fats, easy to digest. More importantly, our bodies scream for fat, especially when fasting. I like walnuts because they are a great brain food, good for people with ADHD. (That would be me.) Almonds are great too, but if you are on a budget, you can substitute peanut butter or peanuts for the nuts. Cheap and healthy. I ONLY eat if it's necessary. A fast is a fast.

<u>Two more recommendations:</u> If I'm fasting **all day**, I also drink a glass of warm salt water. Most of us get too much salt, but when you fast and drink *Healthiest Lemonade*, you don't get enough. We lose salt whenever we go to the bathroom and when we sweat (or glisten). We have to replace the lost salt to be healthy. We just need a little but PLEASE DON'T USE WHITE TABLE SALT! I buy *100% Himalayan Mineral Salt Crystals*. You can get this from most grocery stores or from Amazon. These salt crystals have 84 minerals, and six trace elements. Can you believe it? Salt that's good for you! You can also buy something called *Real Salt*, sold in most major shopping centers. It has brown and tan speckles and almost as good as the *Himalayan Salt*. Either way, I just put ½ to 1 teaspoon of these salt crystals in two cups of warm water and pretend that it's broth, sipping throughout the day. (Use more if you sweat a lot.) Sometimes I put a ½ teaspoon in a little glass dish. I lick my finger, dip it in, and lick again. Makes me feel like a kid. Some people stir their salt in the *Magic Lemonade*. Tastes like *Gatorade*, but I don't like salty lemonade.

The other recommendation when fasting is green tea and lots of it. It also is loaded with antioxidants, vitamins and mineral, regulates your blood sugar, balances insulin, but best of all it is known to increase your metabolism, increase energy and decrease your appetite. It's been used for years as a weight-loss trick. However, **never mix green tea with milk or milk products.** Milk decreases the efficacy of green tea. (Efficacy is a fancy word for effectiveness.)

<u>Before I fast</u>, I have a question I need to ask myself. **"Why am I fasting?"** Is it for spiritual reason? Health reasons? Weight loss? It's important for me to understand why I'm doing it. If it's for spiritual reasons, I never cheat. It's like a promise to God and I want His blessing. After I answer that, I need to ask myself, "How long will I fast?" Finally, I have to figure out what type of fast I will do. All decisions are connected.

<u>A mini-fast:</u> I do this baby-fast twice-a-week, mostly to keep me from gaining, not spiritual. It's pretty simple. Nothing after 7:00 p.m. and nothing before 11:00 the next morning, except for *Healthiest Lemonade*. I call it "The 7/11 Fast." During this time of hunger, I plan my meals and snacks. When I'm done with that, I find something to do, so I don't start eating. I've done these mini-fasts long enough that it's just habit. I sort of look forward to it.

<u>A one-day fast</u> is what I usually do when I've fallen off the diet wagon, or I'm up a few pounds and can't seem to get rid of it. A one-day fast helps puts me back on track and it's a quick weight-loss trick. I also do a short fast if something is weighing heavily on my heart. Then, it's more for spiritual reasons. That answers the "why" and "how long."

When I do a one-day fast, I make a pitcher of *Healthiest Lemonade* and drink it throughout the day. Later in the day, I have a cup of vegetable soup, and a few nuts and seeds. I also drink a lot of tea and take my vitamins. Occasionally, I add some cooked vegetables or a piece of fruit. Altogether, this is about three-hundred calories. It gives me a little bit of everything, and plenty for someone who is fasting! It's more than most other fasts. Some don't allow anything but water. My fast gives me enough energy to get through my busy day and keeps me from fainting. Occasionally, I will have a light supper before bed so I can sleep better.

<u>Longer fasts:</u> I do these twice-a-year, for spiritual reasons. A long fast is very different than a short one. The first one is on January first, my friend's church fasts-and-prays for three weeks! I always fast with them and then go to their healing service at the end of three weeks. The power and presence of God is amazing.

The second fast of-the-year is Lent which lasts for forty days. This was started in the Catholic church to prepare a person's heart for Easter, to celebrate the resurrection of Christ. Many churches followed their lead. It's a wonderful idea.

These fasts are more like a sacrifice than a fast. I don't stop eating. Instead, I just give up a few foods, usually sugar, wheat, potatoes, and corn, also known as "The Fatal Four." It may not sound like much but it seems like an eternity whenever I do. However, it has a strange but powerful impact on my spiritual life. It's something I can't put into words. Just a feeling of being closer to God. Whichever way you decide to fast and for how long is entirely up to you.

<u>Now for the bad part.</u> When I fast, I get hungry. Most people do, but if you read my chapter on "I Get Too Hungry," then you know that hunger isn't a big deal most of the time. When I'm hungry, I know I'm losing weight. Hunger isn't my goal. Weight-loss is, but I refuse to let hunger stop me from my goals. If I want to find sympathy, I can look it up in the dictionary, somewhere between stupid and syringe.

The other problem with fasting is that it can be dangerous. Although fasting has numerous medical benefits, it can lead to low blood sugar, a diabetic coma, and even death, which is why I encourage all people to **talk to their physician before fasting.** I also want you to eat or drink something with nourishment in it throughout the fast, either *Healthiest Lemonade* or *Horrible Soup* (in the recipe chapter), or both.

I don't recommend eating nothing, unless your name is Moses or Jesus. Something to consider about these two amazing men is this.

When they fasted, they didn't chase kids or do housework. Instead, they sat quietly and prayed. Don't try to do a lot when you fast. Keep in mind that although you will be getting a lot of vitamins and minerals though the lemonade, you won't be getting 100%. Instead, you will get a little bit of almost everything.

Overall, I believe that fasting is not only an important part of weight-loss, but the missing component. It's also a great benefit to our health.

Finally, fasting feels good spiritually. When I fast, it adds strength to my prayer life and I feel closer to God. That's joy.

SIXTEEN

Five Pounds by Friday

Have you ever said, "I'm going to lose five pounds by Friday"? Please don't tell me I'm the only one. I used to set these ridiculous, unrealistic goals, then was devastated when I couldn't reach them. The Bible says, *"Hope deferred makes the heart sick* (Proverbs 13:12, NASB)." This Scripture made me angry. I felt like I was getting heart sick from not losing enough the weight I wanted. One time I was upset, so I asked God, "What does this verse mean, God? I keep hoping, but nothing happens." I felt God whisper to my heart, **"Stop hoping."** What? God doesn't want me to hope? He says faith, hope, and love are great! However, **He wants me to stop hoping for something ridiculous or something that's not in His will.** Since "hoping" is a thought, that must mean I can control my thoughts!

But I had to wonder, *Can I really control my thoughts?* Apparently, I can. It's in the Ten Commandments. "Thou shalt not covet…"(KJV). The word "covet" means to "deeply desire." That can be translated, "You are not supposed to have a 'deep desire' for things that aren't in God's will." God will supply what you need. Consequently, it's not healthy to constantly brood about something that He doesn't want for you.

A NEW PERSPECTIVE ON DIETING AND WEIGHT LOSS

Therefore, I can choose what to hope for. I can **hope** to lose five pounds by Friday, but what happens when I get on the scale and I've only lost one pound? What happens if I keep hoping for something that's not God's will? I get mad and depressed.

Here's what I do now. **I never set deadlines for weight-loss anymore.** Instead, I reach for goals, much different than the old ones. My daily goal is to trust God more and let Him direct me. I know He wants me to eat healthy and to set boundaries on my eating.

Now my goal is to change my habits. That's it. It's all about habits. The habit I want to create is to put boundaries on my eating and do it daily. That means counting calories. The other habit I want to form is to make better choices. That means less junk food and more veggies. If I eat healthy and count calories every day (habit), then I'm bound to lose weight! How much I lose and when I lose it is up to God.

Every day, when I get up, I get to decide what habit I want to work on today. Am I going to wake up and start putting donuts in my mouth first thing in the morning or fresh fruit and a bowl of oatmeal. Am I going to eat a bag of chips or am I going to start with some green tea? Am I going to count every calorie or just make guesses? I have to ask myself, "What habit do I want to form today?" I need God's help to show me.

Another habit is to pray before I get out of bed. I used to stand in the kitchen and thank God for my French toast as it swam in syrup and butter. I prayed that I wouldn't eat more than one. It rarely worked.   Now I pray **before** I get to the kitchen, asking God what He wants me to eat. I stop and listen. Then I ask Him to help me be obedient. I also do better if I write down what I'm going to eat **before** I go to the kitchen. It activates a different part of the brain making it easier to eat right.

When it comes to habits, here is the important thing to remember. **Whatever I do today, I am going to do tomorrow.** It's a simple fact. If I eat a bunch of fattening foods without boundaries today, I'll most likely do it again tomorrow. If I do it tomorrow, I will do it the next day. On the other hand, if I eat healthy, count calories, and pray before I eat today, I will probably do it again tomorrow. Do you see the difference? Instead of setting a ridiculous goal, I'm simply working on creating new habits.

When I used to set weight-loss goals, I was constantly disappointed. It set me up to fail. Determination to form new eating habits gave me a daily choice of what I wanted to do. It gave me control. This gave me hope. New hope.

That way, when I step on the scale, I have some choices. First, if I've been losing, I can stop and thank God, then continue to do what I did the day before (or maybe all week). However, if I am not losing, I can ask God, "What did I do wrong? What habits do I need to change? What should I work on?"

Usually, when I pray this, I get an urge or a thought. "Go look in your food journal. When I do, it's right in front of my eyes. Last time, I did this, I had two days that I hadn't kept track of what I was eating, and three days with too many carbohydrates. It seems like it's something different every time. But when I pray first, I get amazing results.

Sometimes, when I pray, the only answer I get is "Be patient." That translates as "keep on keeping on." Just because I haven't lost any weight, doesn't mean I'm doing something wrong. I have to keep reminding myself: **My goal isn't to lose weight. My goal is to eat heathy, with boundaries, and form good habits. As I change my habits, my weight loss will follow.** How much weight or how fast I lose is up to God. That gives me hope.

SEVENTEEN

Accountability and Support

Accountability and support are not the same thing. "Accountability" is just a fancy word for "don't keep it a secret." Accountability is the opposite of ignorance. Ignorance might be bliss, but it keeps you fat. Ignorance means, "lacking knowledge." Ignorant people either "don't know" or they "don't want to know."

On the other hand, My *World Book* dictionary defines accountability as, "the state of being held responsible for carrying out one's obligations." So, when you go on a diet, you need something or someone to "hold you responsible for carrying out your obligations." In this case, your obligation is to control or change your eating habits which leads to weight loss. The bottom line is that accountability helps you to be honest with yourself and honest with others.

The good news is that you don't have to tell anyone what you weigh, because **the absolute simplest form of accountability is a bathroom scale.** For most of my diet journey, I had a cheap, ten-dollar scale that I bought on sale twenty years ago. However, three years ago, I finally bought a digital scale for $19.99. Either way, my scale keeps me accountable and honest.

I used to hate my scale. It used to yell at me, *Ow! Get off! You're killing me!* It kept telling me that I was gaining, but I wouldn't listen until it said, *Hey, Lady! Did you know that you're two-hundred pounds?* Now my scale is much nicer. It says, *Not bad. You lost another two ounces. Keep going.* It doesn't always say what I want it to say, but one thing I like about it. It never lies!

Usually, when people gain weight or are overweight, they hate weighing themselves so they stop. They don't want that accountability, but it's exactly what they need. A scale forces them to be honest with themselves and their eating habits.

As much as I hate it, I hop on it, daily. It keeps me accountable. Many of the "experts" tell us not to weigh every day, but it's right for me. Like I said in the last chapter, I don't worry if I didn't lose in one day. It's more about habits. **However, if I gain regularly, then I listen to my scale.** My scale lets me know if my eating habits are working or if I need to start a new habit. Sometimes, I hit a plateau. If I weigh the same for three or four weeks in a row, or if I start gaining, my scale helps me to know that I'm doing something wrong and I need to make some changes. A scale is the simplest and cheapest form of accountability. I weigh and record daily, but I also record weekly and monthly. That way I know for sure if I am losing or gaining.

The only problem with a scale is that it's easy to stop if you don't like what it's telling you, and that's what most people do. If you don't like the scale and don't want to weigh yourself, there are three more forms of accountability, a tape measure, a camera and a mirror. They don't lie. When it comes to our weight, most of us do. I was the queen. And the queen didn't like a scale, a mirror or a camera. These three items were discussed in the chapter "I Don't Look That Bad." If you skipped that chapter, you may need to go back and read it. Most of us don't want to know how bad we look. I didn't.

Support:

Support is different than accountability. My *Roget's Thesaurus* has so many words for support it's difficult to list them all, but her are a few: help, assist, nurture, reinforce, lend a hand, boost, stand behind, back up, etc. A support system is more personal than accountability alone. A bathroom scale can only report the truth. It won't applaud you when you lose, or give you a shoulder to cry on when you gain. (Thank God, it won't spank you.) That's where a support system comes to the rescue. Not to spank you, but to support you.

Weight loss groups are the best source of both accountability and support. In my opinion *TOPS* (an acronym for *Take off Pounds Sensibly)* is the best one out there. *TOPS Club, Inc.* is a nonprofit, noncommercial, weight-loss support organization with chapters located world-wide. (For more information go to www tops org.)

I absolutely love my *TOPS* group. I've made some wonderful friends, who have lovingly supported me over the past five years, not only in my weight loss, but in my illness, birthdays, and gifts for my foster children. Not all *TOPS* groups are this supportive, but they all have a few things in common. One thing they all do is weigh you every week. It forces accountability. They DON'T announce your weight to the group. Instead, the "weight-recorders" weighs you and everyone else in the group (privately) once-a-week in a back room. After everyone is weighed, we all get together in a large group. Then the weight-recorder calls role. When your name is called, you tell the group whether you gained, lost, or stayed the same. If you lose or stay the same, the group applauds and says, "Good job." If you gain, the group says, "We're here for you." After roll call, the "biggest loser" (for the week) stands up and we sing *We Have a Winner in Our Crowd.* Then the winner has a choice of either a "pin" or money from the "pig." (Oops. I mean "the treasury.") In addition, we have our "monthly biggest loser," and "quarterly biggest loser," with lots of awards, money, and accolades. **TOPS has so much positive feedback for losing weight, but more importantly, it makes you accountable while giving you support.**

It works for me because I get weighed every Thursday. If I've had a bad weekend with overeating, I start getting really serious on

Monday because I know that Thursday is coming. I'm thinking, *My TOPS group and that scale are waiting (weighting) for me, and I don't want to embarrass myself.* I don't want to hear them say, "We're here for you," because that's what they say if I gain. Worse yet, I don't want to let my group down, because we do a grand total of gains and losses. If our group has gained more than we lost, I don't want to be responsible. When my name is announced, I want to hear the applause (love it) and help the group to have a loss for the week. And every week, I really want to be the "biggest loser." I have to fight tears when they put a crown on my head and everyone stands up and sings to me. It's so cool! Every *TOPS* group is different. Some sing. Some don't. Some have weight-loss games. No matter what, they all give support and accountability.

There are two more things I love about *TOPS*. It's affordable, only $5.50 a month. That's not just affordable. That's cheap! Some popular weight-loss groups charge more than twice that much **per week** (not per month) a 900% increase! The other thing I like about *TOPS* is that they have a diet that they recommend, but you aren't forced to do their diet. If what you are doing isn't working, you can switch to a different diet or if you want you can try the latest fad diet. Better yet, you can just count calories.

Many churches have weight-loss groups that are inexpensive, give you support, and force you into accountability. Most of them make you write down everything you eat, which makes you feel obligated to do your duty, and most of them weigh you. Some offer prayer support. Any reputable weight-loss group is better than just getting on a scale at home, because you have to be honest. When I was fat, I was not honest, at least not about my weight. Besides, I didn't have the support.

If you don't have the time or money to join a group, diet with a friend. People are always talking about losing weight or going on a diet. Next time someone brings it up, ask them if they want a diet buddy. If you decide to do this, make some sort of plan. How often will you call each other or get together? Will you write down everything you eat? How often will you weigh yourself? Will you share your exact weight or just the losses? Plan it out; then write it down. Have some sort of reward system in place. (A hot-fudge sundae isn't a good reward.)

One of the best things you can do for support is to get your family members or someone you live with to diet with you. If you're a single parent, with small kids, this is easy. Just stop buying junk food and start feeding them more nutritiously. Center your meals around vegetables. Then, when you eat, count calories.

For older kids and teens, tell them that you love them and you want them to be healthy. Remind them that junk food causes zits, bloating, and gas. Most teenagers run from that. (Except teenage boys. They love gas.) As the parent, you have the right to say, "I don't want sugar or junk food in the house any more." (They have a way of finding it without your help.) Keep reminding them that you love them and want them to live a long time. Finally, give them five dollars if they will read *Sugar Blues*. (It will scare the sugar out of them.)

Your Spouse:

Ladies, if you can get your husband to diet with you, you are halfway there. Some wives say, "How can I get my husband to cooperate?" And I say, "Don't you know how much power you have?" Your husband loves you and cares about you. He chose you and took vows to love and cherish you.

In addition, a man wants his woman to look good. That's common knowledge. So ladies, go to your husband and put it in the form of a question. "Honey, how would you like it if I lost forty pounds and could fit into that little black dress?" Better yet, "Honey, if I lost enough weight, I would could wear a cute little "teddy" to bed. What do you think?" Most husbands will be thrilled! Wives have a powerful advantage, even more so if he wants to lose a few pounds. Most men want to look good too.

You can also take the "healthy" approach. Tell your husband that you love him and want him to live a long time. Let him know that sugar and processed foods cause diabetes, cancer, high blood pressure, and other diseases. Remind him of the high cost of health care (if that fits). Then bat your eyelashes and say, "Pretty please."

If he's not interested in his own health, let him know that. Tell him that losing weight is important, so you want to get the junk food out of the house. If he complains, tell him, he can stop and pick up some goodies on his way home, but please don't bring them in the house. Then thank him and give him a big, wet kiss. Remember, this is the guy who said, "For better or worse."

<u>Step two for wives.</u> According to the book *His Needs, Her Needs*, one of the things a man wants from his wife, is a recreational companion, someone to do things with. (That means you don't always have to take off your clothes.) He simply wants to hang out with you and do something fun, so if you want to exercise, you have someone right there to work out with. **Some men won't change their eating habits, but most will exercise.**

Which exercise? I don't recommend that you start playing basketball with him, if he's been playing for ten years. Instead, pick a new activity that you would both enjoy. Take a dance class or yoga. Join the Y. Go swimming. Try tennis. Get a bicycle built for two. Learn how to golf. Plan something new. Husbands and wives need a date night once-or-twice-a-week. Why not do something original while getting some exercise? Go for a hike in the woods. That's more romantic than an action-packed war movie.

One of my *TOPS* friends recently started losing a lot of weight. We asked her how she did it and she said that her husband bought a "Wii."

"A what?" asked all the women over fifty. She said something like, "There's Wii Fitness and also the Wii Games. It's so much fun. The fitness one is exercise, and the games are things like boxing, dancing and gymnastics, but they all have competitions to see who's the best.

My husband's always trying to break my record and I'm always trying to break his, and our kids are always trying to beat both of us!" She said that her whole family plays every night. It's brought them closer together, plus everyone is losing weight. If you can't afford a Wii right now, just go for a walk every night after supper. The fresh air is good for you, and walking hand-in-hand is romantic.

Oh, by the way, one of the best forms of exercise is sex. Most husbands won't complain if you suddenly want more sex. It burns calories and it will warm up your marriage.

Finally Ladies:

Ninety percent of the time you do the shopping. Do you realize how much power you have? If your husband doesn't want to join you in dieting, it's okay! When you go shopping, don't buy junk food, but let him know ahead of time. Buy fruits and vegetables. Read the labels. Buy "lite" mayo and salad dressings. Men rarely notice these small changes. Drink 1% milk. If you know your husband wants whole milk, get his milk for him and 1% for you. Milk is fairly cheap. If you are the shopper, you get to choose what to buy. Ultimately, you are in charge of your weight, no matter who encourages you or discourages you. It's up to you.

For Men Only:

Guys, you have it a little harder. You probably don't do the shopping or the cooking. Start by making a plan and then figure out what you want to do, like counting calories or cutting junk food. Take your wife out for coffee and tell her you want to talk to her. (Women love those kinds of things.) When you talk to her, she will probably be thrilled that you want to lose some weight. Hopefully she will want to join you. Most women want to lose a few pounds too, but don't suggest it to her. You could however, tell her how much you love her and you want her to be healthy. Or, tell her that you want to lose some weight and ask, "Could you help me?" Women love to help. That's how God made us. If she agrees, tell her your plans to count calories. Plan some meals and menus with her. Then, ask her if you can go shopping with her. (Oh my gosh! Now she is going to be in heaven.) When you shop, read labels. When it comes to dieting, it's always better to have someone special to lean on. It can be fun.

However, if you have a wife who isn't interested in dieting, you have a choice. You can either do it alone or you can bribe her. If you don't know how to bribe your wife, I can help you. Read the book, "The Five Love Languages." It shows you how to understand her, and what makes your wife feel good. Would she rather hear you say that she's the best woman on earth, or does she want you to give her a massage? Would she like it more if you washed the dishes or if you bought her a pretty pair of earrings? If you don't know, do all four of the things and see which one she responds to the most. "The Five Love Languages" will spice up your marriage, and motivate your spouse. When you find out what your wife likes, shower her in which ever area she responds to the most, but have fun with it.

After a few weeks, take her hand and talk to her again. Tell her that you really want to lose some weight and get healthy. Do NOT say one single word about her weight! Got it? Okay? Okay! You are only going to talk about yourself. Look her straight in the eyes and say, "I need your help. Would you please help me?" Most women will melt. Your woman loves. Tell her exactly what you need. Ask her to read a few chapters from this book especially the chapters on counting calories and prayer.

It is a powerful thing when a husband and wife can come together for love and support, especially if it's to change their life by losing weight and getting healthy.

Warning! Warning! Warning!

If you are going to diet together as husband and wife, DO NOT make it a competition. Here's why. Men have more muscle mass. Muscle burns fat. Consequently, men lose weight faster and easier than a woman. Men will lose three or four pounds to a woman's one pound, sometimes more. It is especially frustrating for the woman. Just count calories and pray. It doesn't matter how much you lose or how fast. It just matters that you don't quit.

Finally:

The all-time best support and accountability is God. He is a shoulder to cry on, and an ear to listen. His heart knows your heart. His hand reaches out to you and His loving arms will hold you. He created every part of you. Best of all, He loves you. He is your support and accountability.

EIGHTEEN

The Whole Enchilada

You've just "digested" a lot of information, so you're probably wondering, *Where do I start?* All of the information in the book is good for anyone who wants to lose weight, but now I will pull out what I feel are **the four most powerful diet tools in this book**. They are (1) prayer (3) planning (3) counting calories (4) accountability, aka weighing yourself.

For the first four years I was dieting, that is all I did. I just planned, prayed, counted calories, and weighed myself. Then the same thing the next day. Plan; pray; count calories; weigh myself. Plan; pray; count calories; weigh myself. That's all. I lost slowly, but I lost.

Now, I look at these four dieting tools like planting a seed. If I want to plant a seed, I need dirt and a seed, but I also need to make a plan and check on it, to check on the results.

That may not sound like much, but look at it this way. **Suppose this little seed you planted was worth ten million dollars. Would you be more interested?** Your body is worth far more than ten million dollars. There is no price on looking good and feeling good. So, what will you do? You are about ready to plant that ten-million-dollar seed. Here's what to do:

Tool # 1. Make a plan.

This was already discussed at the beginning, but it's so important to any diet. Buy what you need before you start. Then make a plan of action. When I plan, I start with my veggies, since I often neglect them. Part of your planning should include when you will start and how long you will diet.

Tool # 2. Write it down and count calories:

The simple act of writing things down will change how you eat. For example, if I'm looking at a pie, I may want the whole pie. Wait! Let me reword that. I know for sure that I want the whole pie, but if I write it down, I'm more likely to eat one piece, maybe two, but not the whole pie. Do I really want to write down, "I ate an entire pie today?"

Then, if I take the next step, counting calories, I'm even less likely to cheat. If one piece of pie is three-hundred calories, do I really want to eat two pieces? That's an entire meal plus some! If I write down ONE piece of pie **and** count calories, I'm even more aware of how much I just ate, which helps me to be honest and keeps me accountable. It's painful, but it works. And of course, I want ice cream with my pie. That's another hundred calories but only if I get the low-cal ice cream! Then, if I ate two pieces with ice-cream, I would have to write down eight-hundred calories! How stupid is that? But if I write it down, and count calories before I eat it, I'm less likely to cheat.

The bottom line for counting calories is this. If you take in (eat) more than you burn off, you are destined to gain. If you burn off more than you eat, **you will lose**. Counting calories gives a clear picture of how much you're eating. Consequently, if you write it down, you can see exactly how and why you are gaining, or hopefully losing.

Tool #3: Prayer

I love to laugh and clown around, but I also know that without prayer, I would still be fat. I know this book wouldn't exist. Through a simple, heartfelt prayer, I finally got started on a real diet. However, continual prayer is a necessary part too.

Here's a good example and true story. When I woke up this morning, I was so famished, I almost ate my pillow because I didn't think I could wait until I got to the kitchen. For some reason, I desperately wanted a bowl of ice cream. After all, it has milk in it, and milk has protein so it's good for me, right? As I walked out of my bedroom, I knew I need help and needed it badly. I was about to splurge. I cried out, *"Lord Jesus, help me!"* I asked Him to tell me exactly what to eat and to give me the self-control to help me to eat what I knew was right. As I prayed, I felt strongly like I was supposed to have a cheese omelet instead. (Lots of protein and healthy fats and filling.) It wasn't what I wanted, but I knew it was right. It was hard, but I submitted. While it was cooking, I ate a pear. It smelled great. As I bit into it, it tasted surprisingly good, but I had to pray again when the omelet was gone. Even though it was delicious and filling, I still wanted to bowl of ice cream, a big bowl of ice cream with hot fudge topping. So, I prayed again. Then I decided instead to have a cup of *Barb's Favorite Tea* with a tablespoon of coconut oil. I also took my morning vitamins. Finally, I was satisfied. There was still a tiny desire to eat ice cream, but when I walked out of the kitchen and got busy with the laundry, that desire faded.

You will notice that God gave me two things. Wisdom and willpower. The first time I prayed, God gave me **wisdom** to know what to eat. Some people think it's just mind-over-matter, but when I don't pray, those thoughts don't pop into my head. Besides, it's been happening to me for so many years that I've learned to listen to the gentle voice of God, answering my prayer. Seems logical that if you talk to someone Who loves you, that they would talk back and answer your cry for help. It's not complicated. I ask for wisdom. He answers. The Bible says in the book of James that He gives Wisdom to ANYONE who ask for it.

Remember, I have never heard God speak out loud. Instead, after I pray, I get a strong impression in my brain about what I'm supposed to eat and to my frustration, what I'm not supposed to eat.

When I pray I also have **will power.** Dieting is hard. Resisting my favorite foods is harder, but less difficult when I pray. Notice, I didn't say easy; just **less difficult.** I still have a free will. It's like living with a devil that I can't seem to get rid of, but when I pray, he loses his power. His voice fades. When I pray, he takes a short nap, but I don't trust him. I know he's coming back with a vengeance. I have to keep praying in order to keep him at bay. What's really dumb is when I choose not to pray or forget. When I do that, it's like I'm chasing a little devil around with a bag of chips in one hand and a Hostess *Ding Dong* in the other, yelling and screaming at him, thinking that the little imp is going leave. Instead, he's taunting me. All I have to do is pray. It's so simple, yet I don't always remember.

We have a loving Heavenly Father who wants to help us. We don't want our kids to be fat and unhealthy, and God doesn't want us to either. But remember, God not only fights off the enemy. He empowers us!

It's like when my granddaughter visits for the day and wants a cookie, I say, "Maybe after dinner." She understands that I love her and have her best interest at heart. She has peace. She knows that I'm not going to starve her. In the same way, we have a God Who created us, loves us, and knows what's best for us. He's just waiting for us to ask and wants us to trust Him. He gives us willpower, but also, we have peace after praying. Both are helpful for dieters.

What amazes me is how much willpower I suddenly feel after I pray. Often, after I pray, a cookie doesn't even sound good. Who says God doesn't still do miracles? It's the simplest, easiest thing a dieter can do, but we all seem to forget, even me. Praying works so well that it feels like I'm cheating.

Tool # 4. Weighing yourself:

Wouldn't it be silly to plant a seed, and never go back to see if it's growing, especially if it's worth a million dollars? It's the same with dieting. You need to know if your diet is working. Weighing yourself is the simplest and quickest way to do that. You don't have to tell anyone. You are the only one who has to know. I weigh every day, but you can do it whenever you want. Weighing regularly keeps us all honest and shows us how our diet is working. You can also use a tape measure, but you need something to see how you are doing. A scale is best.

Now What?

Okay. You've planted your seed, and it started growing. You check on it. It sprouts. Success! You get excited. You see the beauty and changes, but suddenly, your little flower stops growing. It looks droopy. Something's wrong. It's dying. Now what? This is where most people give up. They quit. Why bother dieting if I'm not successful?

The first three years of my diet, I lost eight pounds a year. The next two years I didn't lose anything, but I did keep off what I had lost. You are probably thinking, "That doesn't sound good; too darn slow!" But it's like the tortoise and the hare. Remember how the hare laughed at the tortoise when the tortoise challenged him to a race. The hare thought that was just plain stupid. At the beginning, the hare ran fast and was doing great. But he stopped trying. He took a nap. But the tortoise hung in there; didn't quit, and finally beat out the humiliated hare. That's the best way to win at dieting. Keep on, keeping on. Don't give up. The moral of the story was, "Slow and steady wins the race." I have a choice. Do I want to be a humiliated hare or a victorious tortoise?

I started counting calories years ago. I just kept hanging in there, counting calories, praying and checking my progress. That's it. That's all I did. By doing that, three things happened. First, I stopped gaining. That's a success. Second, I lost weight, slowly, but I lost. Finally, I didn't gain back what I lost. Isn't that the three main goals? It has taken a long time, but I'm almost there!

I have friends who are constantly looking for a new or better diet. They want a diet where they can lose quickly. They try something for a while. It works. Then it stops working, they go another diet. When that quits working, they go to another. They are always looking for a new diet or something magical that will get the weight off fast. They are like the hare. They go full-force into a new diet. They do great for a few weeks. Then, for different reasons, they quit. Finally, they start something new, taking it on with a vengeance. They take quit again. Then they try something else. Just like they hare, they lose. I'm more like the tortoise. Slow, but sure wins the race. So, the one last thing you have to do is this. DON'T STOP!

I have a dear friend who's a drug and alcohol counselor. He tells his clients, "Never stop stopping." No matter how many times they go back to their addiction, he still keeps telling them the same thing. "Never stop stopping." He has a high success rate and his clients love him.

I'm taking his lead and saying to you, "Never stop dieting." If you stick to your diet for three days, and fall off for two, you're still better off than if you did nothing. **Something is better than nothing.** The more you diet, the easier it gets, and the more it becomes a part of you. Keep on keeping on.

Just like in the movie *The Titanic*, Jack begged, "Never give up, Rose. Never give up." Then he died. Watch the movie. Memorize the speech, but pretend Jack is talking to you about your diet. It will inspire you, and Jack will not have died in vain.

Hitting a plateau isn't bad, but it's frustrating: When I diet, I often hit a plateau where I don't gain, but don't lose. Sounds bad, but technically, it's wonderful. Most people who lose weight, gain it back within a few months. If you lose weight and keep it off, it's a victory! Pat yourself on the back! You're doing great!

On the other hand, it can be frustrating. When I get stuck at one weight, I've won the battle, but not the war. I haven't reached my goal, but I'm not gaining. That's when I have to do something different. It requires prayer. "God, I've put boundaries on my eating, but now I'm not losing. What now?" Sometimes I know what He wants me to do. Other times, I have to use some common sense and ask myself some questions. Am I eating healthy? Am I including vegetables in my diet? What you do and how you do it is between you and your Creator.

This book has dozens of ideas about enhancing your diet. If you count calories and pray, you will lose weight. But when you stop losing, you might have to do raise the bar. You could give up sugar or wheat. Maybe you could count carbohydrates AND calories. The rule of thumb is this: if you reach a plateau, ask God what else you need to do. Ask Him to show you or tell you what's next. He loves you and wants to help, but we are all different. What works for one person, may not work for another.

One of my co-workers lost fifty pounds just by taking chromium picolinate, a mineral that balances blood sugar. Thus far, I've never met anyone who has responded that drastically to a mineral, but it worked for her! It was an answer to her prayers and it took her forty years to discover it. Her insight came through prayer.

One of my male friends lost forty pounds just by giving up beer. (So annoying!) Still another friend lost seventy-five pounds by giving up salt. Seriously! I wasn't sure that I believed him, but He made it clear to me that salt was the **only** change he made.

I've met several people who lost weight by giving up wheat, but it doesn't work that well for everyone. **For me, eating more vegetables**

was a turning point, but I still had to count calories. Eating more vegetables should work for everyone, but nothing is perfect for all of us. More recently, I'm aware that I'm eating too many carbohydrates. Even though I've been cutting back, it wasn't enough. My body doesn't like me when I O.D. on carbs. I've also noticed that I'm less hungry when I take my vitamins. However, we are all different. That's why we pray. God meets our individual needs.

Here's how I do it. I rarely do everything the same way twice, but I do have a few regular habits. My day starts with prayer. Not long or drawn out, but a prayer of gratitude and a prayer for help. I also pray for my friends and family. I usually do a short Bible study before I start my day.

I usually make some sort of "healthy drink" just before I go to bed or first thing in the morning. A healthy drink is any drink that includes MSM powder, powdered greens, and carrot juice. I count the calories if it's a smoothie or juice, but if it's just *True Lime* or *Healthiest Lemonade*, I don't count the calories. This drink (with all the extras) helps keep me on track, and I know I'm getting a lot of vitamins and minerals. I also take the vitamins I mentioned in the chapter on vitamins. Just before the first meal of the day, I eat a piece of fresh fruit. This has a cleansing effect and a great way to start my day.

I allow myself unlimited green vegetables throughout the day. This usually means at least one bowl of vegetable soup or a large salad. I also have a cup of berries. The vegetables and one piece of fruit are free, but I count calories of salad dressing, butter, and other extras. I usually drink a pot of tea, (watered down) and several glasses of water. If I'm having a good day, it's usually because I'm praying throughout the day.

Now for the important part. I count calories and carbohydrates. My goal is to eat 1,000 to 1,400 calories and 50 to 60 grams of carbohydrates. That may sound low, but with my vegetables, fruit, and berries, I get an extra 200 calories and another 30 or 40 carbs. I also subtract the fiber from the carbs, another 30 or so there. That's about half of the recommended daily allowance, but plenty for me. Too many carbs make me gain weight. I've learned the hard way.

This is what my journal looks like when it's blank:

Day _____ Date ____ ____ __ Wt _____ Goal _____

H.D. ____ Vites ____ ____ Pray ____ ____ Bible _____

Veg _____ _____ _____ _____ _____ _____ _____ _____

Water _____ _____ _____ _____ _____ _____ _____

Time Amt Item Cal Carbs

· · · · · · · ● · ❋ · ● · · · · · · ·

This is what my journal looks like at the end of the day:

Day <u>M</u> Date <u>10/1/17</u> Wt <u>160</u> Goal <u>150</u>
H.D. <u>X</u> Vites <u>X</u> Pray <u>X</u> Bible <u>I John & Prov</u>
Veg <u>X X X X X X X X X X</u>
Water <u>X X X X X X X X</u> ____ ____

Time	Amt	Item	Cal	Carbs
6:00		Woke up		
7:00		Healthy drink/vites	0	0
9:00	1	Small apple	0	0
	1 tbls	Almond butter	95	2
	1 cup	Oatmeal	150	13
	1/4 cup	Milk	25	3
11:30	½	Turkey sand	185	18
		Smoothie	125	8

A NEW PERSPECTIVE ON DIETING AND WEIGHT LOSS

3:00	1 cup	Hot chocolate	100	13
	1 ½	c. Broccoli/rice	235	26
	1 Tbls	Butter	100	0
6:00	1 slice	Veg Pizza/tomatoes	250	20
8:30	2 cups	Green tea/vites	<u>0</u>	<u>0</u>
Total			1,270	99

As you can see, I did well with my calories, but went overboard on the carbs. I have zero for my apple, because I allow one small piece of fruit a day for free and zero for my healthy drink. However, no cookies or candy, and only one slice of pizza. (I used to eat the whole thing.) A small amount of wheat. Here's what's important. **My worst day is when I don't write down anything.** Something else you need to know is that I don't always do everything exactly the same way every day. I do however try to remember to plan, pray, and count calories and I never forget to weigh myself even if I had a bad day. It keeps me honest.

You can do it however you want, but I suggest that you start with planning, praying, counting calories, and weighing yourself. That's all. Plan. Pray. Count calories. Weigh yourself. Plan. Pray. Count calories. Weigh yourself. That's what I did for the first three years. You may not want to wait that long.

Once you are comfortable with counting calories and praying, you can add other things. Use some of the tips and tricks in this book. When you find one that works for you, hang on to it and use it, but don't stop counting calories and don't stop praying. As you continue to diet, you will begin to know and understand your body and what works for you and what doesn't.

Remember, plant your flower and don't let it die. Maybe it needs more water or sun. Keep praying. God will show you. Never give up. That's it.

PART IV

Leftovers

1

My Favorite Recipes

1. My Seven Favorite Tea Recipes
2. My Seven Favorite Smoothies
3. My Seven Favorite Oatmeal Recipes
4. My Seven Favorite Soup Recipes
5. My Seven Favorite Salads (some dressing too)
6. My Seven Favorite Main Dishes
7. My Seven Favorite Quick Snacks
8. My Seven Favorite Desserts

Just a quick note. I figured out the calories, then rounded up. (I never do anything exactly.) As long as I write it all down and count it, I don't worry about perfection. It's much better than when I used to just stuff food in my mouth and say, "I don't eat that much."

One more short note. I never use milk when I can substitute coconut milk or almond milk. When it's mixed with other ingredients, it tastes like milk. It's lower in calories, carbohydrates, easier to digest, and much healthier. One of those perfect foods for people who want to lose weight.

My Seven Favorite Tea Recipes

When I was a little girl, I lived in England, and the English people make the most nectarous tea. (So do the Canadians.) They get frustrated with us American coffee-drinkers who make feeble attempts at making tea. A Canadian lady once told me, "You Americans do NOT know how to make tea!" She held up a cup and said, "You Americans put a tea bag in a cup, run it under hot water and call it 'tea.' That's not tea!" I remember thinking, *Sounds like tea to me.* Then she made the best cup of tea I've ever drank.

She taught me two important things about tea:

1. **The water must always be brought to a rolling boil!** Always! Always! Always!
2. **You must always set a timer for 3 to 5 minutes.** Always! Always! Always! (I do five.)

Since then, I've learned the proper way to make tea, I've played with different recipes. Now, I can make tea that would make the Brits break into a flash mob.

1. Barb's Favorite Tea:

(I drink this almost every day. I made it into ice tea for my son's summer wedding. Big hit!)

2 bags Constant Comment
2 bags green tea (decaf if desired)
3 - 5 cups BOILING water (filtered)
2 - 4 packets Stevia
Place all ingredients in a pretty tea pot.

- Cover.
- Brew for five minutes.
- Remove tea bags.
- Pour into a fine bone china tea cups.
- For stronger tea, use less water. Weaker tea requires more water.

Makes 3 - 5 cups. Zero calories. Zero carbs.

2. Peaches and Cream Tea:

2 bags *Bigalow* Perfect Peach tea
3 cups BOILING water
2 - 3 packets Stevia
6 tablespoons half-and-half
1 cup **hot** almond or coconut milk
Place all ingredients except half-and-half and milk in a pretty tea pot.

- Cover.
- Brew for five minutes.
- Remove tea bags.
- Add milk and half-and-half.

- Pour into a fine bone china tea cups. Drink in front of a roaring fire.

(For Raspberry-and-Cream Tea, use raspberry tea bags instead of peach tea. Yum!)
Makes four cups, about 25 calories and 2 carbohydrates per cup

3. Cherry-Pie Tea

2 bags *Wissotzky* Cherry Tea (You can use any type, but this is the best.)
3 cups BOILING water
2-3 packets Stevia
1 teaspoon almond flavoring (the secret ingredient)
Pour boiling water over tea bags.

- Cover.
- Brew for five minutes.
- Remove tea bags.
- Add almond flavoring.
- Pour into a fine bone-china tea cups. Share with close friends.

Makes three cups. Zero calories. Zero carbs.

4. Apple-Cinnamon Tea

2 bags apple tea
2 cinnamon sticks
3 cups BOILING water
2-3 packets Stevia

- Pour boiling water over tea bags and cinnamon sticks.

- Cover.
- Brew for five minutes.
- Remove tea bags.
- Add Stevia.
- Pour into a fine bone china tea cups. Share with close friends.

Makes three cups. Zero calories. Zero carbs.

5. Favorite Chai Tea

3 Chai tea bags
3 cups very hot almond milk
2 cups boiling water
6 tablespoons sugar-free vanilla creamer
2 - 5 packets Stevia

- Pour boiling water over tea bags.
- Cover.
- Brew for five minutes.
- Remove tea bags.
- Add hot almond milk and creamer
- Pour into cute mugs that say something clever. Makes a lot, so invite your friends.

(I use this one as dessert. Yum!)
Makes six cups, about 30 calories and 2 carbs each.

6. Salted-Caramel Chai Tea:

2 Chai tea bags
2 cups very hot almond or coconut milk
2 cups boiling water

4 tablespoons Smucker's sugar-free caramel topping
2 - 4 pkts Stevia (optional)
½ teaspoon pink Himalayan sea salt
Pour boiling water over tea bags.

- Cover.
- Brew for five minutes.
- Remove tea bags.
- Add hot milk, caramel topping, and Stevia.
- Stir.
- Makes about eight cups.
- Add more salt or caramel if desired, but count the extra calories.

(This has a Halloween/Christmas flavor to it. It's also a lot of fun to take on camping trips.)
Makes 4 servings, about 55 calories, and 10 carbs per cup.

7. Spicy Christmas Tea

2 bags green tea
4 bags *Constant Comment*
4-6 cups BOILING water (depending on how strong you like it)
3 cinnamon sticks
3 whole cloves
Sprinkle lightly with ginger and nutmeg if desired
¼ cup Stevia (or sweeten to taste)

- Pour boiling water over all ingredients.
- Cover.
- Remove tea bags, cloves and cinnamon
- Pour into Christmas mugs.

(Drink in front of the Christmas tree with someone you love. This one is very healthy and makes your house smell like Christmas.)
Makes three cups. Zero calories. Zero carbs.

My Seven Favorite Smoothies

My smoothie recipes all say "almond milk" or "coconut milk." I use the milk that says "30 or 40 calories" on the front of the box. They have some with more calories that are a little richer. If you use those, add the extra calories. Sometimes, I add a raw egg to my smoothie for extra protein, but the FDA keeps telling me it's going to kill me. I'm still waiting. You can add yogurt to any of these. It gives your drink a thicker, richer consistency. Yogurt contains "acidophilus," an amazing probiotic necessary for intestinal health.

To turn your drink into my *Healthy Drink* (a.k.a. *H.D.)* add carrot juice, MSM, and powdered greens. I try to get these three items every day. Those were mentioned in the chapter on vitamins and minerals. It's also in drink number seven.

Please remember, if you are giving this smoothie to growing kids, or if you are an active person, you need to add a few tablespoons of half-and-half, or coconut oil. Kids and active people need a little fat for energy and for their health. Some thin people need extra fat too, but you still have to be nice to them.

1. Basic Smoothie

1 cup of almond or coconut milk
1 cup frozen berries (any kind, your choice)
2 tbls carrot juice

1 teaspoon vanilla
½ cup plain fat-free yogurt
1 - 3 packets Stevia

Blend all together in a blender on high for 60 seconds.
(I drink this one regularly because it's low calorie, filling and healthy.)
Makes two servings. About 40 calories and 5 carbohydrates each.

2. Pina Colada Smoothie (Virgin)

2 cups very cold almond or coconut milk
1/3 cup frozen, condensed pineapple juice
1 banana
½ teaspoon coconut flavoring
½ cup crushed ice or very cold water
2 - 4 packets Stevia

Blend all together in blender on high for 60 seconds. Your taste buds will smile.
Makes 3 servings. About 90 calories and 19 carbs each.

3. Orange Cream Cycle Smoothie

2 cups almond or coconut milk
1/3 cup condensed frozen orange juice
½ cup crushed ice
1 packet single-serving size orange-flavored *True Lime or True Lemon*
1 teaspoon vanilla
1 banana (optional)

Blend all together in a blender on high for 30 - 60 seconds.
Makes 3 servings. About 85 calories and 12 carbs each without the banana.

If you add the banana, then add 30 extra calories and 7 extra carbs for each serving. Bananas make it thicker, but adds calories and carbs.

4. Chocolate Banana Smoothie

2 mashed frozen bananas
4 cups almond or coconut milk
1 small box sugar-free chocolate pudding mix

Blend all together in a blender on high for 30 to 60 seconds.
Mash bananas the day before. Then freeze in an ice-cube tray. Save for smoothies.
Makes 6 servings. About 65 calories and 11 carbs. Very filling!

5. Berry Surprise

2 cups frozen mixed berries (or your favorite berry)
1 cup plain yogurt
2 cups almond or coconut milk
1 cup crushed ice
2 packets single-serving raspberry *True Lime* (raspberry flavor)
(Please notice that it's the **single-serving** size)

(The *True Lime* gives it a unique flavor.)
Blend all ingredients in blender on high for 30 to 60 seconds.
Makes 5 servings. About 40 calories and 4 carbs each.

6. Coffee Milkshake Smoothie:

2 tablespoons instant coffee (decaf if you like)
1 tablespoon hot water
2 cups almond or coconut milk
3 tablespoons sugar-free hazelnut coffee syrup

½ cup crushed ice
2 - 4 packets Stevia
4 tbls. cream if desired

- Dissolve coffee in hot water.
- Mix all ingredients in blender.

Makes two servings. About 50 calories and 3 carbs each.
If you use the cream, add another 40 calories per cup. No extra carbs.

7. Healthiest Smoothie That Tastes Great

Make your favorite smoothie, then add the following ingredients:
2 - 3 tbls. carrot juice
1 teaspoon *Raw Greens Whole Food Powder* (I get mine from Amazon)
1/4 teaspoon MSM powder

Whizz it up in the blender.
The calories depend on which smoothie you decide to make.

My Seven Favorite Oatmeal Recipes

Oatmeal is an amazing food. It's one of the few foods that contains soluble fiber and insoluble. BOTH! That's why it's so good for you. Dr. Oz says "oatmeal makes healthy poop." Probably because of the fiber. Oatmeal is known to lower your cholesterol too.

All of my oatmeal recipes included flax, chia seeds and oat bran because they are so healthy. The oat bran gives me the extra fiber I need and makes me feel full. The chia seeds calm my appetite. The flax offers the heathy fats, but I need to count the extra calories.

Please notice that **none** of the recipes include the calories from the milk. That way, you get to choose skim milk, 1%, half-and-half, almond, or coconut milk. The calorie-count for your milk is on the carton. Some of these recipes for oatmeal are so delicious, that I don't use milk.

All recipes start with the same six ingredients.

1. Smooth-Move Oatmeal

2/3 cup boiling water
1 teaspoon chia seeds (optional)
1/3 cup old-fashioned rolled oats
1 tablespoon oat bran

1 tablespoon ground flax seed
dash of *Real Salt*
1 tablespoon molasses
1 packet Stevia
1/3 cup your favorite milk (optional)

- Boil water.
- Add oats, oat bran, flax, chia, and salt.
- Boil 1 minute.
- Cover. Remove from heat.
- In five minutes, pour into a pretty bowl.
- Add molasses and Stevia.
- Add milk if you like.

Serves one. About 225 calories and 34 carbs without the milk.

2. Crunchy-Chewy Oatmeal:

2/3 cup boiling water
1 teaspoon chia seeds (optional)
1/3 cup old-fashioned rolled oats
1 tablespoon oat bran
1 tablespoon ground flax seed
dash of *Real Salt*
6 almonds or walnuts chopped
2 tablespoons craisins or raisins
1 or 2 packets Stevia
1/3 cup milk or almond milk (optional)

- Boil water.
- Add oats, oat bran, flax, chia, and salt.
- Boil 1 minute, then add the nuts and fruit
- Cover. Remove from heat.

- In five minutes, pour into a glass dish.
- Add Stevia and milk if you like.

Serves one. About 325 calories and 33 carbs, without the milk.

3. Chocolate-Almond Oatmeal:

2/3 cup boiling water
1 teaspoon chia seeds (optional)
1/3 cup old-fashioned rolled oats
1 tablespoon oat bran
1 tablespoon ground flax seed
dash of *Real Salt*
1 tablespoon almond butter or peanut butter
1 teaspoon cocoa powder
1- 3 packets Stevia
1/3 cup milk or almond milk (optional)

- Boil water.
- Add oats, oat bran, flax, and salt.
- Boil 1 minute.
- Remove from heat.
- Add nut butter and cocoa powder.
- Stir and cover.
- In five minutes, pour into your favorite bowl.
- Add Stevia and milk if you like.

Serves one, about 220 calories and 19 carbs, without the milk.

4. Pecan Pie Oatmeal:

2/3 cup boiling water
1 teaspoon chia seeds (optional)

1/3 cup old-fashioned rolled oats
1 tablespoon oat bran
1 tablespoon ground flax seed
dash of *Real Salt*
1 tablespoon real maple syrup
5 chopped pecans
1 - 2 packets Stevia (optional)
1/3 cup milk or almond milk (optional)

- Boil water.
- Add oats, oat bran, flax, chia, and salt.
- Boil 1 minute.
- Cover.
- Remove from heat. In five minutes add syrup and pecans.
- Pour into your favorite bowl.
- Add Stevia and milk if you like.

Serves one, about 280 calories and 29 carbohydrates without the milk.

5. Cinnamon/Raisin Oatmeal:

2/3 cup boiling water
1 teaspoon chia seeds (optional)
1/3 cup old-fashioned rolled oats
1 tablespoon oat bran
1 tablespoon ground flax seed
dash of *Real Salt*
2 tablespoons raisins
1/2 teaspoon cinnamon
1/8 teaspoon maple flavoring (optional)
1-2 packets Stevia
1/3 cup milk or almond milk (optional)

- Boil water.
- Add oats, oat bran, flax, chia, and salt.
- Boil 1 minute.
- Cover. Remove from heat.
- In five minutes add cinnamon, maple, and Stevia.
- Pour into your favorite bowl.
- Add Stevia and milk if you like.

Serves one, about 210 calories and 33 carbohydrates without the milk.

6. Apple Pie Oatmeal:

2/3 cup boiling water
1 teaspoon chia seeds (optional)
1/3 cup old-fashioned rolled oats
1 tablespoon oat bran
1 tablespoon ground flax seed
dash of *Real Salt*
½ apple, chopped into small bite sized pieces
1/2 teaspoon cinnamon
1-2 packets Stevia
1/3 cup milk or almond milk (optional)

- Boil water.
- Add oats, oat bran, flax, chia, and salt.
- Boil 1 minute.
- Cover. Remove from heat.
- In five minutes add apple chunks, cinnamon and Stevia.
- Pour into your favorite bowl.
- Add Stevia and milk if you like.

About 150 calories and 18 carbs without the milk.

7. Peaches and Cream Oatmeal:

2/3 cup boiling water
1 teaspoon chia seeds (optional)
1/3 cup old-fashioned rolled oats
1 tablespoon oat bran
1 tablespoon ground flax seed
dash of *Real Salt*
1 fresh peach, cut into bite-sized chunks
1/2 teaspoon cinnamon
1-2 packets Stevia
1/3 cup milk or almond milk (optional)

- Boil water.
- Add oats, oat bran, flax, chia, and salt.
- Boil 1 minute.
- Cover. Remove from heat.
- In five minutes add cinnamon, peach, and Stevia.
- Pour into your favorite bowl.
- Add milk if you like.

Serves one, about 150 calories and 18 carbs without the milk.

My Seven Favorite Soups

I eat soup three or four times a week. Filling and nutritious. Great place to hide veggies.

1. Super Simple Vegetable Beef Soup

½ pound extra lean ground beef
1 small onion
salt, pepper, garlic powder
(to taste)
2 tablespoon palm oil
1 large can condensed vegetable beef soup
1 can water
1 16-ounce can green beans, drained (or 1 cup favorite cooked vegetables)

- Sauté onion in oil on medium heat for about ten minutes.
- Add ground beef, salt, pepper, and garlic.
- When ground beef is no longer pink, add the soup, water, and vegetables.
- Heat though.
- This soup has lots of protein, vitamins, and fiber, without the calories.
- Simple, filling, and healthy.

(If I leave out the onions and garlic, I give this one to my little dog, but ask your vet.)
Makes about six cups at 100 calories and six carbs each.

2. Horrible Soup:

This is the soup that people eat if they want to lose weight quickly or fast.

(I've looked at a lot of recipes. This one was the least horrible of them all. In fact, it's pretty good, but after three days it kinda gags me.)

1 whole onion chopped
2 green peppers
1 cup chopped mushrooms
2 tablespoon palm oil
1 cup baby carrots cut in half
1cup chopped celery
½ head of cabbage (about 2 cups)
2 pkg. Lipton beefy onion soup mix
½ cup chopped parsley
8 - 10 cups clean water
1 tablespoon fresh garlic
1 tablespoon Worcestershire sauce
1 - 15 ounce can Italian tomatoes (optional)
Salt and pepper to taste

- Sauté the onions, peppers and mushrooms in palm oil for about 10 minutes.
- Add all of remaining ingredients.
- Cover. Boil for 40 – 50 minutes.

Makes about 12 cups. I don't count the calories or carbs on this one. It's mostly fiber and water, two things that won't make you fat. Eat as much as you want.

3. Healthy Beef Stew with Lots of Veggies

Follow the recipe for *Horrible Soup* (above) but add 4 small potatoes cut into bite-sized pieces. (I don't peel them. Peelings are good for you.) Then boil with the soup about 20 minutes.

While soup is boiling, fry 1 pound **extra lean** ground beef. Season with salt, pepper, onion powder, and garlic powder.

When soup is done boiling, add beef. Heat through. Makes about 15 cups.

If desired, substitute 1-pound of beef stew meat for the ground beef. Fry it in 2 tablespoons palm oil. When dark brown, add to vegetables and boil.

About 105 calories and 6 carbohydrates per cup.
(If desired, top with low-fat sour cream, but be sure to count those calories. Yummy!)

4. Chicken and Rice Soup

½ cup chopped onions
2 tablespoons palm oil
2 chicken bouillon cubes
1 teaspoon salt
1 tablespoon dried parsley
1 teaspoon sage
10 baby carrots cut in half

5 cups water 1 cup chopped celery
½ instant rice (or brown rice already cooked)
dash pepper
1 cup leftover chicken (cooked)

- Sauté onions in oil on medium heat for about seven minutes.
- Place all ingredients except chicken, rice, and pepper in a large pot. Cover.
- Boil about 40 minutes.
- Add pepper, rice and chicken. Boil another 3 minutes. Cover.
- Remove from heat. Let stand five minutes. (To lower the carbohydrates, leave out the rice. It tastes great and cuts the calories in half.)

Makes about eight cups, about 80 calories and 8 carbohydrates each.
To change this to chicken noodle soup, substitute ½ cup cooked noodles for rice. It's yummy, but I rarely eat wheat. (You can use wheat-free noodles if you want.)

5. Chicken Taco Soup

1 medium onion
2 tablespoons palm oil
3 cups leftover cooked chicken
(or 1-pound lean ground turkey, fried)
1 (1 1/4 ounce) package hidden valley ranch dressing mix
1 (1 1/4 ounce) package taco seasoning mix
1 can black beans (rinsed and drained)
1 - 15 ounce can stewed tomatoes, chopped (Mexican flavor)
4 cups water

- Sauté onions in oil on medium heat for about 10 minutes.

- Add remaining ingredients.
- Boil all for about 15 minutes.

Makes about 8 cups, 120 calories, 13 carbohydrates each.
Some people add 1 cup frozen corn but add the calories and carbohydrates.

6. French Onion Soup With Veggies and Meat (Oh YUM!)

1 small onion chopped
2 tablespoons olive oil or palm oil
1 pkg. Lipton Beefy Onion Soup Mix
8 baby carrots cut in half
½ cup chopped celery
5 cups water
½ pound lean ground beef (about 3% fat)
1 Tablespoon Worcestershire sauce (optional)
2 tablespoons Braggs amino acid (optional)
1/4 teaspoon garlic

- Mix soup-mix, carrots, celery, and water. Cover.
- Boil on low for 20 to 25 minutes.
- While that's boiling, sauté onions in oil on medium heat for about 15 minutes.
- Add ground beef to fried onions. Fry until hamburger is no longer pink.
- Salt and pepper to taste. (It may not need salt. There's plenty in the soup mix.)
- Add all ingredients together.
- Boil for one minute.

Low in calories, fats, and carbs, and still tastes awesome! Hard to believe. For extra flavor, add a tablespoon of butter, but be sure to count the calories.

Makes 7 cups, about 50 calories and 2 carbs per cup.

7. Cream of Broccoli Soup

It was hard to turn this into diet soup since I like it with heavy cream and lots of butter, but this soup is so good, I worked at it until I got it so it's yummy!

1 medium-sized onion, finely chopped
1 tablespoon palm oil
2 heads of broccoli (chopped up into bite-sized pieces)
1 32-ounce carton chicken broth (low sodium is best)
1 can fat-free evaporated milk (12-ounce size)
2 tablespoons real butter
1/4 cup *Brummel and Brown Lite Butter*
2 tablespoons heavy cream
2 tablespoons Braggs liquid amino acid
1/8 teaspoon nutmeg

- Sauté onion in palm oil on medium heat for about 10 minutes.
- Stir in chopped broccoli. Sauté another five minutes.
- Add chicken broth. Cover. Simmer about 15 minutes.
- Set aside 2 cups of this soup mixture.
- Puree the rest in the blender, but CAUTION!! It's hot and the lid can blow off the blender. Hold it down. Do not fill the blender more than half full.
- After all the broccoli is thoroughly blended, return to pan.
- Add canned milk, butter, amino acid, and the reserved soup mix.

- Heat through. Serve hot.

Makes 9 cups, about 85 calories and 6 carbohydrates each. You will feel so stuffed!
To make it for company, add a whole stick of butter. Add the calories, of course!

8. Onion Mushroom Soup:

I know I said seven, but I just had to throw this in. Quick. Easy. Low in calories and oh, so good. In fact, I think it's the best soup I've ever put in my mouth. (Oh dear. I'm bragging.)

1 onion chopped up
2 tablespoons palm oil
1 cup fresh mushrooms
1 packet Lipton Onion Mushroom soup mix
3 cups water
1 tablespoons butter (optional)
1 - 2 tablespoons Bragg's liquid amino acid

- Sauté onion in oil on medium heat for about 10 minutes.
- Add mushrooms. Sauté for another five minutes.
- Set aside.
- In another pan, add soup mix to water.
- Boil for three minutes.
- Add remaining ingredients.
- Boil all for another three minutes.
- If desired, add butter for flavor but count the calories.

Sometimes, I top each serving with a tablespoon of FRESH Parmesan cheese. So filling! So delicious!
Makes three cups, about 35 calories and 5 carbs each.

My Seven Favorite Salads

But first an important word about salad dressing:

I water down all store-bought salad dressing with *Braggs Apple Cider Vinegar.* **Apple cider vinegar may be the healthiest food on the face of the planet.** I have a friend who drinks 1/4 cup straight every day and she's never been sick. YUK! Apple cider vinegar makes claims of healing sore throats, helps with digestion, heals mouth and gums, and a dozen other illnesses. Some people say it helps with weight loss. Maybe a little bit, but losing weight is hard work. There is no magic potion.

The most important thing about apple-cider vinegar is that it balances your pH. That may not sound important, but **all sick people have an imbalanced pH**. In fact, the sicker you are, the worse the imbalance. (This subject is another book, but you get the idea.) Apple cider vinegar WITH THE MOTHER packs a powerful punch. "The mother" is loaded with phytochemicals, a substance that protects and heals diseases and **fights inflammation, another root cause of illness.** ("With the mother" is labeled on the front of the bottle.) Whenever I make salad dressing or thin it down, I always use this special vinegar.

Barb's Favorite Salad Dressing (Italian):

I don't make a lot of homemade salad dressing, but this one is my favorite because it has two healthy ingredients. It has *Braggs Apple Cider Vinegar* (just mentioned above), but second ingredient is **cold-pressed olive oil**. Notice "cold pressed." If it's not cold pressed, then it has been heated. When olive oil is heated, it decomposes and the antioxidants are replaced by free radicals, a by-product that causes cancer and numerous other diseases. Cold-pressed olive oil is a little pricey, but worth it. My favorite salad-dressing has cold-pressed olive oil **AND** healthy vinegar. Here's my recipe for delicious, nutritious salad dressing. (I find pretty bottles and make it for Christmas gifts.)

Barb's Favorite Salad Dressing

1 cup water
½ cup cold pressed olive oil
½ cup Bragg's apple cider vinegar
2 packages of Good Seasons Italian Salad Dressing.

- Place all ingredients in a blender.
- Blend on high for two minutes.
- Store in a glass jar.
- Keeps in the fridge three or four weeks. (Maybe more.)

One tablespoon has thirty calories and one carbohydrate.

Now for My Seven Favorite Salads:

1. Caesar Sala

6 cups Romaine lettuce, cut into bite-sized pieces
2 small tomatoes cut into 1-inch cubes (optional)

½ cup **fresh** grated Parmesan cheese

Lite Caesar salad dressing, watered down with *Bragg's* apple-cider vinegar
Mix lettuce and tomatoes

- Put into three pretty bowls.
- Top each with lite Caesar salad dressing and 2 tablespoons of FRESH Parmesan cheese (not that stuff you shake on your spaghetti).

The lettuce and tomatoes are free. Parmesan cheese has about 25 calories per tablespoon.
Check the bottle of dressing for the calorie count. Measure. Use what you need.

2. CAT Salad

(No! I don't eat cats. It's an acronym for Cucumber-Avocado-Tomatoes.) The vegetables in this salad are so juicy that they make their own dressing.
Just add salt and pepper.

1 medium cucumber peeled and chopped into cubes
1 medium sized avocado cut into 1-inch cubes
2 tomatoes cut into 1-inch cubes
Salt and pepper to taste
Mix all ingredients. I like to top it with a little fresh Parmesan or Feta cheese and a teeny bit of ranch, but it's delicious by itself.

- This must be eaten within an hour or two as the avocados turn brown.

(If you squeeze some lime juice on it, it will stay fresh longer.)
Makes two servings. About 130 calories each serving and no carbs. You can add a little of "Barb's Favorite Dressing." It's so good!

3. Green-Bean Salad:

2 cans green beans (rinsed and drained thoroughly)
1 can black beans (rinsed and drained thoroughly)
3 tomatoes
salt, pepper, onion powder, garlic powder
3/4 cup Barb's Favorite Dressing

- After draining canned foods, mix all ingredients.
- Add spices. Keep tasting it until it tastes just right.

Keeps well in the fridge for a few weeks. It's loaded with vitamins, minerals and protein.
Technically, it's a whole meal.
Makes six one-cup servings. Each serving has about 190 calories and 9 carbohydrates.

4. Broccoli Salad:

3 slices turkey bacon, fried and crumbled. Drain.
4 cups chopped up broccoli, lightly steamed for one minute, then cooled
(Do not use frozen broccoli.)
1/3 cups finely chopped celery
1/4 cup raisins
Mix these and set aside.

Dressing:
1/4 cup light *Miracle Whip*

3 tablespoons light sour cream
½ cup plain non-fat yogurt
2 tablespoons apple-cider vinegar
2 packets Stevia
3 tablespoons grated red onion

- Whip together *Miracle Whip*, sour cream, yogurt, vinegar, Stevia, and onion.
- Pour over broccoli mix.
- Refrigerate at least an hour.

Makes four servings, about 85 calories and 6 carbs per serving.

5. Spinach Salad with Hot Dressing:

3 slices turkey bacon
8 ounces of fresh spinach leaves (I like the packaged stuff)
1/4 cup pitted Kalamata olives, sliced
1/4 cup crumbled feta cheese
1/4 cups grated red onion
1/4 cup apple-cider vinegar
2 packets Stevia
2 teaspoons Dijon mustard
2 tablespoon cold-pressed olive oil
salt and pepper
Fry bacon.

- While bacon is frying, wash spinach leaves, remove stems.
- Tear into pieces. Dry and place in a wooden salad bowl.
- Add olives and cheese to the spinach. Set aside.
- When bacon is brown and crispy, drain all but two tablespoons of bacon fat from pan.
- Crumble bacon over spinach leaves.

- Fry onions in bacon grease for 2 minutes.
- Add vinegar, Stevia, mustard, olive oil, salt and pepper to bacon fat.
- Bring to a rolling boil. (This sweet and sour dressing is so delicious!)
- Pour dressing over spinach mix.
- Add bacon.

Makes two servings, about 120 calories and 4 carbohydrates each.

6. Crispy Crunchy Salad:

1 cup cauliflower, finely chopped (not frozen)
1 cup broccoli, finely chopped (not frozen)
1 cup chopped celery
1 cup chopped or sliced radishes
1 cup baby carrots, cut into small pieces
1/4 cup grated onions (optional)
1 cup *Barb's Favorite Salad Dressing*.
Mix vegetables in a wooden salad bowl. (If you don't have one, use glass.)

- Pour dressing over veggies.
- Refrigerate overnight.

Makes 5 cups, 20 calories and 2 carbs per cups.
You can turn this into a fun macaroni salad.
Just add three cups of macaroni (cooked and cooled) to the vegetables. Then add another cup or two of dressing. (Maybe a little extra salt and pepper too.)
It's a crispy, crunchy macaroni salad, healthier than other mac salads, but be sure to add the calories from the macaroni and extra dressing.

7. Cucumber and Onion Salad:

5 cucumbers peeled, chopped
1 red onion
½ cup apple-cider vinegar
½ cup water
4 packets Stevia
Salt, pepper, and garlic powder
Slice onion VERY thin.

- Place onions and cucumbers in a bowl.
- In a separate container, mix vinegar, water, Stevia, spices.
- Pour over onions and cucumbers.
- Cover and refrigerate overnight.

I don't count the calories or carbs on this one.
(It's mostly water and fiber. Eat as much as you want.)

My Seven Favorite Main Dishes

When it comes to main dishes, I always try to figure out how to get more vegetables in it and less carbohydrates. That way you can eat more, with fewer calories.

1. Broccoli/Carrots/Rice/Cheese (Quick and simple)

1 box Broccoli & Cheese rice mix
3 tablespoons *Brummel and Brown* margarine
2 1/4 cups hot water
1 pound fresh or frozen broccoli cut into bite sized pieces
20 baby carrots cut in half
½ cup shredded cheese

- Sauté rice in *Brummel and Brown* margarine on medium heat for about 5 minutes, stirring frequently.
- Add water, seasoning mix, carrots and broccoli.
- Reduce heat. Cover. Simmer about 20 minutes, or until water is absorbed.
- Remove from heat. Add cheese. Cover and let stand five minutes.

Makes about 6 cups, about 220 calories and 24 carbs each.

2. Asian Vegetables and Shrimp (or chicken)

2 packages frozen Asian vegetables (without noodles)
1-pound fresh shrimp (peeled)
1 8-oz. can water chestnuts drained and slivered
4 tablespoon sesame oil (or palm oil)
2 tablespoons lite soy sauce
2 tablespoons Braggs liquid amino acid
1 cup cooked rice

- Sauté vegetables, shrimp, and water chestnuts in oil and soy sauce for 10 minutes (or until completely heated through).
- Add rice and amino acid
- Heat through.
- If it needs more salt, add soy sauce or amino acids instead.
- If desired, substitute 1 or 2 cups of cooked, cubed chicken for the shrimp.

Makes about 6 cups. About 95 calories and 22 carbs per cup. (Most of the calories and carbs come from the rice.)

3. Healthy Spaghetti Sauce

1 large onion, peeled and finely chopped
1 tablespoon finely chopped garlic
2 tablespoons palm oil
4 - 8 ounces chopped mushrooms
1 chopped green pepper
½ pound extra lean ground beef or low-fat ground turkey
3 cans Italian tomatoes (15oz)
1 - 2 teaspoon Italian seasoning mix
½ teaspoon oregano
2 tablespoon dried parsley

salt and pepper to taste

- Sauté onions and garlic in oil about 10 minutes
- Add mushrooms and green peppers.
- Sauté another 10 minutes.
- Add ground meat. Fry until meat is no longer pink. Set aside.
- Put tomatoes in blender on high until blended.
- Add seasonings to the tomatoes and blend another 10 seconds.
- Combine all ingredients together in a pan. Simmer for 15 minutes.
- (If you or your family doesn't like the taste of mushrooms or green peppers, put them in the blender with the tomatoes. No one will know.)

Makes nine cups, about 80 calories and 3 carbohydrates each. Better yet, each cup has 4 servings of vegetables!
You can pour this over rice or pasta, but whatever you do, be sure you add the calories.
I pour my sauce over French-cut green beans instead of pasta.
BTW, *Bed, Bath and Beyond* has a gadget that turns zucchini into spaghetti noodles.
Simple and it's only $15.00.

4. Super Healthy Veggie Quiche (minus the crust)

1 bell pepper (sliced and diced, no seeds)
1 green pepper (sliced and diced, no seeds)
1 small onion (diced)
1 tablespoon chopped garlic
1/2 teaspoon thyme
salt and pepper to taste

1/2 cup mushrooms (sliced thin)
1 tablespoon palm oil
6 eggs
1/2 cup cottage cheese
1 cup low-fat mozzarella cheese (grated)

Preheat oven to 350 degrees.
Fry peppers, onion, garlic, and seasonings in palm oil on medium-high heat for 5-6 minutes.
Add mushrooms and fry another 1-2 minutes.
Set aside to cool.
Beat eggs vigorously.
Add milk and cottage cheese and beat again.
Gently fold in veggies and cheese.
Add more salt and pepper if desired.
Pour all ingredients into a lightly buttered glass baking dish.
Bake for 45 minutes or until a knife comes out clean.
Cut into eight equal pieces.
About 120 calories and 2 carbs per serving.

5. Cheesy Chicken and Rice Casserole

1 can Campbell's Condensed Cream of Chicken Soup (98% fat-free)
1 1/4 boiling water
½ cup long grain white rice (uncooked)
½ teaspoon onion powder
1/4 teaspoon black pepper
1 package frozen California mixed vegetables
2 pounds boneless skinless chicken breast (uncooked)
½ cup shredded cheddar cheese
Heat oven to 375 degrees.

- Mix soup, water, rice, spices and vegetables in an 11 X 8-inch baking dish.
- Top mixture with meat. Cover tightly with aluminum foil.
- Bake 1 hour or until chicken is cooked through, and rice is tender.
- Uncover. Top with cheese. Leave uncovered.
- Bake another 10 minutes.

6. Inside-Out Unstuffed Cabbage Rolls:

1 large onion chopped up
1 tablespoon fresh garlic (comes in a jar)
2 tablespoons palm oil
1 pound extra lean ground beef or low-fat ground turkey
1 small cabbage chopped
2 cans (14 oz) diced tomatoes
3/4 cup water
1 teaspoon sea salt
1 teaspoon pepper

- Fry onion and garlic in oil for about five minutes.
- Add hamburger and fry until it's no longer pink.
- Add the rest of the ingredients. Bring to a boil.
- Cover and simmer for 30 minutes.

Serves 8; 190 calories and 8 carbohydrates each serving.

7. Chicken Veggie Stir Fry:

4 boneless skinless chicken breasts, cut into bite-sized pieces
2 tablespoons palm oil
1 small onion chopped up
1 tablespoon fresh garlic

2 cups shredded green cabbage

1 tablespoon cornstarch

½ teaspoon ginger

1/2 cup water

1 small can crushed pineapple (not drained)

3 tablespoons lite soy sauce

1 small can sliced water chestnuts (DRAINED)

- Heat oil in LARGE skillet.
- Fry onion and garlic for about five minutes.
- Add chicken pieces stirring constantly until no longer pink.
- Add cabbage and water chestnuts. Sauté for about three minutes.
- In a separate bowl mix cornstarch, ginger, water, pineapple, and soy sauce until smooth.
- Pour sauce into the skillet, stirring with the chicken and cabbage.
- Cook about 1 minute, until it thickens.

*Serves 8, **about 190 calories and 8 carbohydrates each serving.***

My Seven Favorite Snacks
(which sometimes doubles as a small meal)

1. Quickie Trail Mix:

1 tablespoon sunflower seeds
1 tablespoon of raisins or craisins
2 tablespoons peanuts or 12 almonds

Put all three ingredients in a zip lock bag.
Makes one baggy. Has about 175 calories and 5 carbs.
(I like to make up ten or fifteen bags, so I can grab and go.)

2. Smoked Salmon and Cream Cheese:

1 tablespoons of half/and/half
8 oz. Neufchatel cream cheese (room temperature)
1 tall can (15 oz) salmon (drained)
1 teaspoon smoke flavoring (optional)

- Whip all ingredients together in a bowl.
- Cover and chill.

2 tablespoons is about 80 calories and 2 carbs.
This is delicious on celery. No extra calories.

Tastes amazing on rice crackers, but I have to count the calories in the crackers.

3. Not a Peanut-butter Sandwich:

1 tablespoon almond butter or peanut butter (softened)
2 tablespoon *Brummel and Brown* margarine
1 tablespoon honey

Mix or whip all three ingredients together.
About 200 calories and 17 carbs
I love this on a rice cake. They have 35 calories 7 carbs. Good on celery too.

4. Chips and dip:

½ cup low-fat cottage cheese
1 oz reduced-fat *Pringles*

Use the cottage cheese as a chip dip. Cheap and filling.
About 250 calories and 14 carbs.

5. Great snack or meal

1/4 cup refried beans
1 tablespoon water
1/2 stick celery, finely chopped
1 tablespoon onion, finely chopped (or 1/8 teaspoon of onion powder)
Salt, pepper and garlic powder
2 tablespoon grated cheese
2 tablespoons low-fat (lite) sour cream
1/4 cup fresh salsa
18 ice crackers

- Mix beans, water, salt, pepper, celery, onion, and spices.
- Top with cheese.
- Place in microwave for 30 seconds.
- Remove from microwave.
- Pour salsa over all.
- Top with sour cream.
- Use rice crackers to scoop up beans.

Serves one person. About 200 calories and 17 carbs.

6. Simple and filling:

1 hard-boiled egg (salt if you like)
6 radishes
1 cup sugar-free hot chocolate

Peel eggs. Eat, drink, and enjoy.
Serves one person. About 180 calories and 12 carbs

7. Coke float and a salad

1 cup sugar-free Coke or Pepsi (I know. It's not healthy.)
½ cup lite vanilla ice cream
Salad: one cup lettuce, one small tomato. Little dressing.

Put Coke in a tall glass.

- Stir out some of the bubbles.
- Drop in ice cream.
- Serve with a tall spoon and a straw.

About 110 calories and 5 carbs. If you put dressing on your salad, add it in.

My Seven Favorite Desserts
(Actually Eight)

You didn't think I would leave out dessert, did you? If I go on a diet and can't have anything sweet, I quit. I tried to make these healthy, low cal, and delicious, but it's hard to do all three.

Sometimes I use these as a snack.

1. Pert-near Pumpkin Pie:

(This is almost like pumpkin pie, low fat and low cal, and only takes a few minutes!)

1 large box sugar-free butterscotch pudding (not healthy but good)
1½ cups of cold 1% milk
1/3 cup canned pumpkin (I freeze the rest in an ice-cube tray)
½ teaspoon cinnamon
1/4 teaspoon ginger
1/8 teaspoon nutmeg (optional)
3 or 4 packets Stevia

- Pour milk into glass bowl.
- Add pudding mix.

- Beat well for 1 minute, scraping sides of bowl with a rubber scraper.
- Add pumpkin and spices.
- Beat again for one minute. Continue scraping sides.
- Refrigerate at least 1 hour.

Serve in pretty brandy glasses. (If desired, top with sugar-free *Cool Whip*.) Yum-O, and a great way to get your vitamin A! (Most of us are deficient.)
About 80 calories and 12 carbs per cup, without the Cool Whip.

2. High Protein Jell-O

(Gelatin is great for your fingernails, hair, and teeth, and a delicious way to feed them.)

1 small package sugar-free lime *Jell-O*
1 cup boiling water
4 ice cubes
1 small can crushed pineapple (not drained)
1 cup cottage cheese

- In a glass bowl, stir *Jell-O* into boiling water.
- When *Jell-O* is completely dissolved, add remaining ingredients.
- Stir well.
- Chill for 2 - 3 hours.

If desired, top with *Cool Whip*. Some people call this "salad." I call it delicious!
About 80 calories and 10 carbs per cup.

3. Almond Butter and Chocolate

(Extremely healthy. Extremely delicious, but be careful. It's high in calories.)

2 squares Godiva 72% Dark Chocolate
1 Tablespoon almond butter or peanut butter

- Spread the nut butter on the chocolate. Eat it with a cup of hot tea or coffee.

Makes 1 serving, about 215 calories and 18 carbs.

4. Almost Strawberry Ice Cream

1 cup strawberries, sliced or diced
1 cup plain nonfat yogurt (very cold)
½ teaspoon vanilla
2 - 3 packets Stevia

Mix all together.
If you are craving ice-cream, this is a great substitute.
Makes 2 cups, about 100 calories and 12 carbs each. Read the label on your yogurt. Strawberries are free.

5. Almost Apple Crumble and Ice Cream

6 medium sized granny-smith apples peeled, cored, cut into eighths
5 - 8 packets Stevia
1 cup water
1 teaspoon cinnamon
1/8 teaspoon nutmeg (optional)

- Place all ingredients in a saucepan. Cover.
- Boil all for ten to fifteen minutes.
- Remove from heat. Do not mash apples.
- Pour into glass serving dishes. Serve hot.
- If desired, add 2 to 3 tablespoons ½ & ½.

Makes six servings, about 90 calories and 12 carbohydrates.
Instead of ice cream, I pour two tablespoons of half-and-half over it while it's hot. (about 40 calories and no carbs).
For a "crumble" topping, I sprinkle a little granola on top.

6. Dairy-Free Chocolate Pudding

1 1/2 cups coconut milk (30-40 calories)
1/3 cups chia seeds
1/3 tablespoons cocoa powder
1/4 cup Stevia (or to taste)
Dash of cinnamon
½ teaspoon vanilla
Dash of salt

- Mix all ingredients in a tall glass jar.
- Shake vigorously
- Refrigerate overnight.

Makes three servings, about 40 calories and 3 cars each.

7. Strawberry Cheesecake:

1 container of sugar-free whipped topping (unhealthy, sorry)
1 8-oz. block Neufchatel cream cheese, **softened**
3 - 5 packets Stevia
Fresh strawberries

- Whip together topping, cream cheese, and *Stevia* until smooth and creamy.
- Chill at least two hours.
- Dip strawberries into cheesecake mix.

This is fun to take to a potluck.
The cheesecake mixture is about 80 calories and 15 carbs per tablespoon. Strawberries are free.

8. Black Bean Brownies

1 - 15-ounce can of black beans, rinsed thoroughly and drained
3 tablespoons unsweetened cocoa powder
½ cup old-fashioned oats
1 egg
¼ cup flour
1 tablespoon chia seeds
dash of *Real Salt*
½ cup real maple syrup (it's expensive)
2 packets Stevia
1/4 cup coconut oil
2 teaspoons pure vanilla extract
½ cup chocolate chips (optional)

- Preheat oven to 325 degrees.
- Put beans, syrup, egg, and coconut oil in a blender or food processor.
- Blend well and put in a mixing bowl.
- Add remaining ingredients.
- Mix well.
- Put in a greased 8 X 8 glass baking dish.
- Bake 16 - 18 minutes.
- Let cool 20 minutes before cutting.
- Cut into 16 pieces.

Drink with a cup of coffee or tea.
Each brownie has about 12 carbs and 110 calories without the chocolate chips.
Better yet, they are healthy and have a lot of carbohydrates.

Definitions

<u>morbidly obese:</u> anyone who weighs more than twice what they are supposed to; another definition is anyone more than 100 pounds overweight. (I've heard both.)

<u>empty calories:</u> foods that have calories, but very little vitamins or minerals or anything healthy.

<u>stevia:</u> a healthy sweetener made from the stevia plant, however the FDA doesn't allow anyone to call it a sweetener, even though that's what it is and that's what it does.

<u>herbalist:</u> Sort of like a naturopath except less schooling and not allowed to write prescriptions. Oh yes, cheaper and more effective in my opinion.

<u>carbohydrates a.k.a. carbs:</u> A nice name for sugar. There are good carbs and bad carbs, but if you get too much, your body still sees it as sugar.

Shopping List

Shopping Guide:

My favorite foods are those that are reasonably priced, healthy, and low in calories. The prices listed are what I spent the last time I went shopping.

Look for the foods that have three *** and only one $. Prices vary depending on the season and weather changes. This list isn't complete, but it's a good start.

Mediocre Diet Food	*
Better Diet Food	**
Best Diet Food	***
Cheap	$
Not too expensive	$$
Not so cheap	$$$

Fruit:

Strawberries (fresh or frozen) ***	$
Any and all berries (fresh or frozen) **	$$
Any fresh fruit in season **	$
Bananas *	$
Fresh or canned pineapple *	$

Vegetables:

Alfalfa ***	$
Cooked cauliflower ***	$
Steamed or boiled broccoli ***	$
Romaine lettuce ***	$
All other lettuce ***	$
Spinach (fresh, frozen or canned) ***	$
Green beans (fresh, frozen or canned) ***	$
All lettuce ***	$
Cucumbers ***	$
Carrots **	$
Tomatoes **	$$
Any vegetable except the starchy ones ***	$

To save money, watch for the vegetables in season. In the summer, tomatoes are usually dirt cheap. During the winter they're expensive. Pick up the newspaper or ask for a copy of the specials when you go to the store. Watch for the sales. You can afford vegetables. All vegetables are low in calories, carbs, and fat, except for potatoes, sweet potatoes, yams, peas, corn, beans, hominy, and soy products. Eat lots. Save money. Get thin.

Meat:

Tuna ***	$
Fish ***	$$
Boneless, Skinless Chicken Breast **	$$
Turkey **	$
Lean Ground Turkey **	$$
Eggs ***	$
Lean Beef (only if you are type O blood)*	$$

Dairy:

Skim or 1% milk **	$
Non-fat plain yogurt ***	$
Low-fat or non-fat cottage cheese ***	$
Low-fat or non-fat sour cream *	$
Low-fat or skim Mozzarella cheese*	$$

Grain:

Old fashioned oats ***	$
Steel-cut oats ***	$
Oat bran ***	$
Ezekiel bread *	$$
Brown rice **	$
Barley **	$
Udi's Bread **	$$
Rice cakes **	$
Rice crackers **	$$
Quinoa **	$

Juice:

Organic carrot juice **	$$
Organic lemon juice ***	$$
Organic lime juice ***	$$

The juices look expensive, but they last for several months, sometimes longer. I only use two tablespoons a-day.

Nuts:

Nuts and seeds are loaded with vitamins, minerals and healthy fats, but they are high in calories. (That's why they only have two *'s instead of three.) You can't eat nuts unless you weigh and measure them first.

Peanuts **	$
Walnuts **	$
Almonds **	$$
Cashews *	$$
All other nuts *	$$
Sunflower seeds **	$
Pumpkin seeds **	$
Peanut butter **	$
Almond butter **	$$

Beans: $

Black beans ***	$
All beans except kidney beans **	$

Fats:

You need fat in your diet to be healthy, but please weigh and measure, and count calories. They add up fast.

Coconut oil ***	$$
Cold-pressed olive oil ***	$$
Organic palm oil***	$$
Avocado oil ***	$$
Low cal salad dressing **	$
Lite *Miracle Whip* **	$$
Avocados ***	$$

Brummel and Brown margarine ***	$$
Real butter *	$$
Ground flax seeds ***	$$
Chia seeds***	$$

Dessert:

Sugar-free pudding **	$
Sugar-free *Jell-O* **	$
Tapioca**	$
Lindt dark chocolate 90% cocoa **	$$

Drinks:

Almond milk (low calorie, low fat) ***	$$
Coconut milk (low calorie, low fat) ***	$$
True Lime singles to go ***	$
True Lemon singles to go ***	$
Sugar-free hot chocolate *	$
Tea ***	$$

Sweeteners:

Stevia ***	$$
Wild local honey **	$$
Real maple syrup **	$$$$
Molasses **	$

Canned foods:

Vegetable beef soup ***	$
Canned green beans ***	$
Canned spinach ***	$

Miscellaneous:

*Real Salt*** $$
Pink Himalayan salt crystals** $$
These salts seem expensive, but they last a year or more.

Herbs:

Almost any and all. Most are affordable. Check the ads.

Recommended Reading
(a.k.a. Books You Can't Live Without)

The T-Factor Fat-Gram Counter

Dr. Miriam E. Nelson *Strong Women Stay Young*

William Dufty *Sugar Blues*

Jessica Seinfeld *Deceptively Delicious*

Perscription for Nutritional Healing (my other Bible)

Peter J. D'Adamo *Eat Right for Your Type*

Reese Dubin *Miracle Food Cures from the Bible*

Stanley W. Jacob, M.D., Ronald M. Lawrence, M.D., Ph.D., Martin Zucker *The Miracle of MSM (The Natural Solution for Pain)*

www.ingramcontent.com/pod-product-compliance
Lightning Source LLC
Chambersburg PA
CBHW071427070526
44578CB00001B/21